Women, Crime and Ju
England since 166

COLEG MORGANNWG
LEARNING
RESOURCES
CENTRE
ABERDARE

D0303452

WITHDRAWN
FROM
STOCK

32380A

Gender and History

Series Editors: Amanda Capern and Louella McCarthy

Published

Trev Lynn Broughton and Helen Rogers (eds)

Gender and Fatherhood in the Nineteenth Century

Shani D'Cruze and Louise A. Jackson

Women, Crime and Justice in England since 1660

Rachel G. Fuchs and Victoria E. Thompson

Women in Nineteenth-Century Europe

Angela Woollacott

Gender and Empire

Forthcoming

Paul Bailey

Women and Gender in Twentieth-Century China

William Foster

Gender, Mastery and Slavery: From Europeans to Atlantic World Frontiers

Laurence Lux-Sterritt and Carmen Mangion (eds)

Gender, Catholicism and Spirituality: Women and the Roman Catholic Church in Britain and Europe, 1200–1900

Perry Willson

Women in Twentieth-Century Italy

Gender and History Series
Series Standing Order ISBN 978–14039–9374–8 hardback
(*outside North America only*)

You can receive future titles in this series as they are published by placing a standing order. Please contact your bookseller or, in case of difficulty, write to us at the address below with your name and address, the title of the series and the ISBN quoted above.

Customer Services Department, Macmillan Distribution Ltd, Houndmills, Basingstoke, Hampshire RG21 6XS, England

Women, Crime and Justice in England since 1660

Shani D'Cruze and Louise A. Jackson

COLEG MORGANNWG
LEARNING
RESOURCES
CENTRE
ABERDARE

palgrave
macmillan

© Shani D'Cruze & Louise A. Jackson 2009

All rights reserved. No reproduction, copy or transmission of this publication may be made without written permission.

No portion of this publication may be reproduced, copied or transmitted save with written permission or in accordance with the provisions of the Copyright, Designs and Patents Act 1988, or under the terms of any licence permitting limited copying issued by the Copyright Licensing Agency, Saffron House, 6-10 Kirby Street, London EC1N 8TS.

Any person who does any unauthorized act in relation to this publication may be liable to criminal prosecution and civil claims for damages.

The authors have asserted their rights to be identified as the authors of this work in accordance with the Copyright, Designs and Patents Act 1988.

First published 2009 by
PALGRAVE MACMILLAN

Palgrave Macmillan in the UK is an imprint of Macmillan Publishers Limited, registered in England, company number 785998, of Houndmills, Basingstoke, Hampshire RG21 6XS.

Palgrave Macmillan in the US is a division of St Martin's Press LLC, 175 Fifth Avenue, New York, NY 10010.

Palgrave Macmillan is the global academic imprint of the above companies and has companies and representatives throughout the world.

Palgrave® and Macmillan® are registered trademarks in the United States, the United Kingdom, Europe and other countries.

ISBN-13: 978–1–4039–8972–7 hardback
ISBN-13: 978–1–4039–8973–4 paperback

This book is printed on paper suitable for recycling and made from fully managed and sustained forest sources. Logging, pulping and manufacturing processes are expected to conform to the environmental regulations of the country of origin.

A catalogue record for this book is available from the British Library.

A catalog record for this book is available from the Library of Congress.

10   9   8   7   6   5   4   3   2   1
18   17   16   15   14   13   12   11   10   09

Printed and bound in China

Contents

List of Tables and Figures

Tables

Figures

Abbreviations

BPP	British Parliamentary Papers
BUF	British Union of Fascists
CD Acts	Contagious Diseases Acts
CID	Criminal Investigation Department
CLA	Criminal Law Amendment Act
JP	Justice of the Peace
OBP	Old Bailey Proceedings (online)
MP	Member of Parliament
NA	The National Archives
NUWSS	National Union of Women's Suffrage Societies
RWCI	Royal Western Counties Institution
VDL	Van Diemen's Land
WSPU	Women's Social and Political Union

Acknowledgements

The authors and publishers wish to thank the following for permission to use copyright material:

ITV Global Entertainment, for the production still from *Good Time Girl* (1947) © ITV Global Entertainment.

Mary Evans Picture Library, for the illustration *A Harlot's Progress* by William Hogarth (1732). Reproduced courtesy of Mary Evans Picture Library.

The British Library, for the illustration *An Authentic Narrative of Miss Fanny Davies* by Anon. (London: R. Jameson, 1786) © British Library Board. All Rights Reserved (613. k. 12. (11.))

Every effort has been made to trace copyright holders for the Papers of Miss G. M. West (Chapter 6); the authors and the Imperial War Museum would be grateful for any information which might help to trace those whose identities or addresses are not currently known.

Every effort has been made to trace all copyright holders but if any have been inadvertently overlooked the publishers will be pleased to make the necessary arrangement at the first opportunity.

Introduction: 'Vice' and 'Virtue'?

This book aims to provide an overview of women's relationship to the criminal justice system and to explore key issues in the regulation of 'respectable' and 'deviant' femininities over the last four centuries. Three phenomena relating to women and criminal justice have been recently highlighted as matters of social concern. Firstly, reports have drawn attention to the rising number of women in England's prisons: between 1992 and 2002 the female custodial population increased by 173 per cent.[1] Secondly, it has been noted that women's experience of rape is rarely likely to lead to successful prosecution: only 5.6 per cent of reported cases resulted in successful conviction in 2002.[2] Thirdly, academic studies have commented on the ways in which the involvement of teenage girls in criminality, including a gang culture of bullying and violence, has been sensationalised as a growing trend in the newspaper press.[3] Yet in order to understand contemporary debates and concerns we need to turn to the past. The 'newness' of recent patterns and trends can only be fully assessed by placing them in a broader historical context, enabling us to comment on continuity and change across time. There is no doubt that criminal justice has become highly politicised as increases or decreases in crime rates are viewed not merely as a barometer of the failure or success of government policy but as evidence of the state of the nation. As we shall show, however, the process of 'counting' is riddled with difficulties, particularly when our main subjects – women – have often been hidden not merely from 'history' but also in part from the mechanisms of criminal justice.[4]

The allegorical veiled figure of 'Justice' was commonly depicted as a woman, bearing a sword and a set of scales to symbolise the equality of all before the law. Drawn from Classical iconography, this is the statue that was chosen to grace the dome of the new Old Bailey court building in London, officially opened in 1907. Yet, for most of the period we shall be examining, women were excluded from official roles within the law, police and the courts as well as other public and commercial roles. These structural inequalities between men and women were justified by referring to essential biological differences in temperaments, behaviours and roles. Women appeared before the courts as a minority of those charged with offences across the period as they do now. Yet women's behaviours were closely monitored and regulated across a range of sites, including the private worlds of household and family, or through the related spaces of the workplace (domestic service was the single largest employer of women until the First World War). From the eighteenth century onwards these were joined by a growing number of semi-penal institutions such as lock hospitals,

Magdalen asylums, psychiatric hospitals, rescue homes and inebriates' reformatories that attempted to reform 'deviant' women through custodial measures not sanctioned by the law. Thus the book deals not merely with 'crime' (any act that is contrary to statute law) and the 'criminal justice system' (institutions of law enforcement); it also recognises the broader regulatory frameworks, both formal and informal, cultural as well as structural, that have defined and shaped women's behaviour across time. The term 'deviancy' is used here to refer to the processes through which women's behaviours have been viewed as outside of accepted social parameters and, indeed, as the opposite of behaviours that were likely to command honour, respect and social status. Thus we include behaviours that have been legislated as 'criminal' as well as those that were not technically illegal but which placed some women on the margins of the community.

Whilst the normative stereotype of 'the criminal' has been gendered as masculine, women have been associated with specific types of transgression that have led to moments of heightened anxiety at different points in time. Witchcraft (in the Early Modern period), prostitution and infanticide (both nineteenth-century concerns) were sex-related in England since they have been primarily associated with women and, more specifically, with women's sexual and reproductive functions. Infanticide (the unlawful killing of newborn children) was assumed to contradict women's 'natural' maternal instincts. Although associated with older women, witchcraft allegations often involved narratives of poisoning contrary to women's role as nurturer and feeder; they also referred to the suckling of 'familiars' and to sexual intercourse with the devil (although this feature was less widespread than in Europe). Prostitution-related offences such as soliciting were (and are) illegal, whilst the transmission of venereal disease was a central cause of concern in wartime leading to legal measures to inspect, detain and medically treat female prostitutes as vectors of disease. These three forms of transgression have continued to colour popular perceptions of women's criminality. Yet 'witchcraft' was formally taken off the statute book in 1736, prostitution itself has never been 'criminal', and most instances of infanticide were explained in terms of *post partum* psychosis by the early twentieth century (the last woman was executed for new-born child murder in 1849). Effectively, then, they have come to be viewed as non-offences. Yet their continued cultural resonance is illustrative of the way in which women's deviancy tends to be sexualised even though, as this book will show, the vast majority of women across time (and now) have ended up in the courtroom charged with minor property offences.

We demonstrate throughout this book that women's relationship to crime has been viewed in ways that are distinct and different from that of men. Across the modern period women's social roles have been defined in terms of motherhood and household, their social status assessed in relation to sexual respectability. Indeed, we return repeatedly to the discussion of sexuality – and the opposing categories of 'vice' and 'virtue' – as underpinning formal and informal modes of regulation. Women who actively engaged in criminality tended to be pigeon-holed as irreconcilably 'bad' or, with the growth of a gendered psychiatric discourse that linked mental illness to reproductive function, as 'mad'. The latter was apparent in the Victorian development of the klepto-mania diagnosis, which was associated with hysteria and menopause, as well as with emerging interpretations of prostitution in terms of, first, nymphomania and, subsequently, 'mental deficiency'. During the nineteenth century 'virtu-ous' women were (like children) increasingly positioned as passive innocents, requiring the protection of chivalrous males. Indeed, women's victimhood and suffering had become a campaigning issue for both evangelicals and feminists by the 1880s. This meant women's vulnerability or susceptibility to influence might be accepted as explanation for involvement in offending, effectively detracting attention away from criminal agency. We are not suggesting here that criminal justice responses can be reduced simplistically to harshness or leniency. Rather, responses to women's offending were varied and complex; but they were shaped by gender ideologies and by cultural assumptions about social roles that were shifting subtly across time. The nuances of this dynamic will be teased out across the chapters of this book.

Women, Crime and Justice in England Since 1660 is concerned with the broad historical period associated with the growth of the modern nation state, with the move from a predominantly rural population to a predominantly urban one, and with the emergence of the regulatory mechanisms and institutions (includ-ing the criminal justice system) that we know today. The main bulk of the text begins around 1660 (with the restoration of the monarchy following the period of the Civil War and the protectorate) and ends around 1960 (before gay liber-ation and women's movements of the late sixties led to a partial reconfiguring of ideas about gender and sexuality); where appropriate, however, it also looks beyond this chronology and it emphasises striking continuities into the present. It focuses specifically on England (although national statistical profiles when given relate to England and Wales as a whole). Scotland, Northern Ireland and Eire have been largely excluded from this account because of their separate legal and criminal justice systems but also because they have been remarkably understudied by historians of gender and crime. Broader comparative work on the four nations that make up the British Isles is clearly needed to enrich the study of women, gender and criminality and to further contextualise our under-standing of the specificity of England. In this brief introduction to the book we outline the methods and approaches that have been developed by histori-ans who have studied the relationship between women and criminality. We also outline the thematic approach that we shall adopt here, as well as offering an overview of the strengths and weaknesses of the types of primary source material (historical documents) that we use as our evidence base.

Criminal justice history and the social history of crime

For the nineteenth-century historian Thomas Babington Macaulay, transfor-mations in criminal justice were presented as part of a broader narrative of civilisation, progress and social improvement in which 'we have, in the course of ages, become, not only a wiser but also a kinder people'. The brutal punish-ment of women in particular was seen as symbolic of the barbarism of the past: 'Gentlemen arranged parties of pleasure to Bridewell on court days, for the purpose of seeing the wretched women who beat hemp there whipped.'[5] The development of the criminal law, policing and the court system were charted in the 1870s by Luke Owen Pike and then, in substantial depth, by Sir Leon Radzinowicz in the mid-twentieth century; in both cases their analyses were based on similar arguments about humanitarian improvement.[6]

For social historians, however, the subject of criminality as an area of investigation is a comparatively recent phenomenon. In the 1970s it became a central focal point for the school of Marxist historians associated with E. P. Thompson at Warwick University, who were interested in the relationship between the law, criminality and class conflict. In an essay published in the famous collection *Albion's Fatal Tree*, Douglas Hay depicted the 'manipulation' of the eighteenth-century criminal justice system as 'a ruling class conspiracy' designed to protect the interests of men of property through a smokescreen of 'justice', 'mercy' and 'majesty'.[7] The contributors to the book were interested in offences such as poaching, smuggling, wrecking and bread rioting which, they argued, were condoned by the people who were defending their customary rights. The approach adopted in *Albion's Fatal Tree* raised a number of very important issues that are highly pertinent to the study of women and crime and other periods than the eighteenth century. Firstly, it highlighted the ways in which 'crime' (like 'deviancy') was a socially constructed category and, indeed, subject to contestation. Secondly, it asked vital questions about which social groups benefited from or, indeed, were in 'control' of the criminal justice system. Thirdly, rather than assuming that criminal justice could be labelled as either 'brutal' or 'kind' on a sliding scale, it drew attention to the ideological effect of the law in reinforcing the hegemony of an elite group, legitimating and naturalising their value system. Finally, the interest in law-breakers (poachers, smugglers, bread rioters) as well as law-makers signalled the need to pay attention to the agency (understood in terms of autonomy, self-determination, ability to act and respond) of those previously viewed as marginal ('history from below'). *Albion's Fatal Tree* demonstrated that an understanding of the workings of law and criminal justice was central to the project of social history. If criminal justice history focused narrowly on the administration and operation of the law and related institutions, the 'new' social history of crime of the 1970s saw definitions and experiences of criminality as located within a broad complex of social relationships.

Hay's thesis, in particular, proved controversial and, by way of response, historians of crime and the law turned to quantification and to social science techniques in the 1980s to identify who, exactly, was involved in decision-making in the English court system. It is important to note here that it was not until the nineteenth century that prosecution by police officers gradually replaced the older system in which private individuals brought cases to court (the role of the police was finally taken over by the Crown Prosecution Service in 1985). Peter King's work on data samples relating to the eighteenth-century Essex courts has shown that the poor as well as the rich were none the less able to bring cases to court. Although the bulk of prosecutions were brought by those of 'the middling sort', he has convincingly suggested that access to criminal justice was to some degree a 'multiple use right' in Early Modern England.[8] In *Women, Crime and Justice in England Since 1660* we shall consider a range of questions relating to the category of gender which are pre-empted by these earlier considerations of the significance of social class. Did the law and the mechanisms of criminal justice reflect and bolster male hegemony in a society in which women were unequal to men? Did women use the courts to resolve disputes and to what extent were they excluded from participation? Were they able to demonstrate agency? Finally, to what extent is it possible to uncover the experiences of women enmeshed in the criminal justice system? We shall also demonstrate that women's class position as well as gender shaped their experiences.

Women's history and gender history

The emergence of women's history from the early 1970s onwards was an important component of the identity politics of feminism and the women's movement. In Britain, however, it was also influenced by Marxism and the interest in 'history from below' that focused on socially marginal groups. Recovering women's past involved recognising and valuing their contribution (agency and experience) and was, thus, about retrieval and celebration. The researching of women's history was also, however, of central importance in for-mulating feminist theory. In order to understand women's oppression it was necessary to examine the historical processes – including both 'capitalism' and 'patriarchy' – that had shaped the contemporary world. Women's history was extremely interested in the ways in which formal and informal methods of regu-lation limited and, indeed, socially constructed women's roles and expectations. Studies of middle-class Victorian women, for example, focused on the gender ideologies at work within religious, medical and psychiatric frameworks, which were used to sustain the belief in 'separate spheres' of activity for men and women.[9] Research on working-class Victorian women examined the ways in which women had been excluded from the workplace as the result of the pater-nalism of male Trade Unionists.[10] The American historian Joan Kelly argued that periods of time characterised as progressive from a male perspective took on a very different gloss from the vantage point of women.[11] This was espe-cially apparent if the cultural and political achievements of the Renaissance were set alongside the phenomenon of the Early Modern European witch-hunts. For radical feminists, the persecution of women as witches was evidence of the misogyny endemic within Western culture and part of a continuum of sexual violence through which men (had) kept all women in fear.[12] Polemical inter-pretations of the past were joined by important empirically grounded histories of rape and sexual violence that were informed by feminist theory rather than driven by it.[13]

The feminist interest in the witch-hunts coincided with a growing interest in magic and folk belief systems amongst historians of popular culture influenced by anthropological frameworks.[14] It is worth recording here that in England witchcraft was defined as a crime punishable by execution from 1542 until 1736, with the last known hanging for the crime taking place no later than 1685.[15] The most reliable estimates suggest that comparatively low levels of prosecution and execution took place in England (in contrast to Europe), with up to 2500 individuals being tried of whom around 20 per cent were hanged; most cases involved individual local prosecutions (with the exception of the witch-hunts of 1645 associated with self-styled 'witch-finder general' Matthew Hopkins). Approximately 90 per cent of those accused were women.[16] There is an extensive historiography relating to witchcraft prosecutions and it is not our intention to review it here.[17] Of particular note, however, is the way in which attempts to analyse the witch trials as prosecution/persecution have highlighted the fluidity of categories of 'offender' and 'victim'. As we shall stress further elsewhere, these are labels that reflect understandings of intentionality or passivity, and hence of agency or its lack, although they are of course technically unavoidable for purposes of clarity in some legal contexts. If crime is socially constructed as the phenomenon of witchcraft persecution so strongly suggests, the very categories of criminal justice require deconstruction.

Women's history focuses on women as a group, distinguished by their biological sex, as its subject of study. Gender history, on the other hand, can be characterised as a methodological approach that makes use of the category of 'gender' as a tool for analysis. Within both feminist theory and its off-shoot of masculinity studies, 'gender' has been defined as the cultural construction of difference between the sexes. In contrast to the terms 'male' and 'female' that invoke biological sex, the terms 'masculinity' and 'femininity' relate to the performance of cultural roles. Thus one finds references to effeminate (or feminine) men or to manly (masculine) women. Gender relates to the process of meaning-making, through which physical bodies and behaviours are interpreted and evaluated. It also relates to identity as individuals make sense of self in relation to others. The meanings attached to gender have shifted across time; moreover there may be plural models of behaviours – 'femininities' and 'masculinities' – that are coexistent or competing. Anna Clark's work, for example, has argued that a more restrained and chivalric model of masculinity became dominant in artisan as well as middle-class circles in the first half of the nineteenth century, challenging an older libertine model of manliness that had prized pugilism and sexual conquest.[18] Indeed, dispositions towards violence and sexuality have acted as sometimes crucial defining points of gendered identities, and these have in turn impacted on the framing of the criminal law.

Joan Scott also makes the important point that gender has been 'a primary way of signifying power' in that it has acted as an important metaphor for social and political relationships.[19] This is evident of course in the use of the statue of virtuous femininity to represent 'Justice' itself. Moreover, as feminist criminologists commented as they challenged the gender biases within their own discipline in the 1980s, the law itself is not neutral; rather it reflects normative assumptions about gender difference. As a text, it too requires analysis and deconstruction.[20] Approaches influenced by gender history have now been incorporated into the social history of crime alongside the continued recognition of the significance of social class. Edited collections such as Arnot and Usborne's *Gender and Crime in Modern Europe* and D'Cruze's *Everyday Violence* have show-cased a range of work on both masculinity and femininity, whilst recent monographs by leading criminal justice historians Martin Wiener and Clive Emsley have focused specifically on masculinity.[21]

In centring this book on women as our subject of study we are writing women's history that is also gender history. Of course, it is neither possible nor desirable to focus on women or femininity in isolation. Moreover, as some critics of women's history have argued, it is not necessarily meaningful to talk about all women as a group compared to all men as a group. Class or wealth, 'race' or ethnicity, age or lifecycle stage, religion or geographical location, as well as a proliferation of other factors impact upon individual experience and serve to construct differences between women as much as to unite them. However, as we argue here, women's status before the law was significantly different from men's and this in turn impacted upon their experiences of criminal justice. Our approach, then, is to offer a gendered history of the relationship between women and criminality that is situated in a comparative context, that makes use of recent studies of men and masculinity, and that attempts to deal with difference as well as commonality.

Foucault, feminism and the 'cultural turn'

Awareness of the role of labels (and hence language itself) in constructing social perceptions of gender difference was crucial to feminist thinking of the 1970s and 1980s as we have seen. Other related philosophical and theoretical trends of the post-war period also converged with feminism to produce a critique of the ways in which 'knowledge' circulated within modern societies. In relation to the study of crime and 'deviancy' the work of French scholar Michel Foucault has been both influential and much criticised.

In summary, Foucault was interested in understanding how modern subjects were both regulated and, simultaneously, implicated in regulating themselves and others within increasingly democratic western nation states. His 1975 book *Surveiller et Punir* (translated into English as *Discipline and Punish*) examined the 'birth' of the prison not only as an institution but also as a metaphor for other forms of social regulation that emerged to deal with increasingly large populations.[22] Emblematic of this for Foucault was Jeremy Bentham's design for the 'Panopticon' prison, which had involved the careful organisation of space to guarantee maximum visibility (hence *surveiller*) at all times (whether or not anyone was actively watching). Foucault saw this 'gaze' or 'eye of power' as present across other institutional spaces (workhouse, factory, school, courtroom) as well as in attempts to broaden city thoroughfares and introduce street lighting. Of particular note here is Foucault's argument that it was not possible to analyse the criminal justice system in isolation; rather it was part of a broader 'technology of power'. Rejecting (like Hay and Thompson) the simple narrative of humanitarian progress that had shaped early criminal justice histories, he saw the move towards non-corporal punishment as more invasive than whipping, torture and execution; the strategic effect of a custodial sentence was to reform the soul or self. Foucault drew attention to connections between criminal justice policy and other forms of 'knowledge' such as religious, medical and psychiatric 'discourse', which offered sometimes competing 'truths' about the world. So, whilst he highlighted the physical presence of institutions and the organisational role of structures, he argued that 'power' and 'knowledge' (claims to truth) were implicitly related and indeed mutually constitutive.

Foucault's interest in the effects of 'power and knowledge' on the conduct of the most intimate and personal aspects of everyday life led him to focus further on the history of sexuality. Far from being 'repressed' about sex, he argued, the Victorians were actively involved in discussing, debating, categorising, normalising and prohibiting sexual behaviours in such a way that it became a core defining point of modern identity.[23]

The nineteenth century saw, in particular, the construction of extramarital sex as 'dangerous' as well as the categorisation of (male) homosexuality as perverse. Whilst Foucault's work did not use gender as a category or focus specifically, it chimed with feminist awareness that sexuality was not merely a biological given; rather norms and expectations had been constructed culturally over time within a dense network of power relations. For women, in particular, as we shall show further in this book, ideas about respectability and deviancy were often highly sexualised.

For Foucault's critics, many of the trends that he identifies do not withstand detailed empirical investigation. In Britain, for example, sustained attempts to rehabilitate prisoners through a programme of work and training were rarely effectively introduced (except in relation to institutions for juveniles). The suggestion that the 'gaze' of surveillance was omnipresent does not accord with feminist research which stresses that the private enclave of the family (and indeed the authority of husband or father) continued to be beyond effective scrutiny during our period of study, leading to the under-reporting of domestic violence involving wives and children. None the less, the trends he highlights can be seen as suggestive, rather than conclusive, in enabling us to identify the forms of regulation that have tended to emerge within the modern bureaucratic state. Moreover, the key concepts that he developed have been widely adopted and adapted as a method of analysis.

Indeed, Foucault's emphasis on 'discourse' and 'knowledge', in drawing attention to the role of language in mediating 'reality', was one component of a 'cultural turn' within historical study. In speaking of the 'cultural turn' we are referring to a move away from positivist approaches that involved the measuring of social phenomena through quantifiable indicators. These were replaced with hermeneutic analysis of the symbolic effects of texts, narratives and other forms of visual representation or material culture.[24] The 'turn' was also a result of the interdisciplinary engagement of some historians with linguistic theory, anthropology and literary studies. Some of these methodological shifts – as well as the broader relationship between historiographical trends and the history of women and crime – can be further explored by looking at the work of the historian Judith Walkowitz, who has taken as her focus the relationship between gender, sexuality and the law in Victorian England.

Walkowitz's *Prostitution and Victorian Society*, published as a book in 1980, drew on research that she had begun ten years earlier. The book was a study of the introduction of the Contagious Diseases (CD) Acts which, during the 1860s and 1870s, required the medical inspection of women deemed to be prostitutes and, should they be found to be suffering from venereal disease, their forcible detention in lock hospitals. It examined medical and evangelical views on prostitution, the work of middle-class campaigners (such as Josephine Butler) who lobbied for the repeal of the laws, and also the effects of the Acts on the lives of 'poor "outcast" women' who resorted to prostitution in Plymouth and Southampton. Thus the study drew on traditions of social history and 'history from below' in its interest in social class and in the lives of those on the margins, explored through the use of local case studies. Social and economic profiles of the women were constructed through nominal record linkage, whilst reports of court trials were used to ascertain the social networks in which they moved.

Prostitution and Victorian Society was an important study in the context of the growth of women's history in the 1970s: not only in its exploration of the lives of women of different social groups but also in its interest in women's political activism. Finally, the book was also substantively concerned with the regulation of sexuality: as a central target of state policy and law enforcement, and as a subject of prolific public debate. Walkowitz drew on Foucault's work whilst also developing it further through her case studies, demonstrating that: 'although the CD acts created a "technology of power", they also generated a formidable social and political resistance'.[25] Her methods included a careful analysis of the rhetoric of social commentators and campaigners. She drew attention, for example, to the ways in which medical writers used a vocabulary of 'sin' and 'purity', alongside references to disease and pollution, thereby positioning women's sexual agency as in itself contaminating and dangerous to men.[26]

Walkowitz's interest in narrativity – that is, in literary devices, forms of emplotment, symbolic repertoires, and hence meaning – was demonstrated in her 1992 book *City of Dreadful Delight*, which is often viewed as a key example of the writing of the 'new cultural history'. Its aim was to map out 'a dense cultural grid through which conflicting and overlapping representations of sexual danger circulated in late-Victorian London'.[27] Whilst a huge range of popular 'true crime' books have, since 1888, sought to 'solve' the murders of six 'outcast' women by an unidentified murderer who soon came to be labelled 'Jack the Ripper', Walkowitz sought, instead, to study the construction of the Ripper myth. She was interested in what it told her about late-Victorian social relations including 'fears and antagonisms' linked to 'gender, class and ethnic relations'.[28] She also suggests that the use of gothic and melodramatic tropes served to further construct the city (and, more specifically, the East End) as dangerous and monstrous to vulnerable women, further enforcing the gendered 'segregation of social space' particularly at night time.[29] These myths were deployed yet again in relation to press coverage of the 'Yorkshire Ripper' between 1975 and 1981 (in May 1981 Bradford lorry-driver Peter Sutcliffe was convicted of the murder of 13 women and the attempted murder of seven others).[30] Walkowitz argued that the very 'real' effect of the packaging of the 'Ripper' story as a 'narrative of sexual danger' has been to 'cast women in the role of victims requiring male protection and control', as well as to sensationalise/glamorise violence against women as the acts of a monster rather than an ordinary man. She nevertheless emphasised women's agency in resisting these constructions, both in 1888 and again in the late 1970s.[31]

Women, Crime and Justice in England Since 1660 is informed by the types of cultural approaches that have been exemplified here, in recognising the power of language to shape social reality. The gender historian Joan Scott has argued that even the concept of 'experience', which was so central to 'history from below' as well as to women's history, must encapsulate the process of significa- tion. For Scott, material and physical events are only constituted as 'experience' through processes of naming, remembering, retelling and assigning meaning.[32] Whether one described oneself as a 'victim' or 'survivor' of crime may, thus, be constitutive of experience and identity. For feminist historians of violence, how- ever, the focus on language also raises significant problems. In centring only on rhetoric, we are in danger of ignoring pain, fear, sorrow, bodily injury or harm. Rather than discounting Scott's arguments, we suggest that a recogni- tion of the complexity of the construction of 'experience' is assumed, in which the presence of the extra-textual (emotions, physical sensation, etc.) is fully acknowledged.

Gender, violence and the 'civilising process'

Issues around gender and violence are interwoven in much of our discussion of women and crime and not infrequently intersect with the theme of women's sexuality. One of the historical effects of gendered power relations has been that although many more women have been tried for property offences, women committing violent crime have often had greater cultural visibility. Conversely, the dominant gender order has meant the obscuring or erasure of violence to which women have been subjected, not least within homes and families. Placing the historical experience of women – and its signification – at the centre of our analysis leads us to interrogate what is currently the best used paradigm in the historiography of violence. Deriving from the work of Norbert Elias, this per- spective suggests that there was a long-term 'civilising process', evident in the conduct of elites by the later eighteenth century and later generalised to other social sectors, through which interpersonal violence from the brawl to the duel ceased to be an acceptable means of social interaction.[33] According to this nar- rative, since the Early Modern period, the growth of comparatively centralised states in Western Europe involved more than the suppression of insurrection and direct challenges to state authority by elite violence. It also involved the management and reduction of 'private' interpersonal violence, eventually across society as a whole. This historical interpretation argues that over the *longue durée*, 'civilised' behaviour as a social practice became internalised by ever-wider social groups. This was achieved through complex interactions between social, cultural and psychological processes.[34]

The 'civilising process' has been critiqued and revised from several direc- tions. Historians now tend to focus on its potential effect over shorter time periods and, as Elias himself came to argue, perceive such a process as uneven and even reversible.[35] Research is showing the Western state to have been a far less unitary and co-ordinated entity than this model implies. The precise mecha- nisms of how state attempts at coercion related to individuals' internalisation of less violent behaviour is difficult to reconstruct. Furthermore, any reduction in interpersonal violence in Western societies now needs to be set against the far freer uses of violence of all kinds in colonised societies, not least as an instrument of governance. Perhaps most relevant to women's and gender history, the now accepted persistence of domestic violence and the ways that it has, at least until very recently, been seen as 'private' and outside the realm of criminal justice practice irrespective of the written law indicates that the adoption of non-violent behaviour was at best a very selective process.[36] Nevertheless the civilising process remains a useful framework for historians seeking to explain the changes in the visibility of certain kinds of violence in West European societies.

Recent versions of this argument have related the decline of violent and disorderly conduct in London to a broader cultural shift in behaviour caused by the changing conditions of social life in the fast-growing eighteenth-century metropolis.[37] Social groups that based claims to status not least on their 'civilised' conduct had by the mid-nineteenth century distanced themselves from the interpersonal violence of the mob. Abstention from violence was also used as an element in national identity.[38] Respectable masculinities continued to be associated with legitimate uses of violence. These could range from warfare to the punishment of offences to honour. As late nineteenth-century fiction was so fond of underlining, many a bounder 'deserved a good thrashing' and it was the role of the honourable man (or boy) to administer it.[39] Violence, within certain bounds, was also assumed to be legitimate in administering 'correction' to women and children. It was the prerogative of authority, and of course many women also punished their children with a beating.[40]

Martin Wiener has explored the 'civilising offensive' of the nineteenth-century upper courts in punishing serious interpersonal violence; Victorian judges were keen to enforce the increasingly comprehensive statute law on violence.[41] Whether or not they were the root cause of behaviour change, different kinds of 'top-down' civilising strategies were introduced across the nineteenth and into the twentieth centuries. These were aimed as much at property crime as violence and included the patrolling of the streets by more modern police forces and the significant growth of summary justice to deal with petty violence and disorder, as well as the increasing penal severity towards many perpetrators of more extreme violence. However, given that far more men than women came before the courts charged with violent crime, such 'civilising' projects were principally concerned to police the shifting boundaries of the acceptable uses of violence by respectable men and were therefore raced and classed as well as gendered. Historically, the criminal justice system has perceived violence according to paradigms of masculine conduct. Consequently, it could find violent women problematic to deal with and reacted by either trivialising (and/or excusing) or by exaggerating the offence. Given the comparatively low numbers of women on trial for violence, there is little conclusive historical evidence that a civilising process affected women's violence over the long term. Across the period we discuss, violent women disturbed dominant gender relations which, with varying degrees of emphasis, have associated respectable femininities with passivity. Arguably, the criminal justice process has usually prioritised the reassertion of the dominant gender order, which has subordinated women but also positioned them as 'the weaker sex' requiring masculine chivalry as well as control. Violent women's historical experience of the criminal justice process has therefore been uneven both over time and in individual cases, depending on the sociocultural contexts and circumstances.

Sources for the study of crime and deviancy

Whilst historians are able to work with a range of artefacts including visual images and material objects, it is frequently in the form of printed or manuscript text that traces of the past have been preserved for posterity. Issues of authorship, intended readership, genre (whether the document or the process it captures is formulaic), as well as content and context, require careful evaluation in assessing meanings. The 'cultural turn' that we have discussed above serves to remind us that all documents are complex mediations through which actual events, occurrences and lived 'experiences' (however defined) are reduced to words on a page. This is particularly apparent in relation to the history of crime, since sources were invariably manufactured through the bureaucratic cogs of criminal justice itself.

In many cases, historians have only lists (registers of names and charges) or brief indictments (detailed and formally worded charges) as their source material. This can be particularly frustrating if we are searching for the experiences or agency of women enmeshed in the criminal justice system. None the less, there are a number of very rich qualitative sources that contain traces of women's own voices, particularly as witnesses although sometimes as defendants. Clearly any court appearance was 'a "staged event", a social drama largely manipulated by police [by the nineteenth century] and judicial authorities'.[42] Narratives told in the courtroom were particular orderings (usually chronological) of the facts of an event; witnesses were likely to have told very different versions (including emotional and speculative responses) in a more informal setting to friends or family. What was then told in the courtroom was recorded by a third party. It was the business of petty sessions (held before Justices of the Peace, as the lowest rung in the court system) to prepare statements or depositions from witnesses that were then sent on to a higher court as part of the preparation for trial before judge and jury (at Quarter Sessions or Assizes). Until comparatively recently formal transcripts of jury trials were not required. Historians of the modern period must make do, instead, with newspaper reports of trials penned by journalists; those who work on the Early Modern period may turn to popular ballads and pamphlets that recorded versions of the lives and activities of 'notable' criminals. In relation to London only, the *Old Bailey Sessions Papers* (discussed in more depth in Chapter 1) provides invaluable insights in offering published transcriptions, recorded at time of trial by a shorthand clerk. Whilst we must be aware of processes of filtering and distortion, these materials nevertheless offer us a unique connection with the historical past, linking us to the lives and viewpoints of the poorest members of society (in some cases the illiterate).

The self-articulated experiences of women convicted of offences or subjected to custodial sentences are few and far between, although we may have a sense of the ways in which their past lives were ordered or institutionalised through records collated within penal regimes. In relation to the contemporary period, the criminologist Pat Carlen has used personal testimony and interviewing techniques to work with women in prison.[43] Victorian and Edwardian auto-biographies penned by former 'prisoners' have been collected and studied by Philip Priestley. Revealingly, however, those produced by women mostly relate to the experiences of suffragettes imprisoned for their participation in militant political protest.[44] The general perception that suffragettes were middle class is misplaced, since a number of those who wrote their memoirs were drawn from working-class backgrounds. Nevertheless, they were distinguished from other women prisoners through their high levels of literacy as well as the offences for which they were sentenced. Joan Henry's later text *Who Lie in Gaol*, published in 1952, is a moving as well as disturbing account of her experiences of the harsh regime at Holloway Prison and then of the more benign Askham Grange. She was aware throughout that she was different from other prisoners because of her middle-classness, although she describes a real sense of commonality and, indeed, community amongst women, engendered from the shared experience.[45] It is also possible to read or interpret officially generated sources 'against the grain', that is, to look for the ways in which those subjected to the processes of criminal justice or penality were able to produce moments of resistance. We need to search for 'agency', recognising that it may be frustratingly hard to find. Ultimately, however, historians face clear difficulties in that most documents tell us about perceptions of and attitudes towards criminality rather than about the experiences of those labelled as 'criminal'.

In *Women, Crime and Justice in England Since 1660* we also work with a broad range of source types, including literary fiction and film for insights into popular culture, in order to shed light on the frameworks through which women's behaviour has been regulated across the modern period. Rather than analyse fictional and visual representations separately, we view them as cultural mediations that require evaluation alongside other primary source materials and in relation to the contexts and circumstances that shaped their production. As we shall demonstrate, forms of representation refract, mythologise, and in some ways construct and feed into lived experience. The popular genre of melodrama, for example, might be an indirect reference point in the courtroom as partici-pants were presented or evaluated in relation to gendered stereotypes of 'vice' and 'virtue'.

The book is organised thematically rather than chronologically. Chapter 1 offers an overview of trends across time as well as critically assessing the strengths and weaknesses of the quantitative approach in exploring women's relationship to criminal justice. The next four chapters deal with different types of activity and their gendered construction as 'criminal' or 'deviant'. Official classifications of offences, from the nineteenth century onwards, distin-guished between crimes against the person (including inter-personal violence) and crimes against property. Our organisation reflects these categories as well as problematising them. Given that women were most likely to be indicted for the appropriation of property, we deal with this in Chapter 2, which examines the relationship between women's economic activity (including production, con-sumption and household management) and their engagement in theft, fraud and the receiving of stolen goods. Chapter 3 then considers women's involvement in violence, including homicide, assault, piracy and robbery. The fluidity and permeability of these categories is acknowledged. Robbery and piracy, for example, involved the use of violence as a tactic for the appropriation of property. Whilst the concept of sexuality structures our analysis across the book, Chapter 4 deals specifically with the offences related to prostitution, abortion, concealment of birth and infanticide that have been directly mapped on to women's sexual and reproductive roles. This is not to de-link them from violence but, rather, to suggest that women's sexuality, more so than for men, has structured their relationship with the criminal justice system. Chapter 5 examines the concept of 'political crime' and the moments in which women rejected the rule of law for the purposes of protest, engaging in forms of behaviour that brought them into conflict with the institutions of criminal justice. Women's participation in Early Modern grain riots, in radical political protest in Georgian England, in suffrage militancy in the Edwardian period, and in illegal non-direct action at Greenham Common form central case studies for examination.

For the suffragettes, the law was a legitimate target because it was the tool of a patriarchal state that failed to recognise women's full citizenship, excluding women from the vote and from public office (including positions within criminal justice itself). However, given that they subscribed to broadly liberal notions of equality, many of those who were involved in suffrage militancy argued that the law could be rendered fair if women were represented within the structures of authority.[46] To what extent was this achieved? Chapter 6 addresses this question by focusing on women's incorporation within justice and penal regimes as jurors, lawyers, police officers and magistrates, assessing the power dynamics that were created when women were placed 'in control' of their own sex. Chapter 7 continues with the focus on authority, institutions and structures, looking at the gendering of penal regimes, as well as assessing women's experiences of prison and rehabilitation.

Finally, Chapter 8 focuses on a particular demographic group – young women – and the ways in which they have been labelled and dealt with as 'delinquent' in the modern period. We position it as our final chapter since it engages with themes and issues raised in all previous chapters, whilst exploring the ways in which gendered ideas about childhood and youth impacted upon juvenile justice and penality. For those under the age of 17, deviant or promiscuous sexuality was dealt with through 'social' proceedings designed to protect them from 'moral danger,' but which led them into the same institutions that were used for those who had offended against the criminal law, collapsing once again the categories of 'criminal' and 'victim'. A brief 'Afterword' will link our historical assessment back to contemporary concerns.

1

Women and Criminality: Counting and Explaining

Across the modern period commentators have argued that women as a sex are less likely than men to engage in criminal activity. Yet they have disagreed on the reasons. For the psychologist Havelock Ellis, writing in 1894, there was 'scarcely [...] any doubt that the criminal and anti-social impulse is less strong in women than in men'.[1] In his published memoirs of 1931, high-profile London detective Frederick Porter Wensley explained women's lower levels of participation in terms of social roles rather than instinct: 'women [...] may be just as wicked as men, but their opportunities for crime on a big scale are more restricted'.[2] The collation of criminal justice statistics from the early nineteenth century onwards exposed apparently lower levels of female participation in criminality. Women formed 17 per cent of the prison population in England and Wales in the nineteenth century; this was reduced further to 4 per cent by the 1980s although figures are now rising starkly.[3] Criminality as a concept came to be defined in terms of masculinity. The scientific study of offending behaviour – which has come to be labelled 'criminology' – can be dated back to the analytical work carried out by prison medical officers from the 1860s onwards. These studies focused overwhelmingly on male prisoners and thus the set of characteristics associated with male offenders was viewed as a 'norm' or 'type' against which deviancy was measured.[4] Women's offending has tended to be viewed not merely as unusual, but in extreme cases (including press representations of Myra Hindley or Rosemary West) as 'doubly deviant' in that it contradicts gendered assumptions about 'caring' femininity as well as threatening broader social norms through the act of law-breaking.[5] Indeed, the assumption that certain types of criminal women are exceptionally 'monstrous' can be linked to the dualistic depiction of women as infinitely good or infinitely evil within Judeo-Christian frameworks. This did not mean that all women implicated in offending were treated harshly; indeed, far from it. Rather, notable exceptions to norms of 'womanhood' have been held up as cultural icons of feminine 'evil'.

This chapter will assess whether and to what extent historians have replicated the assumptions that underpinned early criminological investigation in either ignoring women's offending behaviour or assuming low levels of activity. It will begin by assessing the historical incidence of women's involvement in criminal activity, focusing on the difficulties of quantitative analysis, including the problematic nature of data sources. To what extent have women always been prosecuted in far smaller numbers than men? Did they gradually 'vanish' from the criminal justice system and, if so, why? Were women treated with greater or less leniency than men when they encountered the mechanisms of criminal justice? Finally the chapter will assess women's involvement in court procedure as witnesses, prosecutors and complainants. It will suggest ultimately that the trends that are evidenced in criminal justice statistics must be viewed as an important point of intersection between the processes of criminal justice and the behaviours of those accused, but that they must be evaluated carefully and critically. Ultimately, any study of women and crime needs to engage with the broad range of regulatory practices through which femininity has been situated and experienced in the modern period. A focus that is limited to criminal justice itself gives only a blinkered view.

The case of the vanishing female

Historians attempting quantitative analysis of the gendering of offending behaviour are dependent on the survival and accuracy of data generated by the criminal justice system itself. National profiles of the business of the courts are not available for the years before 1805, whilst the classification of offences that is used today was introduced in 1834. With the expansion of the bureau-cratic state and the development of the statistical movement in the nineteenth century, criminal justice and law enforcement agencies were required to submit annual figures to central government; even so, methods of recording the gen-dering of offences has varied. For earlier periods, the business of the Assize and Quarter Sessions (higher courts) can only be reconstructed through painstak-ing examination of individual indictments (formal written accusations, often on parchment, that were prepared as a defendant was committed by a magistrate to stand trial). Moreover, the survival of indictments may be sporadic so that sam-ples need to be constructed of years for which there is a clear run. Such work was pioneered by J. M. Beattie for the counties of Sussex and Surrey between 1663 and 1802.[6] It has been joined by a range of studies including those by Garthine Walker (on Cheshire 1590–1670), Gwenda Morgan and Peter Rush-ton (on the north-east 1714–1800), and Peter King on Essex and London (1740–1820).[7] The business of magistrates or Justices of the Peace (the low-est but very important first rung of criminal function) is only just beginning to receive attention.[8]

Historians of the Early Modern period have often concentrated their atten-tion on the work of the Old Bailey, which acted as an Assize court for London. This is because detailed accounts of the Old Bailey's proceedings (recorded in short-hand by reporters) were published for popular consumption from 1674 until 1913, providing a rich seam of data for historians to mine. Moreover, these sources have recently been digitised (as the *Old Bailey Proceedings Online*), pro-viding a fully searchable and publicly available database of criminal justice cases.[9] The full potential of such an electronic resource is only just being realised and it is likely to generate both extensive and highly innovative studies not merely of criminality but of the daily lives of Londoners. However, the sheer richness of the Old Bailey material can lead to a research bias in favour of urban and, more specifically, the metropolitan experience. Findings for the London courts need to be set alongside continued work on other regions and locales.

Criminal justice historians are inclined to agree that English women tended to be prosecuted for far fewer offences involving violence than men (in contrast to Scotland where, as the work of Anne-Marie Kilday has shown, women were charged with over a third of all offences against the person).[10] Women in England were most likely to appear before the courts in urban areas for theft, drunkenness (or public order offences) and prostitution-related offences (soliciting charges tended to be applied exclusively to women). Historians also agree that English women were more likely than men to be given lesser sentences once convicted. Finally and perhaps most significantly, they agree that women have tended to be prosecuted in fewer numbers than men in England (as elsewhere in Europe). There is considerable debate, however, as to whether a clear decline in the prosecution of women has taken place and, if so, when, where exactly, and why this occurred. In 1991 Malcolm Feeley and Deborah Little published an article, based on Old Bailey data, in which they argued that female offenders had gradually 'vanished' from the criminal justice process across the last three centuries. Using samples taken at 20-year intervals (1735, 1755, 1775, etc), they argued that women's involvement as defendants had fallen from 45 per cent of all those committed for trial in 1735 to a mere 10 per cent in 1895. This, they suggested, was evidence that the marginalisation of women's criminality was a relatively recent phenomenon and that it could be linked to changes in social attitudes and gendered behaviours.[11]

The 'vanishing female' thesis can be criticised from a number of perspectives. Firstly, findings drawn from Old Bailey data cannot be used to provide meaningful conclusions about England as a whole for the eighteenth century. London itself can be viewed as atypical precisely because of the intense urban experience that it offered; young women might move to the capital for work, away from established networks and supports, leading to a period of economic vulnerability. Peter King's extensive research on Assizes and Quarter Sessions in Essex has shown no obvious decline in the prosecution of women across the eighteenth century in what was a predominantly rural county. Rather, females formed around 13 per cent of those indicted for property offences across the period 1740–1804.[12] The work of J. M. Beattie also shows, like King, that the metropolitan urban experience needs to be distinguished from the rural experience. In rural parishes of Surrey and Sussex, women constituted only 11 per cent of those charged with offences against the person for samples obtained between 1663 and 1802; for offences against property, women constituted 14 per cent of those charged in rural Surrey and 13 per cent of those charged in rural Sussex. Urban areas of Surrey demonstrated higher levels of charges against women (22 per cent of those charged with offences against the person and 28 per cent of those charged with property offences).[13] These are not, however, out of kilter with trends for the Old Bailey in the 1790s which King has shown to average around 25 per cent.[14] Ultimately, as King has argued, patterns for the eighteenth century are not distinctly different from that of the late twentieth century in which women have also formed a small minority of those accused (12 per cent of females prosecuted for indictable offences in England and Wales

Table 1.1   Persons proceeded against, England and Wales, by sex

Year	Summary offences			Indictable offences		
	Male	**Female**	**% Female**	**Male**	**Female**	**% Female**
1860	305,625	79,293	21	11,150	3,648	25
1870	427,290	99,579	19	13,353	3,389	20
1880	536,693	126,711	19	11,345	2,763	20
1890	609,638	128,423	17	9,039	1,722	16
1930	546,483	66,592	11	57,751	8,298	13
1950	543,900	60,098	10	109,391	16,203	13
1960	856,552	55,983	6	153,858	20,801	12

Source: *Criminal Statistics, England and Wales* (Police Returns), British Parliamentary Papers (BPP).
(*Note:* Comparable data is not available for the period of the Second World War.)

in 1960 – see Table 1.1). A further problem with the method used by Feeley and Little is the use of 20-year intervals for samples. The years selected are not necessarily representative, whilst the impact of war, which removed a size-able proportion of young male labourers from London's population, is not accounted for.[15]

In relation to the eighteenth century, then, a complexity argument emerges, in which patterns can be seen as regionally distinct, linked to the specific demographic and economic characteristics of parishes, towns and cities. Morgan and Rushton have found that women constituted a half of all thieves prosecuted in Newcastle in the mid-eighteenth century, which they link to women's high demographic representation (57 per cent of the population of Newcastle was female in 1801). London and Newcastle emerge as 'atypical' compared to patterns elsewhere. In many rural areas, women were never prosecuted in high proportions. If there was a 'decline', it is unlikely that the eighteenth century is the period in which this began.

Can the 'vanishing woman' thesis be more accurately sustained for the nineteenth century? As Table 1.1 demonstrates, if we study more serious 'indictable' offences (which could only be tried in the higher courts), women were gradually disappearing from view. Yet we also need to account for the growing role of magistrates (summary justice) and their ability to hear cases previously only dealt with by Assizes and Quarter Sessions. The Criminal Justice Act of 1855 was particularly important in this regard. Along with other legislation it enabled magistrates to hear cases of theft that had, previously, constituted a large proportion of higher court business. Similarly, magistrates were also empowered to try common assault cases. Sue Grace's study of York has shown that women formed 18 per cent of all summary convictions in 1849 but that this rose to 34 per cent in 1860.[16] Thus the contours of criminal justice were themselves changing. Table 1.1 certainly indicates that the percentage of proceedings for indictable offences against females had fallen to 16.0 per cent by 1890 (from 24.7 per cent in 1860). Yet this requires qualification, since females were still appearing for summary offences (before magistrates) in large numbers. Indeed, there was an increase in female appearances for summary offences of around 50,000 (a rise in number of 62 per cent): from 79,293 to 128,423. Prosecution rates for males were simply rising even more steeply. This is one piece of evidence which suggests that the 'vanishing woman' thesis might be more appropriately replaced by a thesis regarding the growing 'criminalisation of men' in the Victorian period.[17]

National aggregates of course conceal local patterns of variation which might be linked to conditions and standards of living. In London's East End, for example, women appeared more regularly as defendants in the police court in the late nineteenth century. A sample of the 2174 cases coming before Thames Police Court between July and September 1888 shows that 27 per cent of all defendants were female.[18] This figure was particularly affected by their prosecution for drink-related public order offences: women formed 46 per cent of those charged in the East End compared to a presence of just over a third in national profiles of summary offences. Clearly alcohol was a coping mechanism as well as an exacerbating factor in lives structured by real poverty, insecurity and overcrowding. Moreover, the overtly 'public' worlds of the East End's destitute women, who inhabited the streets, sleeping rough or making use of lodging houses, brought them under closer police scrutiny. Beneath the national profiles a dense set of local scenarios require unravelling in order to explain why aggregates appear the way that they do.

Women's declining presence in court (in terms of both numbers and relativity to male prosecutions) is a phenomenon of the first half of the twentieth century (see Table 1.1). In relation to summary offences, this decline between 1890 and 1930 can in part be accounted for by a drop in prosecutions for soliciting, which were proving increasingly troublesome to convict, thus showing that strategies of policing, as much as women's actual behaviours, have shaped court profiles. The numerical increase in summary offences by 1960 is wholly accounted for by the growth in motoring offences (linked to car ownership) and for which men were prosecuted in far larger numbers than women.[19] It is worth noting, however, that proceedings for common assault have continued to be taken against females in significant proportions, forming consistently a third of all such cases coming before magistrates in our three sample years of 1930, 1950 and 1960. At the beginning of the twenty-first century adult women constitute around 16 per cent of those arrested by the police for offences.[20] Thus, once again, a simple narrative of increased decline across time appears insufficient.

Explaining women's absence

It is clear, however, that women have appeared in the courtroom in significantly smaller numbers than men, although there have been exceptions to this rule. Reasons for this have been hotly debated. Socio-biologists have tended to emphasise essential hormonal, physical and psychological differences between men and women (what Ellis called 'impulse'), which have made women less likely to display aggression across cultures and societies.[21] In contrast, feminist historians have turned their attentions to stark continuities within social and cultural formations. They suggest that women's association with the household and with domesticity has restricted opportunities for property crime, whilst gendered assumptions about women's caring and nurturing role have meant that women have been socialised to reject aggression as unfeminine. These processes have been most strongly associated with the Victorian period, when cultural assumptions that women were naturally more passive than men came to dominate. Lucia Zedner has also argued that by the end of the nineteenth century, women who demonstrated 'unnatural' behaviour, including aggression, were more likely to be side-tracked into the psychiatric system. The suggestion that deviant women were 'mad' rather than 'bad' was also reflected in the use of the 'kleptomania' diagnosis for theft (see Chapter 2). This was a re-working of Early Modern assumptions that women, particularly older women, were more likely to be associated with witchcraft, either because they were more vulnerable to the devil's temptations or because they were suffering delusions as a result of an over-abundance of the humour of melancholy circulating within their bodies.[22] Like Zedner, Paula Bartley has suggested that women engaged in prostitution were increasingly likely to be classified as 'feeble-minded' by the early twentieth century; the 1913 Mental Deficiency Act enabled them to be detained in semi-penal institutions, taking them out of the purvey of criminal justice statistics.[23] Hence, whilst socio-biology sees the predominance of patriarchal systems as a result of intrinsic biological differences between the sexes, with male aggression acting as a motor for history, feminist historians have tended to suggest that patriarchal ideologies (including medical science) have constructed femininity as 'passive' and thereby prescribed women's behaviours culturally.

Most recently, the historian of violence John Carter Wood has suggested that the relationship between biology and culture might be better understood by making use of insights from evolutionary psychology. 'Nature' and 'nurture' should be considered as interdependent rather than oppositional explanatory frameworks. Drawing attention to 'the universality' of men's 'predominance' in committing acts of violence, he none the less suggests that 'any psychological mechanisms involved are subject to social stimuli such as inequality, threats to personal security, the perceived "legitimacy" of violence, and the social costs of (or potential punishment for) using violence'.[24] He thus throws the ball back towards the cultural sphere as that which requires interrogation by historians (it remains unclear from his article as to how, exactly, the precise interface between nature and culture might be researched in relation to past time). If we formulate similar suggestions in relation to female subjects, we might focus on why, under what circumstances and in what ways women have made use of criminal, deviant or aggressive behaviour. As unusual trends for south-west Scotland and Newcastle indicate, women have in some places and at some times demonstrated equal capacity for criminality. There is some credibility in the suggestion that women's economic (and hence social) equality may lead to higher rates of prosecution; this has some support in contemporary concerns about increases in drunkenness and violence amongst young women in particular. Indeed, one of the paradoxes for contemporary feminism is the possibility that growing equality of opportunity in the late twentieth century might also have led to higher incidences of female criminality or, at least, a hardened criminal justice response.

One of the most significant problems faced by historians of the criminal justice system lies in the impossibility of identifying a clear relationship between levels of prosecution and the commission of all illegal acts whether reported or not. Until very recently the only data collated has related to officially reported crime. Whilst the British Crime Survey now attempts to offer an indication of the prevalence of fear of crime and also of levels of unreported crime, there is no equivalent for the historical past. This has led some historians to contrast reported crime with a 'dark figure' of actual offending behaviour that has not been brought to public account. The metaphor of the 'dark figure' is suggestive of an indeterminate but real phenomenon, rather like an iceberg, only the tip of which is visible above the surface (the mass present beneath, although concealed in terms of size and shape). For historians of gender and crime, the spectre of the 'dark figure' leads to speculation as to whether women were, indeed, committing offences but were simply less likely to be either suspected or prosecuted than men, perhaps because of increasing assumptions about women's passivity and lack of agency (for the doctrine of *feme covert* see Chapters 2 and 6) or perhaps because of sympathy towards women in positions of poverty and vulnerability. It is highly likely that levels of reporting were affected by these phenomena.

There are problems, however, with the concept of the 'dark figure'. In assuming that 'real' crimes can be clearly identified as acts, whether they are reported or not, it loses sight of the process that takes place in the courtroom whereby differing versions of 'the truth' are paraded for assessment. In relation to property offences, ownership of objects or the right to use them may be contested. In relation to violence, who struck whom and where is subject to detailed interrogation. Thus the court hearing involves the negotiation of meaning in assigning culpability. As historians we should not necessarily assume that all those who were convicted 'actually' committed the offence for which they were charged; but neither should we assume their 'innocence'.

Court cases can be seen as mechanisms for resolving disputes or controlling anti-social behaviour that increasingly replaced older informal sanctions such as 'rough music' (also known as *charivari* after French usage of the term). Ritual mockery, which involved the beating of drums and pans outside the house of individuals or couples who had transgressed accepted gender norms had been used in the sixteenth and seventeenth centuries to humiliate 'cuckolded' husbands who had failed to 'tame' adulterous wives. In 1688 a French traveller described his encounter on the streets of London with a noisy mob whose purpose was to shame 'a woman [who] had given her husband a sound beating for accusing her of making him a cuckold'.[25] 'Rough music' was also targeted against wife-beaters or those suspected of sexual offences. As Hammerton has argued, however, *charivari* were conservative in intent in seeking to maintain the patriarchal order and they resulted, on some occasions, in attacks on prosecuting rape complainants.[26] In addition to the ritual of rough music, crowds might also make use of 'rough justice' or mob violence to deal with miscreants. By the nineteenth century this might arise when the courts had acquitted individuals whom the community wanted to see punished. In May 1880 a female mob gathered outside Thames Police Court, threatening to lynch a German

man alleged to have forced a young woman into prostitution (the case had been discharged by the magistrate).[27]

'Rough justice' also resulted when offences were decriminalised by the central state although they were still recognised within some local communities. With the end of gender-related prosecutions for witchcraft in 1736, community violence continued to be directed against women labelled as witches, who subsequently became enmeshed in the criminal justice system as victims of assault (prosecuting their attackers) where formerly they would have stood as the accused.[28] Increasingly, in the nineteenth century, the rough justice of the mob (in which women themselves were often active participants) came to be condemned as anachronistic. Notions of what was a criminal act were subject to contestation, and a range of strategies were available to individuals and communities to settle disagreements or resolve disputes. The criminal law was increasingly seen as the most obvious and accepted step, but it was by no means the only one. 'Rough music' and 'rough justice' might equally be applied to acts that had been criminalised by the state and those that were licit, but viewed as deviant by communities attempting to police their own moral boundaries. Thus reported crime is best seen as the generation of bureaucratic process to deal with allegations relating to a congruence of persons, place, time and action (an 'event'). The search for the 'dark figure' and, indeed, reference to its existence, is misplaced.

The Victorian criminalisation of men?

If our central focus, then, is the bureaucratic process itself, what do its workings tell us about sex and gender? Statistical evidence suggests that women were dealt with more 'leniently' than men across the modern period: that is, they were less likely to be convicted than men and they tended to receive lesser sentences. In a survey of the verdicts delivered by the Old Bailey and Home Circuit (Assizes) for property offences in the late eighteenth and early nineteenth centuries, Peter King found that around 60 per cent of males were found guilty compared to 44 per cent of females.[29] Similarly, Zedner's research shows that in 1857, 53 per cent of women dealt with by magistrates were convicted compared to 66 per cent of men; by 1900 women's conviction rates had increased to 77 per cent, but this was still lower than the figure of 83 per cent for men dealt with by magistrates.[30] The technologies of punishment and sentencing have changed across time but the apparently 'lenient' treatment of women as a group has remained a constant. In the Early Modern period, men were more likely to hang than women, whilst women were more likely to receive the lesser sentence of whipping.[31] By the late nineteenth century women were less likely than men to receive custodial sentences and were more likely to be fined or discharged; in the twentieth century women were less likely than men to be sent to prison and more likely to be made the subject of conditional discharges or binding over orders. The death penalty was still used in the twentieth century (it was finally abolished in 1965) and, once again, women were more likely to be reprieved than men (only 9 per cent of women receiving the capital sentence were executed in the period 1900–55 compared to 58 per cent of men); the vast majority had their sentence commuted to life imprisonment upon appeal. It has been suggested that women might command more sympathy from magistrates and juries because of gendered assumptions about their vulnerability as well as a pragmatic desire not to separate mothers from their children, who might then become a financial burden on the local state (reinforced after the Second World War by psychological concerns about 'maternal deprivation' if mother and child were separated). The flip-side of this argument is that men were dealt with especially severely.

The issue of the gendering of verdict and sentencing in cases of violence has been examined in some depth by Martin Wiener in his aptly titled study *Men of Blood*. Whilst the eighteenth century had seen a clamping down on property crime, violence against the person became an increased target of criminal justice in the Victorian era. Murders were given more prominent press coverage and drunken brawls and fights between males (including the traditional 'duel') were more likely to go to court. Given that violence was more likely to involve male than female protagonists, it can be argued that reform of masculinity had become a key aim of the criminal justice process. Focusing on murder trials (which came before Assize courts), Wiener shows that an increasing number of cases (30 per cent by the 1890s) involved the murder of wives by husbands; this is because wife-killings that might previously have been determined as manslaughter were more likely to be tried as murder. Moreover, men's complaints of provocation (such as wives' unfaithfulness or verbal insults) were less likely to lead to mitigated sentences. If we turn to the crime of new-born child murder (sometimes emotively labelled as 'infanticide') for which women were overwhelmingly held responsible, we find an opposite pattern: such cases rarely led to convictions by the late nineteenth century, and instead evinced considerable levels of sympathy in press coverage of trials. As a model of chivalric and restrained masculinity became hegemonic within middle-class and 'respectable' working-class circles, women (and children) were further defined as vulnerable innocents (and thus potential 'victims') who were in need of protection.

One of the problems with Wiener's work is its concentration on the Assizes and Old Bailey, focusing on homicide (involving fatality) as an extreme form of violence. Most cases of violence dealt with by the mechanisms of criminal justice by the late nineteenth century were in fact more mundane cases of 'common assault' which were increasingly tried by magistrates. Arguably, homicide was handled with exemplary care precisely because it was atypical. Wiener's thesis that aggressive masculinity was increasingly condemned within the Victorian criminal justice system is an important one that requires further investigation in relation to the lower courts.

In attempting to assess how, exactly, gender operates in the courtroom, historians face the difficulty of comparing like with like, given that the circumstances of events are infinitely variable. Did magistrates and judges reveal gender bias in that they viewed women more sympathetically even when accused of similar types of offences? Or was it the case that women were in fact committing offences that might be objectively evaluated as less aggressive or less serious? These questions have formed the central focal point of recent quantitative research by Barry Godfrey, Stephen Farrall and Susanne Karstedt, which examines decision-making in cases of violence that came before magistrates in the period 1880–1920. By examining the detail of individual allegations, as recorded in local newspaper coverage, the researchers were able to classify cases in relation to four categories: resulting injuries; relationship between victim and assailant; strength of evidence in court; and 'culpability' or the individual's role in 'initiating the assault'. In assessing verdict, Godfrey, Farrall and Karstedt found no evidence of gender bias. Rather, women were less likely to be convicted because they were implicated in less-violent offences and in less-serious circumstances. When it came to sentencing, however, men were more likely to receive custodial sentences (and, indeed, longer ones) for involvement in similar types of offences according to the categories used. This leads the researchers to conclude that the courts 'directed their efforts towards "civilizing" dangerous masculinities'.[32]

To some extent this method of assessing the relationship between gender and sentencing (attempted by Wiener and by Godfrey et al.) can only ever be crude. Other criteria such as the respective ages of defendants and complainants, ethnicity, and social class may be as equally significant as gender. Gender has been a significant marker of identity in modern Britain, but it was not the only 'crucial axis of power'.[33] Moreover, the significance of a complainant's relationship to an assailant, of strength of evidence and of 'culpability' are subjective categories that are socially and culturally specific. This is most apparent in relation to an offence such as rape, in which cultural expectations of what constitutes consent, and, therefore, interpretation of the law, have shifted across time.

In arguing that male violence against women was treated with greater severity as the nineteenth century progressed, Wiener cites an increase in the number of rape cases coming for trial as well as a rise in conviction rates (in part a response to the removal of the death penalty for rape in 1841, which made juries less reluctant to convict). Yet he does not mention that the overwhelming majority of 'victims' in rape cases tended to be under the age of consent and hence juveniles rather than adult women.[34] (The age of consent rose from 12 to 13 in 1875 and from 13 to 16 in 1885, thereby leading to the criminalisation of previously acceptable acts as 'unlawful carnal knowledge', sometimes termed 'statutory rape'). Nor does Wiener mention that a significant number of sexual assault cases (rape and indecent assault) were either acquitted by magistrates or dealt with, on a lesser charge of common assault, as suitable for summary trial.[35] Other than where there was clear medical evidence of brutal physical damage, the hearing of rape or indecent assault cases often hinged on an assessment of the reliability of witness and 'victim' testimony. Where historians have factored age and social class into an analysis of the decision-making process in the courtroom, they have tended to argue that cases involving young children were viewed as more serious given concerns about sexual precocity, particularly amongst adolescent girls of the urban poor. Notions of 'respectability' – shaped by perceptions of age, class, status, sexual reputation and thus truthfulness – were an extremely important reference point in the Victorian courtroom. Thus Carolyn Conley has argued that the decision-making process often involved a weighing up of the 'respectability' of the defendant in relation to the 'respectability' of the 'victim'.[36]

Whilst statistical profiles suggest that, overall, women have been treated with apparent 'leniency', historians have also sought to explain why it is that a small number of women have, none the less, received extremely severe sentences. Lucia Zedner has argued that those women found to be truly 'criminal' tended to be viewed as doubly deviant: 'criminal women not only broke the law but also contravened various moral prescriptions about women which were deemed essential to the moral order'.[37] Anette Ballinger has extended Zedner's work by examining the 15 cases in which women were executed in England and Wales between 1900 and 1955. She has argued that ideologies of gender implicitly inform sentencing procedure: 'women who fail to conform to traditional expectations in the areas of sexuality, respectability, domesticity and motherhood are more likely to be the victims of judicial misogyny with the consequent result that they receive harsher punishment than women who conform to conventional models of femininity'.[38] This was most apparent in the trial of Ruth Ellis (the last woman to be hung, in 1955, for the murder of her lover David Blakely), who had worked as a nude model and night-club hostess before bearing a son out of wedlock at the age of 17. However, this is not to argue that women who were reprieved were viewed as 'respectable'. As Chapter 8 will show as it discusses the case of Elizabeth 'Marina' Jones, even when the death sentence was lifted, women's private lives were often still publicly condemned. Where women were accused of murdering spouses or lovers, a weighing up of behaviours took place in relation to gendered ideals of respectability. In cases where women were reprieved, husbands were portrayed as violent, unruly and outside the norms of chivalrous masculinity. Thus, as Ballinger has recently argued, the extension of 'mercy' to women who kill 'can ultimately be understood as a *conservative* strategy which sought to preserve the institutions of marriage in particular, and the existing gender order more widely'.[39] The point made here is that gender ideologies are often naturalised within the courtroom and that their operation cannot be reduced to a simple argument about leniency or harshness; they are played out in complex ways that are difficult to measure in quantitative terms.

Women as prosecutors and complainants

Contemporary feminism makes the important point that to label women as 'victims' in relation to offences such as rape constructs them as passive objects; the term 'survivor', on the other hand, can empower. In their capacity as 'victims' or 'survivors' of crime, women have also been prosecutors, litigants or complainants within the courtroom, terms that suggest significant levels of agency. As private prosecution was replaced by public prosecution (by the police) as the nineteenth century progressed, the term 'complainant' came to replace the term 'prosecutor' to describe the actions of aggrieved individuals. Recourse to the law provided women with a possible way of seeking redress for physical harm or injury, for resolving property disputes or for settling disagreements with neighbours. To what extent did they choose to make use of this resource and what were the constraints that affected their decisions?

Whilst a large number of studies have concentrated on women's presence in criminal justice statistics across time, less attention has been paid to long-term trends in their numerical involvement as prosecutors and complainants. The most significant work on women's role as litigants has focused on the work of the Church (or 'Bawdy') Courts, whose main concern was 'spiritual justice' (although it did deal within this remit with sexual offences such as incest, which was not criminalised until 1908). Laura Gowing's work on the London Church Courts has demonstrated a substantial growth in their business in the early seventeenth century, particularly in relation to hearings for defamation of character that were being brought by a burgeoning number of female litigants. Women came to the 'Bawdy' Court to defend their honour and sexual reputation – a key element of women's status – against those who slandered them as 'whore'. Women formed over half of all litigants in the London Church Courts in 1633, compared to their presence as just 13 per cent of all complainants appearing before the Sussex Quarter Sessions. Thus Gowing argues that the business of the London Church Courts 'testifies to women's maximisation of a rare opportunity of speech, complaint and legal agency' (although it should be noted that they achieved lower 'success' rates than men as complainants).[40] Whilst the work of the Church Courts had significantly diminished by the early nineteenth century (an average of 2.5 cases per year compared to 35 a year in the early seventeenth century), they continued to act as a feminised forum until their dissolution in the 1850s, women constituting 90 per cent of all plaintiffs between 1815 and 1855.[41]

The gradual increase in the types of business that were conducted by magistrates' courts as well as their increased visibility in urban areas meant that women in particular were increasingly using summary justice as a resource by the mid-nineteenth century. As Jennifer Davis has shown in her work on the London Police Courts and as Shani D'Cruze has evidenced in her work on petty sessions in the north-west, the regular and informal style of proceedings attracted women who displayed increasing knowledge and awareness of their use.[42] In addition to hearing criminal charges, urban magistrates heard a range of requests for advice and applications for summonses against third parties. Even the poorest women turned to the police courts in London to complain about domestic violence, despite the fact that the law did not always provide the solution they wanted. In July 1888 Thames Police Court magistrate Montagu Williams told 19-year-old William Donovan: 'you have committed a brutal assault on your sister and given her a frightful black eye. She asks me simply to bind you over to keep the peace, but I shall not listen to that. You will go to prison for six weeks with hard labour.'[43] Any sense of the magistrates courts as a community forum (and, indeed, one easily accessed by women) was lost with the further bureaucratisation of the criminal justice process after the First World War (as prosecuting powers were consolidated in the hands of the police and then the Crown Prosecution Service).

In relation to the higher courts, a crude search of the Old Bailey Sessions Papers shows that, numerically, female prosecutors/complainants were active across the eighteenth and nineteenth centuries although they formed a minority compared to men (see Table 1.2).[44] It is possible of course that their lower level of activity reflected a lower likelihood of being a victim of crime. Furthermore, given that the property of married women was frequently held in their

Table 1.2 'Complainants/victims' by sex, Old Bailey Proceedings, 1725–1899

	Male	Female	Total	% Female
1725–49	10,586	2,129	12,880	16.5
1750–74	11,099	1,781	12,880	13.8
1775–99	17,213	2,272	19,485	11.7
1800–24	29,885	3,081	32,966	9.3
1825–49	52,840	6,963	59,803	11.6
1850–74	16,157	3,441	19,598	17.6
1875–99	11,896	4,393	16,289	27

Source: OBP (www.oldbaileyonline.org, accessed 10 October 2008).

husbands' name, the theft of goods that were used by a woman but not necessarily owned by her might also be concealed within a simple search (by gender) of 'victims'. The profile of types of cases involving female complainants and victims was broadly similar to that involving males (except in relation to sexual offences), with theft being by far the most common accusation across the period of study. A case from 1699 is typical of the kinds of circumstances that might lead women into the courts:

> Mary Pemberton and Jane Chatterton , of the Parish of St. Giles in the Fields, were Indicted for feloniously stealing a silk night Gown, a Quilt, a stuff Petticoat, and a Suit of laced Head Cloaths, the Goods of Ann Malsfret Spinster, on the 21st of September last. The Prosecutor said that she did Lodge in the Room with them, and when she was gone out they took her Trunk and Goods, and went away with them; which were afterwards found upon them. Chatterton said, The Prosecutor gave her leave to use the Goods, and did not steal them; but they being both Confederates, the Jury found them both guilty to the value of 10 d.[45]

The parties in this case were not wealthy; the three women all lodged together in a shared room, so were known to each other. Malsfret had clearly lost her most valuable possessions, a set of best cloths, which she kept in her trunk, the only personal or private space available to her. Pemberton and Chatterton disputed the theft; clearly the matter had not been resolved informally amongst themselves to Malsfret's satisfaction, so she pursued litigation to redress the 'wrong'. The case reinforces Peter King's thesis that access to the courts was viewed as a 'multiple use right' to which the poor turned to resolve disputes amongst themselves rather than the exclusive preserve of the rich, or indeed, of men.[46]

Women were more likely to use the law in some situations than others. In general, cases of family and sexual violence were less likely to be brought to public attention because of shame, taboo and damage to a woman's reputation (bound up as it was with codes of sexual morality). Women were less likely to make formal complaints relating to assaults on themselves and rather more likely to use the courts to protect their daughters from the assaults of strangers. Moral panic surrounding the sexual exploitation of very young women led to a sudden increase in reports of 'statutory rape' in the years after 1885. In cases of incest, where the reputation, status and income of the family might be affected if cases were dragged through the courts, women were still unlikely to report husbands even after 1889, when the legal impediment that had stopped women from giving testimony against husbands (other than in cases in which they were them-selves the 'victim') was finally removed. In relation to sexual offences, informal sanctions continued to be used by communities well into the twentieth century, whilst adult women's prosecution of rape remained low.[47]

Statistics for recorded cases of sexual assault on females (rape and the inde-cent assault of women or girls) are suggestive of a gradual increase in reporting levels across the twentieth century. In 1900, for example, 950 such cases were recorded in official criminal statistics for England and Wales; this rose to 1960 in 1930; to 6992 in 1950; and to 10,178 in 1970.[48] It is important to bear in mind, however, that many reported cases across the period may have been 'no crimed' by investigating police officers; that is, they were not included in data for 'recorded crimes' because it was assumed they were false allegations. Where crimes were 'recorded', they often related to young females under the age of consent, reflecting anxieties about child 'molestation' and abuse as it resurfaced at various points in the twentieth century. Between 1946 and 1954 policewomen in Dartford, Kent, recorded in their station diary that they had taken statements in 122 cases of indecent assault involving minors; they had dealt with only four complaints of rape/attempted rape involving adult women, only one of which was pursued further.[49] The seventeenth-century judge Sir Matthew Hale had argued that, although rape is 'a most detestable crime', it 'is an accusation easily made and hard to be proved, and harder to be defended by the party accused, though never so innocent'.[50] This argument was still deployed within police culture in the mid-twentieth century to argue that false accusations were common. Whilst there have been significant attempts to trans-form the ways in which rape complainants are dealt with by the police and the court system (including the granting of anonymity to rape complainants in the 1970s), a 2005 Home Office report has suggested a continued 'culture of scep-ticism' both within policing and amongst the broader public serving as jurors. Approximately a quarter of cases were 'no crimed', only 14 per cent actually reached trial, and, of these, rates of acquittal were twice as likely where com-plainants were adults rather than those under the age of 16.[51] There have been clear shifts in sensibilities surrounding rape, as Wiener has demonstrated for the nineteenth century. The eighteenth century argument that it was impossible to rape a healthy adult woman is no longer cited in legal texts. Yet its legacy remains in the form of a plethora of cultural myths surrounding rape, which means that there are striking continuities in the ways in which adult rape complainants have had 'justice' dispensed to them across time.

The example of rape is also significant in terms of our wider discussion because it exposes the inadequacies of statistical evidence relating to the busi-ness of the courts, as well as the difficulties that have beset complainants who have invoked the legal process. Whilst it is often claimed that criminal justice records provide an accurate measure of homicide levels, given that bodies – by their very nature corroborating evidence that a crime has been committed – are difficult to conceal, the example of rape lies at the opposite end of the spectrum. As a sex-specific crime that can only be committed by males (defined in terms of penile penetration without consent), its meaning historically has been negotiated through highly gendered discourses relating to sexuality, agency and reputation. In terms of the regulation of rape, the courts have provided a strategy that has been rarely used by women.

Conclusion – writing women in

It can be argued that one of the most significant problems with the quantitative approach adopted within criminal justice history has been its narrow focus on the institutions of criminal justice alone. In other words, it has been hampered by the ways in which it has followed and thus reinforced the logic of its data sources. An alternative approach lies in offering an assessment of the broad range of mechanisms that have sought to regulate women's behaviour within the (emerging) modern state. Criminal justice policy cannot be separated from other forms of social policy. Rather, the mechanisms of criminal justice constitute one of a range of technologies through which individuals have been regulated and, indeed, learnt the techniques of self-regulation. Perceptions of appropriate gender roles have meant that women's sexuality in particular has often been an area of anxiety in relation to constructions of deviancy; this is apparent both in accusations levied against women and also in cultural attitudes towards rape that have made it difficult to convict. At some points in time 'deviant' sexuality has been subject to criminal justice mechanisms whilst at other points it has been dealt with through psychiatric frameworks, as the example of prostitution indicates.

As subsequent chapters will also show, criminal justice needs to be viewed in relation to other social institutions and regulatory practices if we are to move beyond the search for the 'vanishing woman'. Moreover, we need to refocus our attentions on women's involvement in acts or events that came to be labelled as criminal. As Kilday has argued in relation to the Scottish material, there is a need for more studies of 'the active agency of women'.[52] A broader social history of women and crime seeks to analyse the sites, circumstances, relationships and cultures that have led to contested actions or events. Whilst subsequent chapters will make central use of statistical data to identify trends and patterns of prosecution, they will also use qualitative analysis of a broad range of sources to address the difficult problems of locating women's agency and of uncovering the experience of crime, criminality and 'deviancy' in terms of everyday lives.

2
Women and Property Offences

Daniel Defoe created an intimate but cynical portrayal of the relationship between gender and an emerging consumer society in his depiction of Moll Flanders, the most famous female thief in English literature (first published in 1722). Tempted to steal a bundle of clothes from an apothecary's shop and a string of beads from a small child, Moll then learns the 'craft' of pickpocketing and shoplifting from an expert accomplice. She explains her shift into criminality in terms of necessity and then greed: 'as Poverty brought me into the Mire, so Avarice kept me in, till there was no going back'.[1] An opportunist involvement in thieving and prostitution is presented as part of an economy of make-shifts through which poor women managed to survive in eighteenth-century London.

Defoe's detailed description of the visibility and availability of luxury textiles and accessories – cambrics, linens, silks, lace, gold watches and periwigs – is also suggestive of the ways in which the desire for commodities was increasingly linked to forms of self-expression. In keeping with older conventions, temptation is presented as an externality – as the work of the devil, rather than an aspect of one's inner self – but the currents of modern possessive individualism are equally apparent. Material aspiration was connected with social mobility and increased status. Moll's ability to dress above her rank and to masquerade as a 'gentlewoman' created significant opportunities for fraud and deception. The fictional Moll was a composite character, based on Defoe's close observations of a number of infamous women tried for theft at the Old Bailey in the early eighteenth century.[2] The text is far from being a 'genuine' or 'authentic' account of a woman's life. Yet it can be read as a social commentary that sought to expose 'the growing Vice of the age', in which sexual and material corruption were seen as intertwined.[3]

Whilst drawing on the techniques of statistical analysis, recent studies of the history of theft in England have sought to locate property-related crime within wider cultures of production and consumption. They have also paid attention to the gendering of space and its reconfiguration over time in terms of household, workplace, shopping emporiums and department stores. The beginnings of 'modern' consumer practices can be tracked back to the Early Modern period. As a result of industrialisation, cheap mass-produced luxury goods – particularly clothing and accessories – were increasingly made available to the mass of the population. Habits of subsistence and restraint were replaced with a more democratic pursuit of fashionability, in which clothes became symbols of individuality and aspiration for even the labouring poor. Across the seventeenth and eighteenth centuries, availability and desire led to the wider circulation of goods through secondhand and black markets as well as through more licit circuits of exchange.[4] The new consumerism – and the spaces it created – provided a crucial context for acts of theft.

This chapter will, therefore, examine the gendering of theft in relation to the changing economic and social practices of 'getting' and 'spending', but also in relation to the symbolic frameworks associated with 'modern' material cultures and with emerging 'modern' identities of class and status. Stereotypes and representations will be discussed alongside actual cases, since each informed the other. We will begin by discussing notable shifts as well as significant continuities in gendered patterns of property-related offending. A more detailed analysis of women's involvement in theft and the receiving of stolen goods will be followed by a consideration of fraud and other forms of deception.

Continuity and change

The vast majority of women who appeared before the higher courts – some 80–90 per cent across the nineteenth and twentieth centuries – were charged with property offences. As Beattie has commented, 'for women even more than men, it was theft and related offences that most often brought them into trouble with the law'.[5] In seventeenth-century Cheshire and eighteenth-century Surrey as well as nineteenth-century England and Wales, women constituted around a fifth of all those indicted for forms of theft.[6] This only dropped to around 15 per cent in the twentieth century.[7] Thus a discussion of women's prosecution for property-related offences is crucial to any broader historical consideration of women and criminality.

Statistical data has suggested a further set of continuities. First, women were more likely to be accused of theft in urban rather than rural areas. In eighteenth-century Newcastle, for example, women were charged with over 50 per cent of all thefts.[8] Second, women have been most likely to appear in the courtroom for simple thefts: often of clothing, textiles or household goods from homes and shops or of larceny from the person (including cut-pursing or pickpocketing to obtain watches and jewellery), rather than offences involving violence (such as robbery). Third, whilst male criminality has tended to be associated with young adulthood, prosecutions involving female defendants have been more dispersed across the lifecycle. Older women have been prominent in prosecutions for the receiving of stolen goods and, in the twentieth century, for shoplifting.

These continuities clearly warrant explanation. As Chapter 1 has elucidated, the relationship between patterns of prosecution and actual offending behaviour is a complex one. The majority of those prosecuted in the courts were drawn from the poorer sections of society. Clearly poverty – for both men and women – was likely to be the most common incentive for theft. Thus the equation of severe economic hardship with theft is obvious. However, given the structural economic and legal inequalities between men and women, it is surprising, then, that so few women ended up in the courts accused of property-related offences.

Women on the breadline have, historically, engaged in a range of activities in order to subsist (depending on age and resources) including sexual barter, the use of customary rights (such as gleaning), the pawning of goods, and the taking in of washing or temporary lodgers. As Garthine Walker and Lynn MacKay have argued, it is insufficient to state that men and women stole for similar reasons.[9] Rather, we have to look at the gendered networks of exchange in which men and women participated in order to understand the experiences and meanings of property-related offences. Across the centuries, women have been held chiefly responsible for the management of domestic economies, entailing proximity to (and knowledge of the value of) household goods. This has, in turn, shaped the kinds of illegal activity in which they have indulged as well as perceptions of their culpability and criminality.

Nevertheless, there have been distinct shifts in the profile of women's property offences linked to social and technological change. The opportunities for cut-pursing or pickpocketing were clearly more numerous in busy urban areas than rural ones. By 1875, larceny from the person constituted nearly a quarter of all property cases for which women were tried in England and Wales.[10] This can be partially explained in terms of the social congestion associated with rapid urbanisation as well as with the replacement of face-to-face communities (in which individuals were known in terms of family and reputation) by the anonymity of city life. The close urban living of nineteenth-century industrial towns and cities facilitated the activities of pickpockets. In the twentieth century, however, the pattern of prosecution changed again. By 1950 women were eight times more likely to be charged with theft from shops and stalls (now a discrete category) rather than larceny from the person. This trend can be explained in terms of suburbanisation and the reduction in urban street crowds (leading to a decline in pickpocketing), as well as in relation to the emergence of self-service chain-stores and supermarkets (which encouraged shoplifting). The changing technologies of transport have similarly impacted on gendered patterns of theft. Indeed, women's declining statistical presence for theft in the twentieth century can be partly explained by the growing popularity amongst male youth of 'joy-riding' (the indictable offence of taking vehicles without consent), of stealing pedal cycles, and of removing items from parked vehicles (summary offences). Such forms of behaviour can be linked to increased male ownership of cycles and cars, their significance for male leisure, and the continued significance of the street as a masculine space. Statistical profiles are clearly relational.

A second important change across time is a decline in accusations against women for property offences involving violence or forced entry. In seventeenth-century Cheshire, women were charged with 41 per cent of all housebreaking offences and 26 per cent of all burglaries.[11] In north-east England during the eighteenth century, women constituted over a fifth of those accused of aggravated property offences. In one particularly brutal case in 1791, Jane Clark and her two daughters were accused, together with William Winter, of the burglary and murder of an elderly woman, Margaret Crozier in Elsdon. It was alleged that the daughters had strangled Crozier in an attempt to restrain her as Winter pillaged the house.[12] By 1875, however, national statistics indicated that women were accused of just 4 per cent of burglaries, 10 per cent

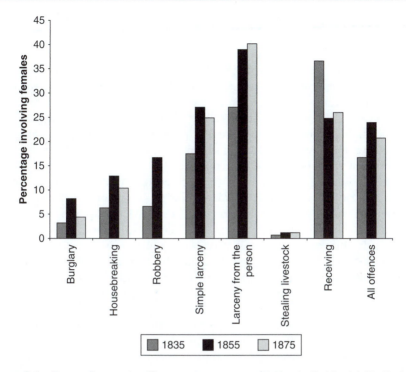

Figure 2.1 Types of property offence: persons committed or bailed for trial in England and Wales (percentage involving females)
Source: BPP, Criminal Statistics.

of housebreaking offences and no robberies (Figure 2.1). By 1950, women were found guilty of just 2.6 per cent of all indicted property offences involving violence.[13] Clearly these trends may be a function of the decisions made by prosecutors as well as actual offending behaviours. It is certainly possible that under the 'Bloody Code' individuals were reluctant to prosecute women for minor property offences, but were extremely persistent in their pursuit of robbers and burglars, irrespective of their sex.

Patterns of offending may also be linked to gendered processes of acculturation and socialisation. As we shall demonstrate, interpretations of women's involvement in theft have shifted subtly across time. Furthermore, the continued association of women with household management (whether as householders or domestic servants), with textiles and skills of needlecraft, and the importance of female networks in sustaining these roles, has profoundly shaped women's engagement in theft.

The thief, the fence and the pawnbroker

In October 1792 Martha Hall was found guilty at the Old Bailey of stealing 20 bed-sheets, a damask tablecloth and other items of clothing and linen from Henrietta Hungerford, whose house she was minding. The goods had been placed with a pawnbroker in exchange for money over a period of months and

Hall still had the receipts. She told the court that she had lost the use of one hand and 'was urged by the greatest distress'.[14] Hall's case can be identified as a typical example. As King has argued, women were more susceptible to theft accusations at certain points in their lifecycle: in their early twenties as they moved away from family for work, as a result of childrearing and dependent offspring in midlife, and in older age when widowed.[15] What is noteworthy, here, however, is the survival strategy that Hall adopted: identifying particular items belonging to her landlady as useful resources to pawn. In so doing, she was drawing upon her knowledge of systems of exchange, and of the monetary value of textiles and household objects.

Men and women have tended to be accused of the theft of slightly different types of objects and artefacts. Women have overwhelmingly been charged with stealing clothing, linen and household goods. Men as well as women were accused of stealing food items, watches, jewellery, money and, around the collieries of the Black Country, coal.[16] Women, however, were rarely accused of stealing livestock, tools, firewood or grain. In May 1911, 17-year-old Amy Checkley was accused of taking a man's suit, a watch, two teaspoons, two blouses and a shirt from the houses of her parents and family friends in Manchester, which she entered after obtaining keys under false pretences. Having refused to live at home, she had been working in a rag-sorting warehouse. Like Martha Hall in 1792, she pawned most of the items, but was wearing the blouses when she was arrested.[17] Clothes were not simply stolen to wear but to exchange as items of significant value that were easily convertible into cash.

Moreover, textiles were closely associated with women's expertise, knowledge and household role across all ranks and social classes. Well into the twentieth century, working-class wives and female servants were responsible for making, cleaning and repairing clothes (and linens), for handing them down to others and for adapting and converting them for other uses (making a tablecloth into a child's dress, for example). As some women moved into paid employment outside of their own homes in the nineteenth century – as seamstresses, domestic servants and as workers in the cotton and woollen mills – the gendered connection between women and textiles was maintained. In London, women's involvement in the sweated trades, through which they undertook piecework for low rates of pay, was based on their skills as needlewomen. Women were able to use their knowledge of the textiles and clothes trade to select items worth stealing and to dispose of stolen goods through networks of exchange to which they already had access. They might also 'disguise' stolen textiles, using their sewing skills, by converting their uses; further, such simple but ingenious adaptations might well have prevented the recovery of stolen goods (and hence prosecution). Indeed, the low statistics for poaching and theft of livestock by women may well have concealed women's involvement in disposing of stolen animals by preparing them as meat for the cooking pot.[18] Metal objects might be harder to dispose of since they were often indelibly marked: Sarah Boram was apprehended in April 1688 after she attempted to pawn a set of stolen gold buttons which had the name of their rightful owner engraved on the underside.[19]

As the desire for fashionable dress, accessories and household linen spread across all social ranks in the sixteenth century with the development of a more popular consumerism, the second-hand goods market expanded for those who could not afford to buy new commodities. These included both second-hand dealers and pawnbrokers as well as those whose dealing were more shady – as receivers (or fences) of stolen goods. As Beverley Lemire has argued 'a good wardrobe could be equivalent to a savings account, as articles of clothing were commonly used as a ready source of cash in emergencies'.[20] In the 1890s, when working-class wives and mothers were largely responsible for the household budget, the ability to 'borrow' foodstuffs or other items from neighbours or to pledge objects with a pawnbroker were all part of the common domestic economy of makeshifts. One's 'Sunday best' might be collected from the pawn-shop on a Saturday after the weekly pay-packet arrived, to be pawned again on Monday morning.[21] Indeed, it seems highly likely that many allegations of 'theft' arose from misunderstandings between women and neighbours or landladies over the loan of items for pawn. In 1792 Martha Hall may well have assumed that she had the right to temporarily place household goods from her lodgings with a pawnbroker; her accuser had originally held her 'in very good opinion' although there had been a later falling out, the reasons for which are not indicated. The pawning of soft furnishings and plate from rented rooms was often a contested area, involving disagreements over the meaning of ownership.[22] It is only in the second half of the twentieth century, which has been associated with increased affluence and the import of cheap ready-to-wear clothing from other parts of the world, that the fetishisation of the 'new' has led to the demise of the pawnshop as a resource for family survival.

The central role of pawnbrokers within the second-hand goods market meant that they often appeared in court as witnesses. 'Respectable' dealers keen to preserve trade reputations sometimes acted as whistle-blowers, returning stolen property directly to owners. Failure to report stolen property might lead to prosecution after receiving was criminalised in 1692. In March 1755 magistrate Edmund Tew summoned George and Margaret Taylor, who ran a pawnbroking and tailoring business in Sunderland, for buying a coat that they knew to be stolen; the coat was returned, the Taylors agreed to pay 'charges', and the matter was settled informally.[23] In their court statements, pawnbrokers and second-hand dealers were careful to stress that they questioned potential clients about the origins of goods (to varying degrees). Mary Bignal told the Old Bailey in 1750 that she ran 'a sort of a broker's shop and a rag shop' with her husband. Mary Williams, who owed her money, had attempted to sell a watch: 'I told her, I would not buy the watch, without she would tell me how she came by it, she said it was her husband's [...].'[24] Women formed a significant proportion of all those indicted for receiving stolen goods across the period (37 per cent in 1835 in England and Wales; see Figure 2.1), suggesting that their involvement in receiving was significant. Yet the overall number of those prosecuted for receiving remained small: only 7 per cent of females being tried on indictment for property offences in 1835, 3 per cent in 1875 and 8.6 per cent in 1938. Ultimately, it was extremely difficult to prosecute cases of receiving, since proof was required that goods were known to be stolen. Thus women's involvement in black markets was suspected but rarely subject to legal intervention.

Workplace theft and appropriation

If women's domestic expertise and involvement in systems of exchange for clothing, linens and foodstuffs created opportunities for theft, so too did their involvement in paid employment. Young women tended to go into residential domestic service in private homes in their early teens, leaving on marriage. However, the employment of older married woman in charring (cleaning), laundry work and in some cases as housekeepers was part of a continuum of domestic employment. 'Larceny by a servant' was often treated as a distinct category of offence, signifying the breach of trust that had been broken between employer and employee. In some court cases, servants had apparently used their place within the household to hoard objects before absconding. In May 1910 a warrant was issued for the arrest of a young woman named Annie Hanshall when her employer, a poor-rate collector in the parish of Dunkinfield, discovered she was missing one Friday morning along with a cash box and jewellery. Hanshall was apprehended in the centre of Manchester, with the missing goods packed in a tin trunk and the stolen money concealed in her stocking.[25] Some servants used their positions as household representatives in negotiations with tradesmen to acquire goods for themselves.

Yet there was often a blurred line between employers' expectations regarding servants' resourcefulness and employees' assumptions that they could 'borrow' objects within the household for their own purposes. In October 1750 a married servant, Elizabeth Smith, was found guilty of stealing and pawning a series of household goods from her master, a widower who lived with his adult son. Claiming a role as housekeeper, Smith argued in her defence that: 'what was pawned was for money for housekeeping; when I have asked him for money, he'd say, what have you done with the money you had before? [. . .] If you have not money, you have money's worth in your hands'.[26] That servants were vulnerable to mistreatment is indicated by the disputes over which the eighteenth-century magistrate Edmund Tew adjudicated. In May 1763 he summoned Ann, wife of Thomas Russel of Shields, to appear before him 'for turning away her servant Hannah Northouse and taking 14 shillings from her box'. The two parties were reconciled by the magistrate without further legal intervention.[27] In other cases where employers had withheld wages, Tew arranged for their payment.[28] Allegations of appropriation by servants were also commonly resolved within households, often by dismissal without references, rather than making recourse to the law. There were clear economic tensions in the master–servant relationship that were subject to negotiation both in and outside the courtroom.

Within the workroom and factory, disputes also arose over the appropriation by workers of materials that some may have viewed as simply 'perks' of the job. From 1777 to the mid-twentieth century the worsted industry employed its own paid inspectorate, which acted as a private police force to investigate and prosecute complaints of work-based theft, initially in the domestic system and subsequently in factories. Whilst women constituted three-quarters of worsted employees in Bradford (the centre of the industry), they made up only 15 per cent of formal prosecutions for workplace appropriation in the period 1844–76. Barry Godfrey has argued that this may have been linked to the more rigorous surveillance of female employees on the factory floor which, combined with occasionally bullying tactics by foremen, reduced opportunities and incentives for appropriation. Clearly, too, the worsted inspectorate chose to prosecute only those cases it thought it would win, as exemplary warnings to the rest of the workforce; it was assumed the magistracy was undesirably lenient towards young women who pleaded poverty as an excuse for their actions.[29] Workplace appropriation was, ultimately, more likely to be resolved through dismissal than the expense of prosecution. Prosecutions for embezzlement (the classic 'white collar' offence) have been predominantly male across the last 300 years given that women were, until comparatively recently, structurally excluded from positions of key financial responsibility in businesses other than family firms.

Pickpockets and shoplifters

The association of pickpocketing with forms of prostitution has been a point of reference across the centuries, occurring as a common narrative in the courtroom as well as being stereotyped in Defoe's *Moll Flanders*. Labouring women were able to make use of a culture of flirtation involving sexual barter or 'treating', in which they exchanged sexual favours for food, drink, goods or money. As with any other economic transaction, trust could be misplaced and intimacy became an opportunity for theft. The women who regularly appeared in the courts accused of stealing watches and rings from drunken men hoping for sex were not necessarily 'prostitutes' in a formal occupational sense. Rather, these women recognised the use of sexuality as a currency or resource within a patriarchal society in which women's bodies were themselves commodities. In 1896 Walter Peyne was accosted by two young women in Oxford Street, Manchester: 'They spoke to me and walked along with me [. . . they] then began messing about and I missed my purse [. . .].'[30] The scandal of a court appearance involving prostitution was in all likelihood a strong deterrent against the reporting of these thefts.

Methods of theft have changed in relation to technology and dress style (as have objects of desire). Obvious examples include the shift from 'cut-pursing' to 'pickpocketing' (as ownership of pocket watches increased), and more recently from handbag stealing to cheque and credit-card fraud. Pickpocketing was viewed as requiring skills of manual dexterity and swiftness associated with women and young people (hence Dickens's depiction of Fagin's gang of pickpocketing children in *Oliver Twist* of 1835). It was also associated with women's ability to trick men through flattery, hence John Gay's depiction of the character of 'Jenny Diver' in *The Beggar's Opera*: 'If any woman hath more art than another, to be sure, 'tis Jenny Diver. Though her fellow be never so agreeable, she can pick his pocket as coolly, as if money were her only pleasure [. . .].'[31]

The voluminous clothing that was fashionable for women in the eighteenth and nineteenth centuries enabled concealment of stolen goods – by both pickpockets and shoplifters. In November 1763 it was alleged that Elizabeth Green and her accomplice Richard Smith had made use of a range of tactics to dupe the shopkeepers and stallholders of Doncaster on market day. Two of the customers in a mercer's shop, William Heaton and John Kay, became suspicious of their activities. Heaton made a formal statement to committing magistrates:

> Smith ask'd Mr Atkinson to look at some black Callimanco and whilst he was showing him the said Callimanco the said Elizabeth Green lean'd upon the Counter with her Elbow & threw her long Cloak over a whole piece of Shalloon and took it up under her cloak. She then asked to look at some Buttons which were shewn her & whilst the Buttons were opening she look'd to the Window & said 'Yonder's Moll gone past and I must go after her', upon which she was going in a hurry out of the Shop [...] John Kay seized her as she was going out of the Door & told her she might well stay & take the Buttons with her upon which she endeavoured to shuffle the said piece of Shalloon on the Counter again but not doing it very readily this Informant took it from her hands.[32]

Depositions such as this are indicative of the procedures surrounding shop purchases as well as the means through which theft might be attempted. Items were produced by shopkeepers and laid out on the counter in response to customers' enquiries; they were discussed and a price negotiated. Where items were left lying around, shoplifters tended to resort to a 'grab and dash' method, as well as attempting to conceal them on their person. The changing techniques of selling in the nineteenth and twentieth centuries – in particular the open display of goods in bazaars, drapers' emporiums, department stores and, subsequently, self-service supermarkets – led to a further feminisation of shoplifting as an offence as well as to its increased prominence amongst women's property offences.

Theft by plebeian women was viewed as understandable if it could be explained as an isolated instance that resulted from ill-fortune, distress and hardship – as 'necessity' – in the seventeenth and eighteenth centuries. The increased prominence attached to 'respectability' by the Victorians led to a distinction between 'deserving' and 'undeserving' poor, the latter being increasingly constructed as a criminal and parasitic underclass, steeped in 'avarice'. This narrative explained a woman's habitual thieving in terms of the bad breeding and environment associated with the vicious poor.[33]

In the first half of the nineteenth century, however, the existence of a small number of middle-class 'shoplifters' began to provoke considerable anxiety and debate, precisely because it was unclear why, exactly, wealthy 'ladies' should steal. The 'genteel', by definition, could not be viewed as either 'vicious' or 'distressed'. Instead, an explanation for 'white-lace-collar' crime was increasingly provided in terms of mental instability. In April 1849 Miss Lydia Dixon, a music-teacher and daughter of a solicitor, was arrested after walking out of a large London draper's shop with a number of items concealed inside her shawl and stuffed down the front of her dress. A search of her lodgings revealed further stolen goods and a range of disguises. It was claimed in court that she was suffering from 'a brain fever' and she was imprisoned for one month, a severely reduced sentence given the value of the goods stolen.[34] The term '*klopé-manie*' was first used in 1816 by the Swiss doctor André Matthey. It was further conceptualised as *kleptomanie* (kleptomania in English usage) by the French forensic specialist C. C. H. Marc, who defined it as a 'distinctive, irresistible tendency to steal'.[35] As the century progressed it came to be viewed as a specifically 'female malady', a product of women's biological propensity to mania and hysteria, which was sexually charged. Where kleptomania was identified in men it was linked to trauma (sustained through injury or illness) rather than to natural disposition. According to the historian Tammy Whitlock, kleptomania had become an accepted defence in 'white-lace-collar' cases by the 1880s, and it was further mythologised as an 'Eve-like proclivity' through *fin de siècle* music hall and popular theatre.[36]

If otherwise respectable women could be reduced to hysterical wrecks in the shopping emporiums and department stores of England's major cities, part of the blame was also seen to lie with store owners, who used opulent and over-extravagant window displays to tempt female customers. Whilst perceptions of the retailer as a corrupt seducer of women reached their apogee in representations of the late nineteenth-century department store,[37] they were familiar concerns. Eighteenth-century commentators had lambasted women for their frivolous expenditure, whilst early nineteenth-century critics portrayed new methods of advertising and display as fraudulent.[38] However, anxieties about the vulnerability of bourgeois women concealed their very considerable roles as arbiters of taste: in selecting soft furnishings for the home and genteel dress for public occasions. It was partly through these displays – of a style that was understated, subtle and eminently 'civilised' rather than flamboyant and 'unrefined' – that middle-class status was projected to others. Acts of theft and dishonesty were clearly out of keeping with a middle-class identity that was constructed around gendered notions of virtue and purity; as Whitlock has argued, the kleptomania diagnosis provided an effective solution to the paradox of the lady thief.

As the criminologist Carol Smart has demonstrated, shoplifting was increasingly viewed as a gender-related offence in the twentieth century. Judicial statistics showed female convictions for larceny from shops and stalls equalling and then overtaking male convictions (46 per cent in 1950, 48 per cent in 1960, and 54 per cent of all convictions in 1970), making this category of offence unique amongst property offences (in which women's overall convictions had declined to 19.3 per cent).[39] Furthermore, as Figure 2.2 demonstrates, age profiles for convictions showed shoplifting to be associated with boys under 14 (the single largest group of convicted offenders) and mature women in their forties (the largest age group of convicted female offenders in 1950 and 1960); from the age of 21 onwards, women outnumbered men in convictions for this offence. Clearly, store proprietors have varied their prosecution strategies, some preferring to warn or bar shoppers as more cost-effective methods of dealing with wastage, thereby avoiding publicity. It is highly likely, however, that the statistics reflect the increasing employment of (often female) store detectives in retail outlets stocking clothes, food and cosmetics, as well as the 'type' of shopper that was likely to be suspected of thieving. London store detectives, interviewed in the late 1950s by the researchers Trevor Gibbens and Joyce

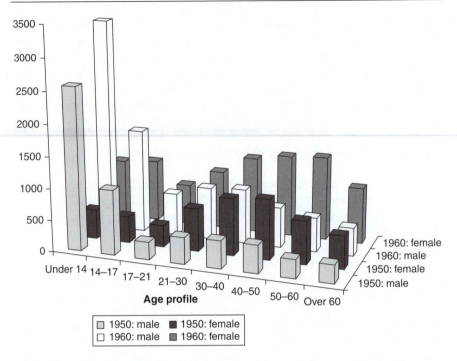

Figure 2.2 Larceny from shops and stalls: offences before magistrates (persons found guilty)
Source: BPP, Criminal Statistics.

Prince, believed that they could intuitively identify a shoplifter: 'a good store detective could "mark her subject" as soon as she comes in the door'. In some areas of the city, store detectives 'said they would particularly "watch" any foreign-looking woman', assuming that other European cultures were intrinsically more dishonest. However, 'all were agreed that there were many more women than men shoplifting'.[40] Thus the stereotyping of the middle-aged woman as shoplifter and her prominence within official statistics were mutually reinforcing.

Forensic psychologists discussed and debated the 'kleptomania diagnosis' into the twentieth century, some associating women's alleged propensity to shoplift with altered mental states arising from gynaecological problems, the menopause, premenstrual tension, pregnancy, sexual excitement and frustration. Thus the 'myth' of the female kleptomaniac continued to hold cultural resonance, although practitioners and researchers were expressing scepticism in its use as a defence by the mid-twentieth century. Writing in 1962, Gibbens and Prince (both psychiatrists) argued that there was a significantly higher incidence of mental illness amongst women prosecuted for shoplifting than amongst the female population as a whole. In most cases, however, women were suffering from forms of neurosis, including depression, rather than personality disorder and compulsive behaviour (which the older term 'kleptomania' had suggested). Most significantly, Gibbens and Prince suggested that women were more likely to be diagnosed as mentally ill for a range of social and cultural reasons. The 'social cage' of femininity, in which women were responsible for the care of the family whilst being in a position of financial dependency on husbands, meant that women were subject to far greater daily stresses.[41] Women were more likely than men to seek medical help for anxiety, whilst solicitors actively encouraged them to do so since it could be used as mitigation in court (reinforcing popular understandings of 'kleptomania'). The relationship between anxiety and shoplifting, possibly as a 'call for help', was spelt out in many examples cited in the report:

> *Case 33.* A woman of 52 stole food from a multiple store, a shirt and socks from another and two ashtrays and children's clothes from a department store. She said she had no reason to steal but it was just the idea she was getting them easily; she had seen others do it. She had worked until one year ago; since then there was no shortage of money but she had felt depressed and bored and had slept badly. Her mother and herself had worrying natures and two years before she had had a hysterectomy. Some years before a son had been killed in her presence in an air-raid; she had felt suicidal for a time after [...].[42]

Thus the reasons for women's theft were complex and multi-faceted. Gibbens and Prince argued that poverty was unlikely to be a determining factor although economic pressures were reflected in patterns of behaviour. Commonly 'the housewife' took 'something extra' when making an ordinary shopping expedition, perhaps as an impulsive tactic to eke out the family income.[43] Their emphasis on the relationship between the social and the psychological began to move analyses away from purely biological models.

The criminologist Pat Carlen presents women's involvement in stealing in the 1980s as the result of a series of experiences including poverty, addiction, the rejection of conventional gender norms, as well as women's 'strong commitment to obtaining a decent standard of living and to defending their domestic and personal space by *any* means within their power'.[44] Yet this interpretation of women's involvement in shoplifting as rational agency has nevertheless been accompanied by continued references to 'kleptomania' in the tabloid press; the increased profile of young women in their twenties in prosecution statistics in the final decades of the twentieth century has also led to the linking of shoplifting with bulimia, anorexia and other gendered forms of mental illness.[45] Perceptions of the female offender as a psychiatric aberration have, thus, proved long-lived.

Frauds and tricksters

If the 'kleptomania' diagnosis had suggested that women's theft might be hysterical and pathological, other persistent cultural myths marked women as essentially untrustworthy because of a disposition towards vanity, wiliness and trickery. In 1615 the misogynist pamphleteer Joseph Swetnam had argued that 'Commonly women are the most part of the forenoone painting themselves, and frizling their haires, and prying in their glasse like Apes to prancke up themselves in their gawdies; like Poppets, or like the Spider which weaves a fine web to hang the flie'. It was assumed that a certain sort of predatory woman used dress and cosmetics not only to trap men into marriage, but also to defraud others out of goods and money, by pretending to be of higher rank or status. Swetnam also praised 'wise, virtuous and honest women'; the issue, for him, was how to tell them apart.[46] Writing over 300 years later, the criminologist Otto Pollak made similar claims in 1950, identifying the 'greater proneness of woman to deceit' as a 'female characteristic' rooted in biology.[47] In assessing continuity and change, however, it is important to pay attention to historical specificity. In this final section of the chapter we shall examine the shifting meanings and contexts in which femininity has been stereotyped in terms of fraud and deception across time. We shall discuss once again the significance of clothing and dress, this time in relation to the evaluation of honour and creditability.

Until their repeal in 1604 in England, sumptuary laws had restricted the wearing of luxury fabrics to elite groups within the social order. Whilst clothing fashions increasingly came to be associated with self-expression and individualism in the seventeenth century, there were those who mourned the loss of these direct indicators of rank. Henry Fielding complained that 'the meanest Person who can dress himself clean, may in some Degree mix with his Betters'.[48] Adapting one's outward appearance could clearly become a route to social mobility. Dress was still a marker of wealth, status and gentility; and taste in clothes was used by individuals to classify others. Manners, physical carriage and deportment were also indicators of gentility. At the same time, however, the reliability of this classification was constantly open to question. As Faramerz Dabhoiwala has commented, there was a 'central paradox' in the construction of female reputations: it was assumed that one should be able to tell a woman's status and honour from her dress and bearing, and yet lack of virtue could be far too easily disguised.[49]

For much of the period of study, household goods were purchased on credit rather than through cash. Reputation and status were vital to gain the necessary trust and credit amongst trades people, to make purchases. In small communities it was vital to preserve one's name as honest amongst neighbours. Whilst a great deal of the secondary literature on defamation has focused on sexual slander, tried in the church courts, it is important to note that women also complained to higher authorities when they were slandered as 'thieves' and 'cheats'. Such cases were often resolved through arbitration. In 1754 magistrate Edmund Tew summoned 'Sarah Stead, widow of Sunderland, for declaring that Margaret Longill sold a pair of boots which she knew to be stolen'. In 1757 he 'granted a special warrant against Isabel Hall of Shields, widow, for defaming Jane Board, calling her whore and thief and declaring she would prove both'.[50] Both cases were settled without further legal action. Notions of economic creditability and moral reputation were closely intertwined; it was important to defend one's name to assure both economic and social standing within a community.

Outside of immediate neighbourhoods and small face-to-face communities, appearance and demeanour were the primary means through which trust and creditability were assessed. Indeed, opportunities for theft and the successful disposal of stolen goods were often dependent on masquerade and impersonation. Arriving in Doncaster in 1753, Elizabeth Green and John Smith were keen to display their assumed gentility, which was, in turn, closely noted by residents. The innkeeper's wife told the court how Elizabeth, 'first pulling on a clean handkerchief apron & cap [... said] she was going into the market & loved to be clean'.[51] 'Gentility' enabled women to enter shops selling expensive commodities and facilitated proximity to desired goods. Similarly, posing as a servant who had been given goods to pawn by a master or mistress was one common response to a pawnbroker's searching questions, since it offered a satisfactory explanation as to how one had acquired goods beyond one's station in life. Servants might also make use of their employers' identities to acquire goods for which they would not themselves have received credit. Most acts of theft involved some form of duplicity or masquerade as part of the process.

Until well into the nineteenth century, popular knowledge of offending behaviour was disseminated through cheap criminal biographies that were sold on the streets in pamphlet form and, subsequently, collated together in works such as *The Malefactor's Register* and *The Newgate Calendars*. The descriptions of female thieves and rogues contained in these narratives often focused on the activities of 'counterfeit ladies', who used gentility as a cover to defraud. Mary Carleton, who posed as 'a German Princess' in order to rise above her humble origins, came to public prominence when she was tried for bigamy in 1663. Numerous pamphlets followed her moral decline as she was transported for stealing a silver tankard in 1671 and was finally hung two years later for the theft of plate.[52] The case of the 'German Princess' clearly influenced Defoe's *Moll Flanders*. Defoe's 'Moll' not only passes herself off as a woman of fortune to contract a bigamous marriage, but also uses dress as a pickpocketing trick to escape suspicion: 'on these Adventures we always went very well Dress'd, and I had very good Cloathes on, and a Gold Watch by my side, as like a Lady as other Folks'.[53] The con-woman and shoplifter, Moll Hawkins, executed for theft in 1703, was described in similar terms in a well-known collection of criminal biographies, first published in 1714:

> She went upon the Question-Lay, which is putting herself into a good handsome Dress, like some Exchange Girl, then she takes an empty Band-box in her Hand, and passing for a Milliner's or Sempstress's 'Prentice, she goes early to a Person of Quality's House, and knocking at the door, she asks the Servant if the Lady is stirring yet [...]. for if she was, she had brought home, according to order, the Suit of Knots (or what else the Devil puts in her Head) which her Ladyship had bespoke over Night; then the Servant going up Stairs to acquaint the Lady of this Message, she in the mean time robs the House, and goes away without an answer.[54]

Men could clearly be frauds too, but women were assumed to adopt a particular mode of duplicity. This was spelt out most clearly in a text that purported to narrate the life of 'Mal [sometimes known as Moll] Cutpurse', the cross-dressing fence and pickpocket. Her ability to combine manly 'resolution' with 'female subtlety in the wily Arts and ruses of that Sex' was commented on with some admiration.[55] As a 'celebrity' criminal of the later eighteenth century, Miss Fanny Davies was depicted as duping a series of male and female lovers by

Figure 2.3 Illustration from Anon., *An Authentic Narrative of Miss Fanny Davies* (London: R. Jameson, 1786) © British Library Board. All Rights Reserved (613.k.12(11.))

passing herself off as both a woman of beauty and modesty 'not much lower than the angels' and 'a very smart youth, deemed too young to be bearded' (see Figure 2.3); in male dress she then took to the Essex roads, where she carried out a series of highway robberies before she was sentenced to hang at the Chelmsford Assizes in 1786.[56] The popularity of these narratives is indicative of anxieties that 'reputation' could be refashioned and negotiated.

Feme-covert to *femme fatale*

Trades people also had to grapple with the problem of a wife's technical inability to make financial contracts (until changes in the law as a result of the Married Women's Property Acts of 1870 and 1882). According to Sir William Blackstone, writing in 1765, a woman's autonomy – legal and economic – was subsumed by her husband through the principle of coverture:

> By marriage, the husband and wife are one person in law, that is, the very being or legal existence of the woman is suspended during the marriage, or at least incorporated and consolidated into that of her husband: under whose whole wing, protection and *cover*, she performs every thing; and that is therefore called in our law-french a *feme-covert*.[57]

This acted both to protect and constrain. Following the doctrine of '*feme covert*', it was argued in the courts that a married woman could not be found guilty of a theft if her husband was a co-defendant. Peter King has further suggested that '*feme covert*' created a grey area surrounding married women, which meant that they were more likely than single women to evade prosecution in the late eighteenth and early nineteenth centuries.[58] Such a legal position rendered married women to a degree 'untrustworthy' – but shopkeepers could not afford to ignore their custom. Whilst married women could not contract debt in their own name, they were nevertheless permitted to contract for 'necessary goods' using their husband's name, and for which he then became liable.[59] What was considered 'necessary', however, was dependent on status and here, once again, shopkeepers found themselves making informal calculations regarding the relationship between appearance and social rank. For some, new silks, gloves and bonnets might be luxuries whilst, for others, they were essential items within the daily business of keeping up appearances. Once again, women's creditability was assessed with regard to levels of gentility. However, as Whitlock has persuasively argued, there was often a fine line between debt and fraud, particularly when wives were separated from husbands and were attempting to make use of 'the law of necessaries' as a way of gaining alimony.[60]

The popular culture of the early eighteenth century, voiced in canting ballads, associated thieves with bravado as they celebrated 'triumph over life's adversities, and especially getting something for nothing'.[61] Similarly, the pamphlets relating to female 'rogues' evinced a qualified admiration for their ability to trick through 'women's wiles'. An increasingly moral discourse came to dominate representations of criminality in the late eighteenth century at the same time that a middle-class femininity was being delineated in terms of purity and virtue. The attributes that had been associated with an active but feminine duplicity were simply recast in the nineteenth century as weakness: first as moral weakness (vice) or victimhood (poverty) and then, in the case of kleptomania, as a form of hysteria or medical infirmity. Women as a whole were viewed as 'less disposed to crime' because of maternal and caring instincts which suited them for a domestic role.[62]

In the 1920s, concerns about female fraudsters began to resurface once again, this time in the context of uncertainty about gender relations that followed the First World War. The popular press voiced concerns about 'idle gold-diggers' and 'flappers "on the make"' as a consequence of 'the shortage of marrying manhood caused by the war'. These were young female 'crooks', who had drifted to London aiming to seduce men and defraud them of their money.[63] It was argued that 'the most successful of trade swindlers are women' because men tended 'to extend towards "the gentle sex" that deference which serves to stupify his common sense and dull his eye-sight'.[64] The belief that men were the naïve victims of women's trickery can be explained in terms of an antifeminist backlash that followed the war, women's suffrage and the appearance in 1919 of the first women lawyers and MPs. The former Scotland Yard detective Cecil Bishop was forthright in his sensationalist condemnation of women's skills of trickery and deception as a result of the 'equality' fought for by 'misguided extremists'. Writing in 1931 he blamed women entirely for an apparent hike in the criminal statistics: 'many efficient gangs, both in London and the Provinces, are led by women, who exploit their sex to maintain control of the men they have gathered around them'.[65] Recognition of women's rights in the twentieth century has, hence, been accompanied by the stereotyping of the predatory *femme fatale* as thief and seductress.

Conclusion

This chapter has argued, following recent scholarship, that women's involvement in theft – as well as the meanings placed on it by contemporaries – can only be understood in the context of their prominent role within a growing consumer culture. Theft was, ultimately a gendered activity. Women were accused of stealing items that were linked to their domestic roles as wives, mothers, and servants; women recognised the value of household goods, made use of opportunities that arose in familiar circumstances, and possessed the knowledge and skills to dispose of household goods effectively. Similarly the gendering of space was reflected in the locations in which women stole: shops, stalls, home or street rather than warehouses or workshops. At the same time, too, gendered discourses served to sexualise women thieves and to depict them as duplicitous by nature. Ultimately, these forms of representation acted as a critique of women's significance as lynchpins within both consumer culture and the household economy.

Clearly the profile of women's prosecuted theft has changed over time, most obviously in relation to the diminution of violence; this can be viewed as a result of the social and cultural construction of a more 'passive' femininity from the nineteenth century onwards; it may also be linked to the demise of the Bloody Code, which affected the decisions of prosecutors. Technological and social change also transformed the methods of appropriation as well as specific objects of desire. We have shown, too, that the nineteenth-century medicalisation of women's thieving, through the kleptomania diagnosis, increasingly presented women's acquisitiveness as both unnatural and unfeminine. This rhetoric was very different from the broadly celebratory stance of the popular criminal biographies of the eighteenth century. Undoubtedly women's legal position also shifted significantly. The notion of *feme-covert*, in which women's economic interests were represented by her husband, was replaced with the extension of liberal citizenship and rights (including the right to contract) to all women, whether married or single. Yet this legal acquisition of autonomy has not obscured or replaced women's economic, social or cultural responsibilities in terms of household and the domestic sphere.

3

Women and Violence

Historically, women have been a clear minority of individuals tried for violent offences. For example, only 9 per cent of those accused of murder at Surrey Assizes between 1660 and 1800 were female.[1] The key historical questions this raises revolve not only around how men's and women's social practice has differed in its uses of violence, but also around how their acts have been differentially recognised by the criminal justice system.

As with property offences, the gendered social contexts of women's lives have often coloured the circumstances in which they have committed criminal violence; family and neighbourhood have frequently formed the background to women's violent offences. Historical and criminological studies have reiterated how, across time, violence has been a common strategy in masculine social practice, in particular to pursue interpersonal disputes and defend male honour. Nevertheless, across the whole chronology we are discussing, although in far smaller numbers, women have engaged in similar kinds of violent social practices as men, and they have been prosecuted across the same range of violent crime, including piracy and highway robbery. Women have also been the majority of offenders in other violent crimes, such as infanticide or witchcraft. Technically, infanticide (the killing of an infant by its mother) is a crime that only a woman can commit.

One approach to violence often adopted by dominant cultures is to see it as deviance, harmful either to the social order or to individuals, or indeed to both. Some researchers, from a range of academic disciplines also take this view.[2] This has certainly been the perspective from which the criminal justice system has criminalised certain violent acts since the seventeenth century, though its definition of social harm has shifted over time. The harm caused by violence was assumed to vary according to the gender of the perpetrator, which has affected how seriously the violence was treated as crime. For example, even during periods when the legal penalty on infanticide was exceptionally severe, in many (but by no means all) cases the sentence was mitigated by the substitution of the lesser offence of concealment of birth.[3]

Another valuable research perspective sees violence as performative, in other words an emphatic means of social interaction and therefore expressive of particular gendered subject positions.[4] A verbally and physically violent neighbourhood quarrel, so frequently the cause of working-class women's appearance in Victorian police courts, is an obvious illustration. Some analyses separate 'expressive' violence from 'instrumental' violence, that is violence for gain, for example in the course of a robbery.[5] However, as our example of women pirates makes clear, even the most instrumental violence derives meaning from its social and cultural context and therefore shifts in significance over place and time. Violence committed by women can therefore be expected to be coloured by the constraints and opportunities available to them within an historically specific gender order, which denies them power in some social arenas but accords them particular (if subordinated) competences and knowledges and may even allow them licence for certain kinds of actions. Verbal violence, in the guise of scolding or barratry, was a recognised offence in the medieval and early modern periods, though less often prosecuted after the seventeenth century. Women were the majority of those accused of scolding, but this in itself illustrated how important they were in adjudicating social reputations through verbal censure and gossip.[6] Women have also used violence in food riots and in other kinds of protest.[7]

Although at first sight a fairly self-explanatory term, violence turns out on further investigation to be more complex. Distinctions between force and violence, between physical, verbal, emotional or indeed sexual violence have been debated by historians.[8] Across time, the criminal justice system has most easily recognised physical violence (along with the more physically violent forms of sexual violence) as a criminal offence, although, as we have argued, it has varied in the extent to which it sought to punish such violence. Before the nineteenth century a good deal of physical violence was perceived as a matter between individuals. At this period, before the establishment of modern police forces, all prosecutions were brought personally by the aggrieved or injured individual and, hence, very often the resort to law was just one of a wider range of informal and formal strategies for settling the matter. It was from the early nineteenth century that much more interpersonal violence, certainly outside the home, was more seriously regarded as a general social threat.[9]

In fact, across the whole chronology we are considering, the law has been selective and historically specific in its treatment of violence as crime. Any historical investigation of violent *crime* needs to recognise how violence has been differently criminalised at different periods. In this chapter we therefore look not only at arguably more expressive violence such as murder and assault, but also at offences such as piracy and highway robbery where the violence is apparently chiefly instrumental (perpetrated for gain). Furthermore, we take account of how and when the law has criminalised practices such as verbal violence and witchcraft – effectively causing physical harm by the manipulation of supernatural forces. Witchcraft is perhaps the most stark example of historically changing legal definitions of violent crime – a capital offence for which the majority of those punished in the sixteenth and seventeenth centuries were women – but which was removed from the statute book in 1736. Nevertheless, even apparently greater continuities in the treatment of physical or sexual violence as crime can be shown to be far more differentiated and uneven.

Dominant ideologies of gender have positioned violence by women as highly symbolically transgressive. Although historically far more women have come before the courts for property offences, women's violent crime has not infrequently acquired high(er) cultural visibility. For one thing, the law as a discursive system has included some exemplary punishments. Whilst a husband murdering his wife was liable for hanging, a wife murdering her husband was guilty of the offence of petty treason and liable before 1790 to be burned at the stake.[10] Her transgression was not simply an interpersonal one, but (like the servant killing his master, or the subject betraying his monarch) threatened the whole symbolic social order. Some historians and criminologists have argued that women criminals have been invariably heavily punished by the criminal justice system for a doubled transgression of both social and gender norms.[11] However, work on both severe and petty violence by women is demonstrating lighter sentencing in many cases. We take up the gender issues around punishment in Chapter 7, finding that criminal justice is only one of a range of formal and informal fields of gender regulation. It is within the historical complexities and contradictions in cultures of penality that explanations are to be found for the variability of treatment of violent women before the law.

The dominance of masculinity has required that femininity should frequently be characterised by weakness or instability, but this in itself has often enabled courts to perceive women's violence as an unsurprising outcome of their weaker natures and therefore less socially threatening. Nevertheless, those same assumptions about weakness and instability, combined as they have been with anxieties about the disorderliness of female sexuality, have also made some violent women seem particularly disturbing. Historical studies point to many cases where a woman has received seemingly disproportionately punitive treatment compared to male offenders, either directly at the hands of the law, or by extra-judicial punishment in the form of ostracism in society or in the press, or through the proliferation of harmful effects on children, family and friends. Our discussion below of women tried for murder, for example, will show some marked contrasts in the criminal justice response to women tried for apparently similar kinds of lethal violence.

Identifying and explaining this unevenness in the experience of women violent offenders before the law is not a straightforward process, and given the difficulties of many of the available historical records is often simply not possible. The criminal law is a flexible discursive system which applies general principles to particular cases and the outcomes for women offenders have frequently depended on a complex interaction between the specific circumstances of their offence and character, the current priorities of the criminal justice system, and wider prevailing cultural concerns over the gender order. The rest of this chapter will review different violent offences for which women have been brought before the criminal law, both those like witchcraft where the majority of offenders have been female, as well as physical violence from common assault to adult murder. We will also consider some of the verbal violence that underpinned civil actions for slander and defamation in the ecclesiastical courts. As well as the broad sociohistorical shifts across the chronology we are considering, which provided the social context for the violence which women committed (or were accused of), our discussion will also take into account historical changes in the criminal justice system which shaped its priorities and response to the women who were brought to court.

Witchcraft

The far greater majority of witchcraft trials in England and Wales took place before the period we consider here, in the late sixteenth and early seventeenth centuries as well as those cases in the late 1640s instigated by the activities of 'witchfinder' Matthew Hopkins. This review of women and violent crime since 1660 therefore considers a period when witchcraft prosecutions were decreasing. The phenomenon of early modern witch trials had arisen out of the confluence of three factors. Firstly, both elite and popular cultures accepted that supernatural causes had physical effects in the material world. Though the patterns of belief in different social sectors varied, there was sufficient overlap for witchcraft to be seen as the cause of harm within both elite and popular social imaginaries.[12] Dominant views combined this with profound anxieties about the forces of evil in the world, that were played out through the complex religious reformations of the period.[13] Secondly, women were thought of as the weaker sex and also particularly unruly and disruptive through the effects of their sexuality. Women were the majority of those accused of witchcraft not because of simple misogyny, but because they were ideologically positioned as the 'weakest links' through which the forces of evil could set to work in the world.[14] Furthermore, there is evidence that some women at least did accept the dominant view and found witchcraft a plausible explanation for their emotional distress and desire to harm.[15] If we take seriously the statements made by many accused witches as a description of a mental world, it seems likely that in their comparatively weak social and material positions some women did experience meetings with the devil in divers forms such as that of a black dog, did practice the rituals of everyday magic (*maleficium*) and, to the extent that harm was the intent, can be held to have committed violence. Thirdly, fluctuations in demographic and economic growth had increased social divisions and tensions in local communities. Although the trials of the 1640s were encouraged by outside agency, all Early Modern witch trials originated in personal accusations. Women were involved not only as the accused but also as witnesses and accusers, and as semi-formal participants in the criminal justice process as juries of matrons who searched for witches' marks. Women had some authority and agency in witch trials though this was to a greater or lesser extent exercised at the behest of powerful men.[16] Not all accused witches were marginal women, but many were in vulnerable positions, often outside family when their material situations were being made particularly fragile due to the wider effects of social and economic change.[17]

From the 1670s witchcraft disappeared as a prosecuted crime because the confluence of historical factors which had created the situation in which witch trials flourished slowly altered. The last execution for witchcraft in England took place no later than 1685 and the last indictment in 1717. Firstly, economic growth and the development of statutory poor relief not only provided some help for the materially insecure but also significantly changed relationships between the poorer and better off in local communities. Relief became institutionalised through parish vestries rather than relying entirely on ad hoc charity and importuning. Secondly, elite views on the supernatural shifted and the developing criminal justice system became rather more materialist in its views of the nature of proof and evidence. Popular beliefs in the supernatural and the effectiveness of *maleficium* persisted, arguably into the late nineteenth century at least, but the criminal justice system was progressively less willing to give them credence in court. Owen Davies argues that the changing attitudes and practices of local Justices of the Peace, who were the first point of access to the criminal justice process in many areas and who, as unpaid officials of some social standing had a good deal of discretion as to how they dealt with particular cases, were especially important in curtailing the access of potential prosecutors to the courts.[18] Gender inequality and dominant assumptions of women's weakness and unruliness hardly weakened. Neither did the frequent social marginality and poverty of women outside familial support systems. However, a greater elite confidence in rational and scientific understandings of how the world worked made the cunning women and men who practised everyday magic seem far less threatening.

Street robbers and wicked ladies

Because London's streets had been designated as 'highways',[19] a good deal of what was tried in London as highway robbery was banal street crime and a small but significant minority of offenders were women. The Old Bailey Sessions Papers show that women were around 10 per cent of those tried for highway robbery between the late seventeenth and early nineteenth centuries. For example, during the 25 years from 1809 and 1834, there were 129 women amongst the 1139 individuals tried for this offence; 114 of these women were tried for the robbery of a male victim. Of these the greater majority (85) were accused along with other people; 52 with one or more other women, 15 with one or more other men and 18 with groups of both men and women. Overall these were mundane London street robberies which followed similar patterns across this period. There are a few examples of women who literally stole the clothes from the backs of women and children. In 1692 Elisabeth Lee was tried for taking the coat from a five-year-old boy who had 'straggle(d) abroad alone into the Fields' in Stepney. She was detected very quickly by someone who met the child then saw her with the coat under her apron. She was found guilty and transported.[20] Given the liveliness of the trade in second-hand clothing, there were plenty of opportunities to sell or pawn a child's coat, though doubtless for much less than the 5s it was valued at in court.[21] However, as the figures cited above show, men were most frequently the victims of street robbery cases involving women at the Old Bailey. Some of these incidents were perfunctory muggings, especially where the thieves were working in groups. In 1726 William Whittle was walking near Whitechapel in the early hours when he was seized by Frances Blacket and two men. They threatened his life if he did not give up his property and Frances Blacket rifled his pockets as the men held him. She made off with his watch and 6d, but was recognised when she tried to pawn the watch. When Whittle came making enquiries, the pawnbroker easily directed him to her usual alehouse where she was caught. The watch was located at another pawnbrokers.[22]

Numbers of these robberies were associated with drink and the lure of sex. Tony Henderson comments that London prostitutes often solicited in pairs.[23] It seems that women also found it advantageous to steal in pairs. Mary Mukes and Jane Dennis colluded to rob Isaac Eastwick of over £7 in 1727. He was out drinking with his cousin. Jane Dennis invited them forcibly into a gin shop where she and Mukes were drinking – according to Eastwick, dragging him in by his collar. By the time he left the shop they had quarrelled and he had been relieved of his money.[24] In 1809 sailor Benjamin Burd had just collected his wages of over £50 in banknotes and had a bit to drink. Late that evening, he was knocked down in the street by Ann Kennington and Matilda Dyer, two women in their thirties, and his banknotes taken. They, too, were fairly easily traced since all banknotes at that period were numbered.[25] In 1780 eighteen-year-old apprentice Robert Carter was walking down Drury Lane at ten o'clock when he was accosted by Jane Morris, who rifled his pockets and took his money and his watch. He called for help but was not answered, then followed her to her room and, with the help of a neighbour, retrieved some of the money, but they had to wait till the following day to recover the half-guinea which she had swallowed. Her story was that he had been drinking gin with her in her room. In the event she was found guilty of the robbery only and escaped with a whipping.[26] The connections between drink, sex and robbery are clear in the patterns of these women's offences, so is their readiness to use fairly low-level violence to hustle the valuables from lone men. Sometimes, particularly when men were included in the group of muggers, the violence could be more serious. In 1718 James Martin was mugged and cut with a sword when he ran into soldier Joseph Shannon and Elizabeth George in St James' Park (a well known pick-up ground for prostitutes).[27] These are all London examples, and in the huge capital city not only was prostitution a comparatively viable living for numbers of women, there were also more developed networks of professional thieves than were common at a time when most property theft was comparatively unorganised.[28] Indeed, many of these examples are comparatively opportunist.

We have reviewed women's property theft in detail in Chapter 2. The key points relevant to this discussion of women's violent crime are, firstly, the consistent presence of a minority of women amongst street thieves, who often worked in small groups and were prepared to treat their victims in a pretty heavy-handed way for the risky profits to be gained from stolen clothes, jewellery or cash. Secondly, there are obvious associations with street theft, drink, prostitution and therefore social marginality. The patterns of street crime in the huge metropolis cannot necessarily be generalised across the country, not only because of London's particular social and demographic profile but also because of prevailing legal definitions. These Old Bailey highway robbery cases illustrate 'everyday' street crime and contrast with the more slippery historical figure of the mounted, armed highwaywoman, who has nevertheless gained a persistent place in the popular cultural imagination since the late seventeenth and eighteenth century.

The disruptions of the Civil War period and the increase of trade and road transport thereafter encouraged the growth of highway robbery in the later seventeenth century. The 'gentleman' highwayman who could afford a good horse and pistols added style to the conduct of robbery with violence and produced a cultural stereotype which has informed popular romantic narratives ever since. How much more intriguing, therefore, when the bold and daring highway robber was a cross-dressed woman? There are a clutch of seventeenth- and early eighteenth-century tales of highwaywomen, at least some of which have external historical verification. We mentioned the 1786 career of Fanny Davies in Chapter 2. A not dissimilar story of the last months and execution of Jenny Voss (alias Jenny Roberts) appears in the Newgate Ordinary's account of 1684. She had been convicted for the theft of a silver tankard. This was one condemned woman for whom pleading the belly (claiming pregnancy) deferred rather than avoided execution.[29] No pardon was forthcoming, no doubt because of her extensive criminal history and previous convictions. Her existence and her exploits, including assisting in the theft of the Lord Chancellor's mace, are corroborated in other Newgate memoirs. One highly sensationalised source claims to recount her biography, beginning with a teenage career as a confidence trickster in the company of a band of gypsies and a period as a fearless, cross-dressed, armed and mounted highway robber in the West Country.[30]

Marcy Clay (alias Jenny Fox) is the anti-heroine of another anonymous pamphlet of 1665 which recounts a similar criminal biography. Beginning as an accomplished shoplifter in London she later took to the 'more manly debaucheries' of cross-dressed highway robbery. The pamphlet comments on her physical courage and skill with sword and pistol. This highwaywoman was also condemned to die at Tyburn after returning to shoplifting in London, but defied the hangman by poisoning herself. Apparently many spectators gathered to view her on her deathbed.[31] Alexander Smith's *A Complete History of the Lives and Robberies of the most Notorious Highwaymen* (1719), a source of dubious historical accuracy, also described Joan Bracey, daughter of a wealthy farmer, who partnered her common-law husband, Edward Bracey, in numerous highway robberies and ran an inn in Bristol before eventually being caught and hanged around 1685. Perhaps the most detailed and enduring legend of an upper-class highwaywoman is that of the so-called 'Wicked Lady' who robbed and murdered near St Albans in the mid-seventeenth century. The most frequently cited candidate is Catherine Ferrers, who married into the prominent royalist Fanshawe family in 1648 when aged only 13. Although the historical evidence for Catherine Ferrers as a highwaywoman is pretty dubious, the legend has become firmly embedded in popular culture. Catherine's malevolent ghost has been sighted on several occasions. In the mid-twentieth century the story underpinned two novels and also the highly successful, melodramatic and lavishly dressed film adaptation of one of these which thrilled cinema audiences amidst the post-war austerity of 1945.[32]

Of this collection of highwaywomen, the best evidenced is Jenny Voss, though indeed her highway robberies are less well documented than her other crimes. These stories all follow an accepted narrative form, a criminal biography which begins with the success of an accomplished thief followed by detection and death, often on the gallows. Cross-dressing, and the sexual attraction to other women of the apparently handsome young 'man' combine (in most of these examples) with the initiation of the highwaywoman into her profession by a male lover – the criminality and violence of the highwaywoman is always eroticised. She assumed the male identity of highway robber through appropriately gendered dress and also by the masculine attributes of bravery, recklessness, skill at arms and a readiness to kill or injure. It is far from impossible that some women were attracted by the profits and adventure of highway robbery. Nevertheless, the pamphlets and the legends of the highwaywoman exceed these historical possibilities. Together they build a sensational narrative which draws on an enduring cultural fascination with cross-dressing, gender play and the eroticisation of female violence. There is, however, another small group of better documented criminally violent women whose activities also resonate with such themes – these are the female pirates of the early eighteenth century.

Women pirates of the Caribbean

The early eighteenth century saw growth in maritime trade and the movement of peoples around the Atlantic world. At the same time the governance of colonies in the Americas was comparatively light and European powers recurrently warred over the control of territories and trade. Especially after the War of the Spanish Succession ended with the Treaty of Utrecht in 1718, numbers of discharged sailors were out in search of lucrative careers. Privateering (the government licensing of private vessels to attack and seize ships and cargos of hostile states) was a highly profitable occupation in the Caribbean. Unsurprisingly, piracy (unlicensed theft of and from vessels by force of arms) also flourished. Historians have identified a Golden Age of West Atlantic piracy between 1710 and 1729, until governments were able to take firmer control of the seaways. Linebaugh and Rediker argue that piracy was a component of a nascent culture of liberty that later found democratic political expression in the founding of the United States.[33] Amongst the many pirates who took advantage of this historical window of opportunity for profitable violent criminal activity were a few women.[34] Mary Harley was found guilty of piracy along with six men in Virginia in 1726, but was released whilst the men were hanged. Mary Crickett was another woman sentenced to death for piracy along with male companions in 1729.[35] Two women pirates in particular gained widespread notoriety, both at the time and in subsequent histories. The fame of Anne Bonny and Mary Read was ensured when, three years after their capture and conviction, their stories were published in *A General History of the Robberies and Murders of the Most Notorious Pyrates* (1724) by Captain Charles Johnson (thought to be a pseudonym for Daniel Defoe). This account is in respects verifiable against the transcript of their trial proceedings and other sources.

Anne Bonny was originally from Ireland, the illegitimate daughter of a lawyer and his housemaid. Mary Read was English, another illegitimate child, born of an affair after her mother's sailor husband had deserted her. Both were raised as boys – Anne Bonny to disguise her parentage and Mary Read as a means of passing her off as an earlier legitimate child of her mother's. Anne Bonny's father eventually moved to Virginia and became a merchant and plantation owner, though he fell out with his daughter over her marriage to a poor sailor.

Mary Read went into service as a boy in her teens and then joined the army in the Netherlands and served as a soldier until she married a man from her regiment. Both these women found themselves in New Providence (later Nassau) in the Bahamas in 1719. New Providence was a haven for pirates, who assembled there in particular numbers that year due to a general amnesty issued by the governor in the hope of controlling piracy. Bonny had arrived there with her sailor husband but soon began an affair with the colourful pirate Calico Jack Rackam. They broke their amnesty and went back to sea as pirates. Mary Read was in the Bahamas because after her husband died she had set sail for the West Indies, been captured by pirates and joined their crew. She later joined Rackam's ship. Bonny and Read 'cussed and swore like sailors, carried their weapons like those well trained in the ways of war and boarded prize vessels as only the most daring and respected members of the crew were allowed to do.'[36] Although they wore female clothing day-to-day, they specifically put on male clothes when the pirates attacked other vessels. They 'wore Men's jackets, and long Trouzers, and Handkerchiefs tied about their Heads, and . . . each of them had a Machet[e] and Pistol in their Hands.'[37]

Because they had broken their amnesty, named warrants were issued for Rackam, Bonny and Read. When eventually their ship was attacked and captured by a privateer, the women were the fiercest in resisting (many of the men were apparently drunk). They were tried in Jamaica in November 1720 along with Rackam and ten men of the crew. The men were executed, but Bonny and Read escaped hanging by pleading their bellies. Mary Read died shortly afterward in prison, probably of gaol fever. Ann Bonny disappeared from the record, but might have been ransomed by her father. Some sources identify her as the woman who in 1721 married a Joseph Burleigh in South Carolina, bore eight further children and died in her eighties, a respectable woman.[38]

Bonny and Read are important to this discussion not least because they are clear examples of women with a capacity and capability for violence who, for a short while at least, made a successful criminal career. They made creative use of the movements of people, things and ideas that constituted the Atlantic world at that point in history to escape from their potentially marginal status as illegitimate, and indeed as women. In part they did so by drawing on a wider if partly submerged tradition of cross-dressing that enabled some women to make opportunities for themselves in a highly gender-unequal world. They, and other women pirates, demonstrate the ambiguity of the law when faced with women who were guilty of 'male' crimes – some women so tried were hung whereas others seem to have been punished far less. Like the highwayman, the pirate was a highly masculine cultural identity. Notwithstanding that research is now showing that women went to sea in various capacities at this period, ships were a culturally masculine world.[39] The work required great physical stamina and hardiness and women were barred, not through any 'unequal opportunities' policy, but because sex was thought to rob men of their capacity to work and to respond to discipline.[40] Of course, men did have sex on board ships but the story of male sailors' same-sex relationships is not one we have space to explore here.[41] One of the reasons why Bonny and Read have fascinated feminist scholars is the possibility that they had a lesbian affair.[42] In the context of the sexual economies of the ocean-going sailing ship, arguably any such relationship would have been read against the same-sex exchanges that were current between (some) men. They also need to be understood in terms of early modern gender identities which operated in the social world in ways less securely fixed to either sexuality or biological sex than became the case in later periods.[43] Bonny and Read became pirates, and were good at it. In that identity they adopted all the pirate's masculine traits, not least that of violent crime. In fact they 'did' violence in masculine ways, rather than the kinds of criminalised violence more closely associated with femininity and its debilities and disorders.

Adult murder

We will discuss the specifically female violence of infanticide in Chapter 4. Neonaticide (the killing of newborns) was a form of violence structured by women's constrained social and economic opportunities. As a crime, it was treated ambivalently by the criminal justice system because the killing of an infant by its mother posed contradictions to dominant gender ideologies. Infanticide seemed to demonstrate both the debilities and the depravities of female sexuality, and so we discuss it alongside prostitution and abortion – other offences where dominant perceptions of female sexuality and reproduction were crucial in shaping how women were positioned as offenders. Our discussion in this chapter will focus on the murder of adults by women.

In the Early Modern period mortality and morbidity levels were high and people of all ages could die suddenly. Early Modern conceptions of legal proof differed from modern rules of evidence. The prime purpose of the law was to uphold social order and this meant recognising hierarchies by class, gender and age. The jury assessed the guilt of an accused person mostly in relation to their social position, so rumour and opinion were relevant as well as fact. Social hierarchy conveyed authority over subordinates, and acceptable violence could be used to enforce that authority. Killing became unlawful where violence had exceeded its legitimate use, and the degree of a killer's culpability depended on how far that line had been over-reached. Men were entitled to use violence to order their households. In Garthine Walker's findings on seventeenth-century Cheshire, no man who beat his wife to death was convicted of murder. The law had already distinguished murder 'with malice aforethought' from manslaughter, which was typically a killing arising from male:male confrontation. Men were expected to defend and maintain their honour and reputation through violence; manslaughter was interpreted as instances where such violence was miscalculated.[44]

Garthine Walker has found that women were a fifth of those tried for unlawful killing in seventeenth-century Cheshire and most frequently killed people from within their own domestic circle. Female sexuality was held to be intrinsically disorderly and could both explain women's transgressions and sometimes make them more threatening. Proportionately more accusations against women than men were dismissed at the pre-trial stages. However, once found guilty of homicide women were far more likely to hang than men. Just over a quarter of men tried for murder were found guilty. The rest were 'either acquitted, pardoned after verdicts of death by misfortune or self-defence or – most common of all – were branded after they were found guilty of a reduced charge of manslaughter.'[45] Manslaughter was essentially not a criminal offence applicable to women. Early modern law treated men's fatal violence as intrinsically different from that of women, producing uneven treatment not only between men and women *per se*, but between different gendered scenarios of killing. These gendered legal precedents coloured the law on murder at least until the Homicide Act of 1957 established a partial defence of diminished responsibility.

By the 1840s capital punishment was effectively reserved for murder and high treason, a situation formally confirmed in the 1861 Offences Against the Person Act. Neonaticide had effectively ceased to attract capital penalties.[46] Consequently adult murder became more clearly distinguished from other kinds of serious violence. The manner and appearance of the accused as well as the circumstances of the case achieved a higher cultural visibility in the Victorian period.[47] Even though juries were now expected to reach verdicts on the evidence with the legal direction of the judge, rather than on the assessments of reputation, they still often took strong views as to the *kind* of person they saw in the dock. Either through their verdict (to the annoyance of judges keen to enforce the more stringent Victorian law) or through recommendations to mercy, juries continued to make ad hoc assessments as to gradations of culpability. The public also regularly intervened through post-sentence petitions for the reprieve of sympathetic murderers. Although, as Ballinger argues, judicial mercy to murderous women was far from the norm, some were acquitted outright or were given signally light punishment. In a number of murder cases there was comparative sympathy for women on trial for adult homicide (particularly for killing nasty husbands and lovers) who could marshal properly respectable feminine demeanours, although uncongenial women killers were readily hung.[48] We can explore these dichotomies a little further by looking at nineteenth-century poisoning cases.

Victorian ideologies of domesticity saw the home, and gender and class hierarchies within it between men, women, children and servants, as an important symbol of social order. The figure of the domestic poisoner, particularly where she was a woman, was guaranteed to trigger cultural anxieties and ensured that the comparatively small numbers of nineteenth-century domestic poisoning cases would attract much public attention. There were a number of highly lethal substances easily available in Victorian homes. For example, arsenic had a range of domestic uses from fly papers to the green colouring in wallpaper. From the 1830s, advances in toxicology made the presence of poison easier to detect. As Katherine Watson points out, between the 1820s and 1850s rapid and uncontrolled urban growth and fluctuating labour markets produced high levels of poverty and material uncertainty for labouring people, which coincided with both a harsher system of poor relief following the Poor Law Amendment Act of 1834 and also the proliferation of cheap burial insurance, in particular that for infants.[49] During these decades a succession of domestic poisonings came to trial. Though the offenders were both women and men, the cases involving poor women seemed to typify the disorder of working-class homes and the transgressive character of working women's femininity. Mary Ann Burdock was hung in Bristol in 1835 after administering red arsenic in gruel to her elderly female lodger, so as to obtain her savings. The forensic tests managed to identify arsenic in the exhumed corpse 18 months after the murder. The same year Sophia Edney was convicted at Taunton Assizes for killing her husband with arsenic in his fried potatoes.[50] From the 1850s, economic change was doing something to ease the immiseration of the labouring poor at the same time as coroners were becoming rather better empowered and enabled to investigate suspicious deaths, and the new police forces increased the regulation of working-class neighbourhoods. Some middle-class poisoners came to trial, both men and women, as well as one particularly notorious case on the earlier model. Mary Ann Cotton was a working-class woman, who, until the trial of Harold Shipman in 1999, had killed more people than any other murderer in Britain. She poisoned husbands, lovers, children and other kin for small amounts of financial gain and was executed in 1873.

Three domestic poisoning cases involving middle-class women hit the headlines in the closing decades of the century. Florence Bravo came to public attention in 1876 when her second husband, Charles, died a slow and agonising death from antimony poisoning. He had swallowed the tasteless poison in the drinking water at his bedside. The Bravos had only been married for a few months that had been marred by quarrels over money – she was a wealthy, young widow and, though a lawyer with a promising career, he had only a small independent income. Florence had earlier had an affair with a well-known doctor, which rankled with her new husband. Because of the upper-class position of the protagonists and because no conclusive evidence against any one person was established, the case never came to criminal trial, but an extended and very public coroner's inquest rehearsed Florence's sexual transgressions with as much energy as it interrogated the possibility that she had poisoned her husband. Bursting into tears and 'sobbing bitterly', Florence appealed 'to the Coroner and to the jury, who are gentlemen, to protect me'. Her appeal to the manliness and the respectability of the jury produced 'applause from the audience, immediately suppressed'.[51] Florence's appeal seems to have shifted the sympathy of the court in her favour. The jury returned a verdict of murder, but refused to suggest who might be to blame. Nevertheless, the case ruined her reputation, already dented by her earlier affair. She became socially isolated and estranged from her family, and died of alcoholism two years later.

Adelaide Bartlett was a lower-middle-class young wife with a dull, cantankerous, invalid older husband and a (probably platonic) lover. She was acquitted of her husband's murder in 1886, for the most part because there was no clear evidence of how the chloroform that killed him had entered his stomach.[52] Three years later, Florence Maybrick was found guilty of poisoning her husband, despite the inconclusive evidence. She, too, was unhappily married and was having an affair. Charles Maybrick was taking arsenic as medicine at the time, some of it self-administered and some of it prescribed by doctors. Although the verdict was so questionable that the capital sentence was set aside, she served 15 years in prison, since her transgressions as an adulteress themselves seemed to call for punishment and prevented her release.[53] Taken together, these three late nineteenth-century poisoning cases illustrate the interactions in court between middle-class women who demonstrated appropriately feminine gentility, their past sexual histories and the increasing role (if not always the effectiveness) of forensic scientific evidence. We cannot say whether Adelaide Bartlett or Florence Bravo did poison their husbands, and we cannot be certain that Florence Maybrick did not. However, these three cases became sensational because they indicated motivations around emotional and sexual relations not so easily dismissed as what could (simplistically) be represented as the mostly materialist impulses of poor women who poisoned for financial gain. They took place during an era when marital relations were in the public eye. Family legislation such as the Married Women's Property Acts (1870 and 1882), the Matrimonial Causes Act of 1878, and provisions of 1886 and 1895 which enabled maintenance for wives separated from their husbands, each in some measure eroded the patriarchal authority of men in marriage and the surrounding debates interrogated the proper uses of such authority.[54] Domestic poisoning required no physical force nor bravery, but seemed indicative of feminine treachery, particularly when associated with the home and family which, according to normative Victorian ideologies should have been emotionally and socially secure.[55] Women who were accused of murder by poison, yet seemed properly feminine, and who had suffered domestic infelicities from inappropriately patriarchal husbands seemed not to fit the established stereotype of the treacherous female poisoner. As Anette Ballinger has argued, where women on trial for murder were able to be positioned as confirming dominant gender norms which reiterated the appropriateness of women's subordination, the law was able to extract rather less in the way of direct individual punishment. Such a woman's very deviance acted as an object lesson that reinforced the dominant gender order.[56]

Into the interwar period, women on trial for murder who had endured a violent or sexually importunate partner continued to receive sympathy from the criminal justice system, whereas if their own sexual transgressions loomed largest in public perception they could still be convicted against the weight of the evidence. In 1922, Mme Fahmy killed her husband Ali Bey Fahmy with his own pistol in their suite at the Savoy Hotel in London. He was an aristocratic Egyptian. She was French, and had had something of a chequered past life. She might easily have been represented as blameworthy, being foreign and having a questionable sexual history. She was acquitted, more or less against the evidence. Mme Fahmy successfully presented herself as a victim, at root because of a public and judicial acceptance that an 'oriental' such as Fahmy might well be capable of bestial violence and perverse sexuality insupportable to white society.[57] In contrast, Edith Thompson was a sexually transgressive women who found her criminal culpability taken for granted. She was hanged in 1922 as was her lover, sailor Freddie Bywaters, for the murder of her husband. Edith took no part in the killing, but the prosecution argued a conspiracy to murder between Edith and Freddie. In court, without any forensic evidence, selective and partial readings from her highly coloured letters to Bywaters convinced both judge and jury that she had been trying to poison her husband.[58]

In May 1935, Alma Victoria Rattenbury (38) and George Percy Stoner (18) were tried at the Old Bailey for the murder of her husband Francis Rattenbury (67). It has been said before that R v. Rattenbury and Stoner

demonstrates the unfairness of the 1935 criminal justice system and the pruri-
ence of the popular press towards a woman brought to trial for murder mostly
because of her sexual behaviour and so far condemned by such patriarchal prejudices that, though acquitted, she was driven to suicide.[59] Her supporters at the
time thought so and the words that she wrote immediately before her suicide
also infer this. She had an elderly, depressive husband and was conducting a
passionate sexual affair with the household's under-aged gardener handyman.
Late one evening a jealous Percy Stoner killed Mr Rattenbury with a mallet.
Finding her injured husband, Alma became hysterical and drank large quanti-
ties of whiskey and soda. When the police arrived she made advances to them
and confessed to the crime. During the early stages of the trial the extent of
Alma Rattenbury's sexual transgression seemed to make it entirely plausible
that she had conspired with her lover to murder her husband. Because of the
age difference, she was assumed to have 'dominated' Stoner and controlled him
through manipulating his immature sexual desire. However, in the dock she
was a frank and attractive witness, conforming to all the requirements of interwar middle-class femininity in fur coat, gloves, hat and a permanent wave.[60]
The judge condemned her heartily for her sexual behaviour, yet he himself
questioned the validity of her confessions since they were made when she was
heavily drugged not only with alcohol but also with morphia administered by
the doctor. Consequently she was found not guilty, yet the extinction of her reputation as well as the emotional collapse she experienced thinking that Stoner
would hang, led her to take her own life shortly afterwards. The example of
Alma Rattenbury illustrates both how appropriately gendered self-presentation
in court could engage the sympathies of the criminal justice system against the
odds and how women's sexual transgressions could be punished in informal
if not in formal ways. Alma Rattenbury balanced on the knife-edge between
attractive and 'depraved' femininity and thus between innocence and guilt.

Alma Rattenbury was not a murderer, but came very close to being punished
as one. The contrasting, and more recent, example of Myra Hindley shows how
a woman who was certainly guilty of extreme and repeated lethal violence has
been represented as the personification of evil to a greater extent than the man
who took the leading role in their crimes. Ian Brady and Myra Hindley were
tried in 1966, shortly after the abolition of capital punishment, for a series of
vicious and sadistic murders of children and teenagers culminating in 1965.
They were sentenced to life imprisonment. Brady and Hindley's relationship
was itself abusive. As well as the sexual and physical violence to the children they
killed, Brady was also guilty of violence against Hindley. This does not excuse
or condone her share of responsibility for the murders, but it does provide an
important dimension to the context for her actions. Even so, this was not a
narrative that was attended to in dominant discourses, either at the time of the
trial or since. Over the ensuing decades, it has been Hindley, rather than Brady
who was repeatedly cited as the prime exemplar of evil, and it has been her image
from the original police photograph that appeared repeatedly in the media until
her death in 2002.[61]

Sensational murder trials highlight cultural perceptions of violence and social
disorder and therefore are useful to analyse as case studies of how gender,

culture, violence and criminal justice have interacted. Certainly, from the Victorian period it is possible to detect the workings of the dichotomy which feminist historians and criminologists have argued has decided how violent women were perceived by the law and the public – as either 'mad' or 'bad'. However, numbers of examples, such as those of Alma Rattenbury or Florence Bravo, show how elements of 'madness' and 'badness' intertwined in specific cases. Murder trials were high-profile events, and the outcome of each depended not only on the events but also the individual characteristics of the accused and the conduct of the case in court. There is also much to be learned from the far more numerous cases of petty violence involving women (both verbal and physical) which have come before the ecclesiastical and criminal courts since the seventeenth century.

Verbal violence and common assault

In the seventeenth century verbal violence and the language of sexual insult had forceful effects in the social world. In face-to-face communities where one's reputation was largely settled through gossip, insults about sex adjudicated social as well as sexual reputation. Men were condemned as cuckolds whereas women, whose reputations hinged on their sexual conduct more directly than men's, were stigmatised as sexually promiscuous. Women readily resorted to ecclesiastical courts to defend against such insults.[62] Over the eighteenth century in London, the growth of the metropolis made for shifting neighbourhoods and even more crowded streets. By the end of that century the need to defend against verbal violence was less imperative since reputations were forged less before the whole local community and more amongst particular social circles.[63] However, in provincial towns where communities were smaller – and in localities where the legal mechanism of the ecclesiastical court persisted and enabled the informal uses of verbal violence to be extended into a formal case – then not dissimilar patterns of use, along with the potential costs and risk of imprisonment that it involved can be seen to continue until the abolition of such courts in 1859. Women's sexuality was not simply an individual matter, but could affect spouses, kin and other close associates. In 1827 one Gloucester woman ambiguously defending her own sexual reputation said; 'I don't go to bed with any man as thy wife does. I don't go to bed with Mr Lloyd for the sake of a glass of gin and water.'[64]

Much male:male interpersonal violence into the twentieth century followed the patterns of the 'fair fight' – a rough and ready set of procedures which for the most part regulated the violence. Violence was about settling disputes and restoring honour. Women could also use the model of the fair fight, and both young and older women settled their disputes by fighting in the street. Women in the late nineteenth century were brought to violence by the myriad annoyances of life in working-class neighbourhoods – about shared taps and privies, about the disruptions caused by children as well as about men or spiteful gossip. In Birkenhead in 1889 people had been standing around talking in the street on an August Bank Holiday when Hannah Carey approached Mrs Bowen who was standing at her door, and 'called me some bad names and challenged me out to fight'. They ended rolling in the gutter and pulling each other's hair. When Hannah's mother and sister became involved the fight became more general. Catherine Gilfoyle was arrested for assaulting Joanna Potter 'out of spite because I would not drink with her on Monday'. The rules of the fair fight and also the importance of complying with rules of sociability in sharing drink are evident here.

Young women also shared in the violence of youth gangs in the same period. The press and the magistrates saw these violent young women as 'degraded' and 'unwomanly' though sentenced them more lightly, clearly seeing their violence as less serious than that of young men.[65] Some women were notable street fighters. Nancy Dickybird is recalled by the novelist Anthony Burgess for being regularly thrown out of his stepmother's pub in interwar north Manchester. The landlady employed a truncheon, knuckledusters and even a loaded revolver. Nancy, Burgess recalls, 'would sail into an ecstasy of foulness, urinate on the floor and then leave'.[66]

According to Police Superintendent Leah, Mrs Elspeth Bispham was 'the most troublesome woman in Crewe – in fact more troublesome to the police than all the people of Crewe together'.[67] This is some reputation. Judging by the three assault cases involving her (in one of these she prosecuted) at Crewe Borough Sessions between 1880 and 1881, she seems to have earned it. She was not only troublesome to the police, but also to her neighbours. Awkward, cantankerous, given to hurling bricks and bad language, she seems not only to have been difficult to live near but also to have become a target for boys' mischief, neighbours' acerbic humour and sometimes more deliberate harassment. She was known as 'the captain's widow' and in court (and doubtless before her neighbours) could wax loquacious about her 'noble captain'. Police opinion was that this was due to the effects of drink. She was hardly overawed by court appearances or the attentions of the police. It was often near impossible to serve a summons on her, as she locked the house and hid inside. The magistrates resorted to minor fines of up to 20 shillings. Aside from one short period in Knutsford Prison after smashing a glass in her landlord's face, there was little relief to the police, the court, or Mrs Bispham's neighbours, for the 'trouble' that she generated. Of course, she was also victimised herself – her vegetable garden was periodically trampled and her windows broken.[68]

Along with other kinds of offence, the levels of recorded violent crime had declined by the later nineteenth century even while the population continued to rise. Therefore, by that period working-class women had become a significant proportion of offenders charged with minor violent offences. Godfrey, Farrall and Karstedt find that women comprised 32 per cent of their 1880–1920 sample of assault cases in police courts.[69] At this period, the police acted as prosecutors and magistrates heard the vast majority of criminal cases in these 'summary' courts in the first instance, referring the most serious on for jury trial. Working-class neighbourhoods were heavily policed and summary courts were readily used by working people.[70] These trends reinforced the visibility of women's minor neighbourhood violence, illustrating yet another way in which the 'civilising process' seems to have been gendered as well as classed. Meanwhile, ideals of femininity in the modern period had placed a new emphasis on passivity, modesty and reticence as criteria of respectability. Such qualities had of course been called for in respectable women for centuries. However, the symbolic dominance of middle-class family forms and their role in guaranteeing social order, alongside the changed social conditions in industrial society and the proliferation of welfare, philanthropic and policing agencies, together made physical violence (against other adults if not against children) something which women striving after respectability resorted to less readily. Consequently, the women who showed up in police courts for fighting seemed irredeemably transgressive and incapable of rehabilitation. Nevertheless, they did not receive particularly heavy punishment. The criminal justice process in that period had few penal measures available for minor violence – only fines or short periods in prison. Violent poor women were instead disregarded, and sometimes mocked because of their lack of respectability. Their violence did not undermine the social order, but in fact underlined their social unimportance because of their poverty and their gender.

Conclusion

This discussion has necessarily ranged wide across the diversity of violent crime committed by women and the differential responses of the criminal justice process. If it is accepted that violence is historically situated and arises out of social interaction, it is perhaps unsurprising that rather than a clear trajectory of change over time, there have instead been different historical moments where women's violence has been perceived as either particularly serious or as comparatively trivial. This effect is perhaps most clearly seen in the case of murder trials where by definition prevailing social questions – about poison, about interwar middle-class marriage, about the disruption of the early modern social order occasioned by husband murder – have been measured both against the law and against the particular people in the dock and their individual stories.

We have been able to distinguish two broad patterns of women's violent crime. There have been particular offences which seemed to the prevailing criminal justice system to be manifestations of women's intrinsic debility ('madness') or their more dangerous disorderliness ('badness'). In such cases, the criminal justice response has been severe where violent women seemed to exemplify the inherent deviance of femininity, but could often be comparatively lenient where violence could be attributed to female weakness and debility. Some women, from early eighteenth-century women pirates to the later nineteenth-century working-class women who employed the rituals of the 'fair fight', have also assumed criminal identities that have been normatively gendered masculine. Such uses of violence have been associated with agency and authority. For the most part they have been the behaviour of men. It is perhaps therefore unsurprising that they have been adopted by women who want to enforce or establish otherwise constrained agency. In the later nineteenth and early twentieth centuries the criminal justice system had few responses to the everyday interpersonal violence of working-class women, and so demeaned them even as it punished them only lightly. Such women transgressed both gender and social norms, but seem at first sight to have escaped the stigma of 'double deviance'. However, punishment for gender deviance can be informal as well as formal. Alma Rattenbury was driven to suicide. Elspeth Bispham continued to be victimised by her neighbours. Furthermore, as we will argue in later chapters, across the twentieth century the growth of welfare institutions itself found ways of disciplining gender deviance that could be punitive, although outside the strict remit of the criminal law.

4
Women and Sexuality

Where women's sexuality has overlapped with crime, gender issues have been to the fore in the criminal justice process reflecting and often symbolising specific and historically shifting social anxieties. Firstly, sexuality in terms of motherhood and reproduction has positioned women offenders differently than men; pregnant women convicted of capital offences in the seventeenth and eighteenth centuries could plead their bellies and defer or sometimes avoid the gallows (Chapter 7). Secondly, perceptions of women's sexuality have helped shape judgements about their culpability or criminal responsibility in a range of crimes, sometimes to their advantage and sometimes markedly to their disadvantage. To recap some of the points made in previous chapters, although the precise timing, spread and mechanisms of the shift are very much debated amongst historians, it is clear that in the Early Modern period female sexuality was more often understood as dangerous because it was active and even predatory. By the mid-Victorian period, although the earlier model could still be applied, especially to lower-class women, the dominant model of respectable female sexuality was one of passivity and submission. Both models saw women as very much constituted by their sexuality and potentially debilitated by its vagaries. Hence, where sexuality could in any way be linked to women's criminal behaviour, the way was open for them to be constructed as either particularly threatening or as in part victims. Either way, their autonomy and agency were undermined. We noted such effects at work in our discussion of female murderers in Chapter 3, and in Chapter 2 saw how shoplifting by women could be attributed to the menopause.[1]

Our main concern in this chapter is the gendered construction of women as offenders in areas of crime which concerned sexuality directly and are specifically or predominately associated with women. We shall focus on prostitution, infanticide and abortion. Although the sale of sexual services by men to men also has a long history and transgender individuals have both bought and sold sex in ways even less visible in the historical record, by far the majority of prostitutes in the period we are discussing have been women and girls – and most of their customers have been men. Furthermore, the dominant and morally inflected cultural identity of the prostitute has named her as a woman selling sex to men.[2] For much of our period the crime of infanticide has been defined as the killing of an infant under a year old by its mother. Abortion, the deliberate termination of pregnancy, produced far more criminal sentences against women than men in the first half of the twentieth century. Furthermore, following the

1861 Offences against the Person Act until the 1967 Abortion Act it was an offence for a woman to try to end her own pregnancy.

Prostitution and crime

Although prostitution is not a universal characteristic of human societies it has nevertheless been present in the West over very long chronologies.[3] The patterns of prostitution or sex work have varied widely. In some ancient societies, so-called 'sacred prostitution' could be a high-status occupation and existed alongside the exchange of sexual services for money or other material benefit. What has counted as prostitution, particularly from the perspective of those who bemoaned it, has shifted by time and place. For the Victorian journalist Henry Mayhew, working-class women who cohabited in pretty stable relationships with men outside marriage counted as prostitutes.[4] The woman who, when asked by a Plymouth court in 1870 whether she was still a prostitute replied, 'No, only to the one man', showed either that she had internalised such norms or that she knew how the court would understand her current relationship.[5] In England, the sale of sexual services has never in itself been illegal. There have been many reasons why the law has never attempted to abolish prostitution *tout court*, not least the impossibility of enforcement. A core ideological reason has been the frequent perception that male heterosexuality was an innate and unstoppable drive; the prostitute therefore provided an outlet which prevented the dangerous venting of male sexual urges in respectable society.

Overall the relationship between prostitution and crime has been a shifting and often ambiguous one. Where prostitutes have also committed theft, fraud or other offences the criminal justice system has been the more ready to assume them guilty.[6] When Elizabeth Herd (alias Racket) was tried for sedition against the King in 1685, 'she appearing to be a common Prostitute, her denial weighed not with the Jury, who brought her in Guilty of the Trespass.'[7] The law has been used to criminalise activities around prostitution such as soliciting, procuring or 'keeping a bawdy house'. Only very recently (particularly since the Sexual Offences Act 1985) and at some very specific moments in the past (e.g., the activities of the Societies for the Reformation of Manners in the later seventeenth century) have prostitutes' customers been brought before the courts.[8] Prostitutes (or women thought to be prostitutes) have also been subject to a range of disciplinary regimes established in the cause of their 'rehabilitation' or because of wider public health agendas. We will review three areas which have defined the relationship between prostitution and crime; firstly the social historical experience of prostitutes and others involved in the sex trades, secondly the symbolic and ideological power of prostitution as a key signifier of deviance and marginality, thirdly the criminal justice and related moves to regulate and control prostitution.

Sex and work

Because our concern here is to explore the intersections between crime and women's sexuality, our discussion of prostitution will have fairly little to say about women who, as courtesans or mistresses, were able to trade sexual and emotional services at a pretty high price and obtain a certain amount of social recognition and status as well, for some at least, long-term economic security. The existence of such women as Catherine Walters, known as 'Skittles', whose long-term liaison with Lord Hartington (later the Duke of Devonshire) exploded into scandal in 1862, frequently offended the moralists,[9] and the possibility of respectable wives and daughters being 'elbowed' whilst walking in nineteenth-century Hyde Park by those well-dressed 'somebodies whom nobody knows',[10] or the difficulties of distinguishing servant girls, prostitutes and respectable women promenading in St James' Park in the eighteenth century, made the social proximity of vice the more alarming to respectable society. However, women selling sex in upscale markets were (for so long as they could retain that position) largely immune from the criminal law. Our concern here is rather with those working-class women for whom commercial sex provided little in the way of social mobility and for whom poverty remained the context of their prostitution. Prostitutes' lobby groups and organisations in the second half of the twentieth century preferred the term 'sex worker', and while this is more difficult to apply in a historical discussion, a sociohistorical understanding of prostitution makes most progress when set alongside the very poor options most working women had for earning a reasonable living across the three centuries we are considering. Contrary to the melodramatic myths of cross-class sexual encounter, most prostitutes and clients were lower class throughout this period. Thus the criminalisation of prostitution impacted on recognised social, sexual and material economies in working-class communities.

Ruth Mazo Karras[11] has described the diversity and small-scale organisation of medieval prostitution, which she sees as a trade organised much like any other. Such diversity continued into the Early Modern period, although the open licensing of brothels did not. In fact, there have been pronounced long-term historical continuities in prostitutes' lives and work. What have changed over time above all have been the systems of criminalisation and regulation that prostitutes experienced. Changes in the historical experience of prostitutes have arisen firstly out of the varying impact of such regulatory systems as well as out of broader demographic and social trends – urbanisation, industrialisation and historically uneven opportunities for women in waged work. The small-scale organisation of prostitution (unlike that which developed under elaborated systems of regulation in continental Europe)[12] embedded it in working-class neighbourhoods; women who let rooms, publicans and beerhouse keepers who sold drink, seamstresses and milliners who provided the finery that moralists found so offensive, all took a certain economic benefit from the trade. Landlords have long been able to maximise their rentals by letting rooms to prostitutes. Prostitution provided young women with a superficially good income, but the wages of sin were insecure, seasonal and bought at the risk of venereal disease, alcoholism, a shortened life expectancy and the risks associated with other kinds of marginality, not least of violence from clients and sometimes from 'bullies' or pimps (though these were not a frequent aspect of the trade in England, certainly before the mid-twentieth century), and heavy-handed interventions by the police and the law including arrest, fines, occasional harassment and imprisonment.

Henderson found that in eighteenth-century London women entered prostitution in their late teens or early twenties. Walkowitz found that around 16 years old was more common in nineteenth-century Plymouth and Southampton and most of the prostitutes identified by Finnegan in mid-nineteenth-century York were in the 15–25 age group, though the diversity of London prostitution in the 1950s meant that Rolph's case studies include a wider age range. Walkowitz argues that prostitution was a transitional stage in women's working lives, though the move out of prostitution was often occasioned by poor health and declining earnings. Given the fluctuating population of sailors in Plymouth and Southampton, some prostitutes could set up a rather more secure existence through longer term relationships with one or more sailors, becoming their common-law wives when they were in port and collecting their half-pay when they were at sea.[13]

Finnegan emphasises the progressive degradation of prostitutes in nineteenth-century York, though her meticulous research in local records inevitably shows up best those who persisted (for want of better opportunities). In some cases prostitution and brothel-keeping was replicated over successive generations in families. Prostitutes in 1950s London included those who drifted in and out of prostitution, and as in earlier centuries, those who stayed tended to be at the most disadvantaged end of the trade. Women who looked to prostitution as a way out of economic constraints, while so many others coped with poorly paid work in domestic service or the needle trades, seem to have been especially detached from family and other support networks. Henderson argues that eighteenth-century London prostitutes were often orphaned or abandoned and had not managed to acquire much in the way of marketable skills or education. Walkowitz's sample in Plymouth and Southampton also contained a high proportion of orphans or had had one parent die. Research on the 1950s, the 1980s and 1990s also show a frequent background of institutionalised childhood, disrupted schooling and few marketable skills among young prostitutes. Most eighteenth- and nineteenth-century prostitutes recorded in available studies were either native to the town where they worked (around 40 per cent in eighteenth-century London) or had migrated short distances from the surrounding countryside, though migration distances were unexpectedly greater into the twentieth-century London trade.[14]

Prostitution had its specific geographies, both nationally and locally. Although prostitutes operated in rural communities, it was urban prostitution that was most highly visible. Different kinds of towns varied as to the numbers of prostitutes they accommodated. Police returns on known brothels for the mid-nineteenth century show the greatest concentration in resort towns and ports (where leisure visitors or returning sailors included paid-for sex amongst their pleasures), but lowest in textile and other manufacturing towns where women could more readily find other paid work.[15] University towns, with their populations of young male students also had a flourishing sex trade.[16]

Within each town or city there were also specific geographies of prostitution. Although prostitutes could be found in many parts of eighteenth-century

London, they unsurprisingly favoured areas where accommodation was cheap and there was plenty of custom; for example, the docks areas or the parishes of St Giles and St James in Westminster. The size of the capital and the different policing jurisdictions also enabled them to shift their territory during periods of heavier regulation; many prostitutes moved out of the City of London in the mid-eighteenth century for this reason, returning from the East and West Ends when control regimes relaxed some decades later.[17] Prostitutes solicited clients in the main thoroughfares or the parts of town associated with leisure. In nineteenth-century York the key location for soliciting was the river bridge that formed the main roadway into the city; in Manchester, Oxford Road (also known as 'Dirty Mile') was well known for both its prostitutes and its gin palaces. In London there have been many such sites, most notoriously in the Haymarket and Piccadilly in the West End of London, where theatres, shops, oyster bars, and other purveyors of alcohol and entertainment proliferated. There has been a striking persistence of the sex trade in this particular area of London, from the eighteenth through to the late twentieth centuries. In the 1950s male and female prostitutes gathered in numbers on the north side of Piccadilly and in 1978 young boys were found to be regularly solicited into prostitution from the Playland Amusement Park in Piccadilly.[18] In most large towns there have been hierarchies in the sex trade, ordered by location and price (and therefore earnings). In London, West End prostitutes have over centuries earned far more than those in the East End.[19]

If prostitutes solicited in central or commercial areas, they tended to live in working-class districts. In York the small, older streets around the Water Lanes were notable for both the appalling state of the housing and for the high concentrations of prostitutes renting rooms in its lodging houses. The association of run-down urban fabric, poor sanitation and the presence of prostitutes was the outcome of poverty and poor urban development, but to moral reformers who readily elided social and moral deprivation, it seemed to indicate the environmental causes of vice. The urban geographies of prostitution provided ideologically inflected explanations for it, and prompted geographies of regulation, which in turn reinforced or sometimes shifted its location. Sanitary reforms to clear slums in York demolished the old Water Lanes and concentrated the city's prostitution in the more outlying Hungate and Walmgate areas by the interwar period.[20]

Social evil?

In medieval and Early Modern society it was held to be unremarkable for young men to pay for sex. Fornication *per se* was a sin and an offence before the ecclesiastical courts even where it did not involve a cash transaction. However, Mazo Karras argues that the late medieval period was a society where some kind of consideration was exchanged for sexual access to women in all sorts of bargains ranging from the marriage dowry to the payment to a prostitute.[21] While this meant that the prostitute was inevitably constituted as unrespectable in relation to other women, was denigrated and sometimes regulated, she was nevertheless accepted as an inevitable if distasteful part of the social order. Henderson describes a not dissimilar situation in eighteenth-century London, where ideological condemnation of prostitution combined with limited toleration and management rather than repression.

Early Modern condemnations of sin and disorder perceived women as naturally prone to lust and lewdness and hence parcelled up prostitution amongst diverse (mis)behaviours from fornication or excessive drunkenness to the religious witnessing of Quakers.[22] The law did not then distinguish clearly between sex-for-cash and lewdness more generally, and targeted the keepers of 'bawdy' houses as much as prostitutes themselves.[23] Following the Restoration of Charles II, royalist political satire used the prostitute and the bawd to satirise the recently lapsed Protectorate. The disorder inherent in the 'common woman' represented the instability of republicanism. Hence, when in 1668 a London mob composed mostly of apprentices rioted and destroyed East End brothels in the so-called Bawdy House Riots, its target was as much the opposing political ideology as the prostitutes and brothel keepers who were attacked.[24] This very specific symbolism was tied closely to the politics of the Restoration, though by the 1690s a new set of organisations, the Societies for the Reformation of Manners, seized upon the image of the depraved body of the bawd to launch their own campaigns to clean up society. Between the 1690s and the 1730s such societies used the law to wage campaigns in London and other cities, prosecuting bawdy houses and prostitutes. However, their main intention was to reform the conduct of (middling and elite) men (since *ipso facto* the lewd woman was irredeemable and of little account) and they also targeted numbers of prostitutes' male clients, even entering brothels to catch men having sex.[25] They also turned their attention to homosexual 'molly houses'.[26] Although periodic riots and the energetic attention of the Societies for the Reformation of Manners made life uncomfortable for eighteenth-century prostitutes, they were hardly extensive or co-ordinated enough to significantly curtail the trade.

By the late eighteenth century, cultural changes associated with the Enlightenment, in particular the idea of 'sensibility' had led to the growth of the so-called 'seduction narrative', which matched a predatory, even rakish male heterosexuality with an increasingly subservient female response, though as with all such cultural narratives, not all fallen women necessarily internalised it.[27] The dominance of such narratives explained extra-marital female sexual predicaments, but sometimes also enabled 'fallen' woman to be constituted as a victim when they transgressed social or even criminal codes through prostitution, infanticide or abortion. By the mid-nineteenth century normative tropes of (respectable) female sexuality emphasised passivity and explanations of sexual incontinence as primarily sin had changed to those that modelled its dangers through discourses of public health. An early nineteenth-century middle-class campaign blamed prostitutes for an apparently spiralling incidence of syphilis amongst urban men, who then transferred the debilitating disease through marital sex into the heart of the Victorian family.[28] Lower middle-class ratepayers could also be persistent in requesting prosecutions of brothels to remove prostitution from their neighbourhoods.[29] Campaigners lobbying for the abolition of prostitution were equally horrified by other kinds of disease raging in the growing cities, in particular cholera.

The city was a risky place because of moral and health dangers and the symbolic figure of opprobrium became the young female prostitute.[30] By mid-century, the impossibility of outright abolition became evident and counter arguments about the utility of prostitutes in diverting men's excessive (or unconventional) sexual demands from over-troubling their respectable womenfolk were persuasive. Demands for abolition gave way to plans for regulation. Public health agendas mapped prostitution onto the spatiality of Victorian towns and justified its medical regulation. Early Modern ideas held illness and bodily discomfort to be the outcome of sin and therefore socially unexceptional and a vehicle of individual mortification and eventually redemption. However, the political economies of population, as well as morally inflected notions of Victorian progress, made it possible to imagine controlling disease – and produced initiatives to regulate prostitution through the control of prostitutes (rather than their clients).

The Victorians had a basic incomprehension of and fascination with such women who (a) had lots of sex at a period when respectable female sexualities were meant to be passive, and (b) engaged in autonomous commercial transactions in an age when the aggressive realm of commerce was increasingly defined as masculine (a construction which ignored the numbers of women who earned wages or ran businesses). Two trends reified these impulses. Firstly, the emerging field of social enquiry (and the masculine professionalisation that eventually went with it) which was often inaccurate and moralistic, but energetically curious about the city and its (more exotic) denizens. Secondly, that of bourgeois domesticity which idealised the middle-class family form and the role of women within it as a key guarantor of social order and at the same time legitimated women's philanthropy and social activism on the platform of maternalism. Such women claimed the moral standing either to speak for fallen women or to discipline them in the cause of social purity and the eradication of social evil. Such ideologies and anxieties catalysed legal change and the intensity with which prostitution was policed.

Prostitution, regulation and crime

As the discussion above has indicated, the legal regulation of prostitution in the Early Modern period was uneven and sporadic. Henderson finds a series of working accommodations between the London policing authorities and prostitutes and brothel keepers. Magistrates could also be flexible and lenient. Despite the illegality of keeping a 'bawdy house' or the lesser charge of keeping a 'disorderly house', the sex trade was able to negotiate a tolerated if disadvantaged existence in the metropolis.[31]

The growing codification of the criminal law from the early nineteenth century and the increasing efficiency of urban policing (the Metropolitan Police were founded in 1829) produced greater powers to control prostitutes amongst other 'vagrants' (Vagrancy Act, 1822). The arguments about the social and sexual utility of commercial sex as well as the unlikelihood of enforcement meant that criminalising the actual exchange of sex for cash was never a possibility, despite the fulminations of abolitionists. Hence in the first half of the nineteenth century, it was for disorderliness, lewdness or for obstruction that prostitutes and bawds came to court. Under the Town Police Clauses Act, 1847, it became an 'offence for a prostitute to solicit or importune in a public place for the purpose of prostitution'.

However, when the dire sexual health of the armed forces sent to fight the Crimean War became apparent, the way became open for stringent regulation of prostitutes on public health grounds.[32] A very vocal medical lobby envisaged a widespread system akin to those already established on the Continent. Parliament acted swiftly and in the spring of 1864 rapidly passed the first Contagious Diseases Act. The Act applied to specific military and naval towns[33] and two later acts in 1866 and 1869 increased their geographical range. The CD Acts empowered local police to arrest any woman *thought* to be a prostitute and submit her to compulsory internal medical examination. If found to have a venereal disease, she could then be compulsorily detained for up to three months to receive medical treatment. All such women were entered into a register of known prostitutes and required to attend for regular medical examinations thereafter. The CD Acts thus enabled an arbitrary curtailment of the civil rights of working-class women, who could be arrested on simple suspicion of prostitution and forcibly detained without having been found directly guilty of any criminal offence. Although the CD Acts are the best known of such systems, similar regimes of compulsory detention already existed in Edinburgh and under the proctorial system of university student discipline in Cambridge.[34]

Into the 1870s such measures attracted increasingly vocal and organised public criticism and pressure for repeal. For those who thought prostitution a 'social evil' which should be eradicated, the CD Acts unacceptably licensed the commission of vice. For those, particularly amongst the nascent women's movement, who were concerned with the state's heavy-handed coercion of working-class women and were shocked at the 'instrumental rape' of the internal medical examination, the issues were more about feminine decency and civil rights. Josephine Butler and her Ladies National Association combined public campaigning with 'rescue' work to rehabilitate prostitutes. Working men's organisations also campaigned, seeing the Acts as yet another means of policing the working class. In 1879, a Parliamentary Select Committee was established and eventually a private members' bill which removed the powers of compulsory medical examination and suspended the working of the CD Acts was passed in 1883. In contrast, regulatory regimes flourished across the British empire, where imperialist views of the diminished humanity of non-white prostitutes combined with the perceived importance of providing a sexual outlet for white men. White prostitutes also found utility in licensed status.[35]

Through the early 1880s the focus of concern on prostitution was shifting from adult women; firstly, to the issue of child prostitution (see Chapter 8) and secondly, to that of the forcible abduction of girls into prostitution, in particular overseas. The child prostitute, whether as an adolescent '£5 virgin' deflowered by a metropolitan, upper-class libertine or sold into 'white slavery' in a foreign brothel, was the more easily cast into the role of victim. The emergent villains in these melodramatic narratives were those who controlled the trade (the female brothel keeper) and the parents (mothers) who sold their daughters into sexual

slavery. The young prostitutes tracked down in continental brothels by concerned campaigners were generally in their mid- to late teens, in other words
at the same age that young women were entering prostitution in England.
A Select Committee of the House of Lords deliberated in 1881–82, but the
decisive intervention came from the popular press. W. T. Stead, the editor of the
Pall Mall Gazette, published a series of articles entitled 'The Maiden Tribute of
Modern Babylon'. This exposé of the 'vice' on London's streets culminated in
a description of the actual procurement of 'Lily', a 'Child of Thirteen', for £5
in a West End brothel. Through his contacts with Josephine Butler and other
campaigners, Stead had been introduced to Rebecca Jarrett, a reformed prostitute, who had been persuaded actually to make the purchase of the girl (Eliza
Armstrong) from her mother. Stead and Jarrett were tried and imprisoned for
the abduction. Nevertheless, the public outcry following the publication of the
story forced the passage of the Criminal Law Amendment Act (CLA) of 1885
and the repeal of the CD Acts in 1886. The key provisions of the 1885 CLA
were to raise the age of sexual consent for single girls to 16 (sexual intercourse
within marriage was legal with a 12-year-old until the legal age of marriage for
girls was raised in 1929[36]) and to increase the legal penalties for brothel-keeping
or for renting premises for the use of prostitution to a £20 fine or three months
imprisonment for a first offence. A late amendment to the Act (the Labouchère
Amendment) also criminalised sexual acts between men.[37]

Following the 1885 CLA, the campaigning coalition that had come together
to oppose the CD Acts reconfigured itself. The resulting 'social purity' activism
was a complex alliance of those who sought to aid 'unfortunate' women and
those who aimed to eradicate vice. Josephine Butler's Ladies National Association renamed itself the National Vigilance Association. Butler soon retired from
its activities as it set about prosecuting brothels, male sexual offenders and sellers of pornography. Their energetic targeting of brothel keepers, many of whom
were small-scale lodging-house keepers renting rooms to prostitutes, forced
prostitutes to work more openly on the street and brought them under even
more direct police surveillance.[38] Police vigilance, doubtless encouraged by the
climate of social purity, led to a couple of scandalous cases when over-zealous
policemen wrongfully arrested respectable middle-class men on the street for
obstruction or indecent acts with prostitutes.[39] A new Vagrancy Act in 1898
also made it an offence for a man to live on the earnings of prostitution or to
solicit 'for immoral purposes'.

The dimension of the 1880s agitation that involved 'white slavery' and
the forcible abduction of English women into foreign brothels shifted into the
twentieth-century concern with foreign men as controlling prostitution. The
high age of imperialism saw greater movement of people, cash flows and legal
and illegal commodities (including drugs such as opium) between colonies and
metropole. The orientalism inherent in the personification of the pimp as foreign enabled the female prostitute to remain something of a victim (or at least a
deluded and debilitated person). Early in the twentieth century Jewish criminal
entrepreneurs were held to control significant sections of the sex trades.[40] In
the 1920s, in a panic around white, high-society young women succumbing to
opium and cocaine habits, the Chinese were seen as the root of the drugs trade,

organised crime and prostitution.[41] By the 1950s the Maltese, in particular the Messina brothers, were the focus of public and media concerns.[42]

The 1950s were in some respects an illiberal decade of reconsolidation following the Second World War, and saw the next major legislative development on prostitution. The Report of the Committee on Homosexual Offences and Prostitution (The Wolfenden Report, 1957) was comparatively liberal on male homosexuality, recommending an end to the provision enacted in the 1885 CLA that had criminalised same-sex acts between 'consenting adults in private'. It was far more restrictive on female prostitution, recommending the removal of the need to prove direct 'annoyance' of any particular person since prostitution was 'likely to cause annoyance even though no particular person was annoyed'.[43] It became an offence 'for a common prostitute to loiter or solicit in a secret or public place for the purpose of prostitution' and police were empowered to arrest without warrant on reasonable suspicion alone. At the same period, prostitutes and prostitution featured in what Frank Mort sees as a series of high-profile moments of anxiety in the transition to the 'permissive' society of the 1960s when high and low culture met. Most of the victims of the serial killer, John Christie, at 10 Rillington Place (1953) were women who were either prostitutes or whose mobility, marginalisation and undeferential sexuality positioned them as prostitutes in the police mind. The Profumo Affair (1963) forced a senior government minister into resignation after a complex scandal when he was held likely to have passed state secrets to the 'call girl' Christine Keeler.[44]

The association of prostitutes with victimisation and vulnerability was underlined again in 1980 with the Yorkshire Ripper series of murders. By this period, however, there was a second-wave feminist discourse to respond and 'Reclaim the Night', and the possibilities of prostitutes organising themselves.[45] A few years later the Sexual Offences Act 1985 for the first time made it an offence for a man to solicit a woman from or near a motor vehicle. However, differential standards of proof still applied. 'Persistence or causing fear' was necessary to prove an offence against male clients for soliciting (Sexual Offences Act 1985 (Eng.), Section 21(1)) though the 1959 Street Offences Act still made it possible to convict a woman of simply loitering.[46] Into the twenty-first century, therefore, English law still chose to penalise the prostitute more heavily than the client, and directly specified that prostitutes were women.

Rescuing or disciplining?

Since the eighteenth century philanthropists have opened numbers of asylums for 'penitent' prostitutes. The first was the Magdalen Hospital in Whitechapel, London, in 1758 and numbers of others were founded mostly in the early nineteenth century. The Church of England ran over 50 'penitentiaries' by 1885, and numerous other organisations from the Salvation Army to the Jewish Ladies Association operated such establishments by the 1880s.[47] The intention was to redeem 'fallen' women by separating them from family and kin, subjecting them to regulation in dress, diet and work, and through religious instruction and moral uplift make them suitable to fill places as domestic servants. Such institutions undoubtedly provided a route out of dire poverty and disease for some prostitutes; Finnegan's work on York shows that most women who applied for admission had been reduced to absolute destitution. However, they achieved this through confinement and discipline. Even those rather more sympathetic initiatives, such as Josephine Butler's, still positioned the prostitute as debilitated and requiring the maternalist guidance of middle-class ladies. Resistance, disruption and absconding was far more prevalent in many such homes than the philanthropic ladies and gentlemen who ran them would have liked.

Treatments for venereal disease in the seventeenth and eighteenth centuries depended mostly on the poisoning effects of mercury. Hospital accommodation was also very scarce. Most hospitals were reluctant to take venereal cases because of the fears of infection. The London Lock Hospital for venereal disease was founded in 1746 in Southwark. Though 'lock' here comes from the French '*loques*' for rags or bandages, the idea of the segregation of infected prostitutes was not fortuitous. More provincial lock hospitals were built in the nineteenth century[48] most of which were primarily intended to isolate prostitutes.[49] In towns under the CD Acts, or elsewhere where compulsory confinement of women diagnosed as having venereal disease was enforced, the demeaning hospital regime as well as the painful medical treatment made the experience pretty punitive.

Bartley argues that there was a shift in the regime of rescue homes in the later nineteenth and early twentieth centuries to positioning the prostitutes they dealt with as 'feeble-minded', that is, lacking reason and autonomy. The construction of 'feeble-mindedness' redefined the marginal women whose chances had been poor enough to turn to prostitution and whose options of getting out were even slimmer. Walkowitz argues that in the towns covered by the CD Acts, the stigmatisation and regulation that was enforced made it the more difficult for women to leave prostitution, and created an 'outcast group' distanced from the working-class communities which had hitherto more or less incorporated them. The criminalisation by the 1885 CLA of those who rented rooms to prostitutes, also created further barriers between prostitutes and working-class neighbourhoods. Walkowitz argues that by the later nineteenth century, prostitutes stayed longer in the trade, were older and more disadvantaged.[50] Unsurprisingly, 'feeble-mindedness' became a plausible explanation of prostitution to those who policed it. It was women such as these, given their greater likelihood to be heavy drinkers, who probably also best fit Zedner's paradigm of the increasing medicalisation of disciplinary regimes for habitual women criminals (Chapter 7).

Institutionalisation was also the preferred welfare solution for juvenile girls, both offenders and those deemed in need of 'care and protection' and judgements about precocious sexuality (and hence the likelihood that such girls would turn to prostitution in some form or other) were key to their positioning as 'delinquent'. We take up the issues around sexuality and crime in relation to juvenile girls in Chapter 8, including anxiety about young 'amateur prostitutes' enjoying good times with the military during both World Wars and the particular remit of the Women Police in combining regulation with social work for such 'wayward girls.' The rehabilitation of prostitutes increasingly focused

on juveniles by the mid-twentieth century, whereas the adult woman prostitutes were regulated by the police and penalised under the stricter 1959 Street
Offences Act.

Recent Concerns

Prostitution of the under-aged (including boys but predominately girls) resurfaced as a concern late in the twentieth century. Often prostitution was still a
tactic for young people isolated from family. As we argue in Chapter 8, a childhood in 'welfare' care proved a good predictor for women's offending in adult
life. Family instability, 'broken homes' and increased sexual activity amongst the
young were blamed in a 1978 *Sunday Times* report on prostitution amongst
schoolgirls in council care.[51] The police cautioning system instigated under the
Street Offences Act of 1959 was proving ineffective. There was a real incentive
for girls to give false names and ages and police attention encouraged absconding and the greater mobility of under-age prostitutes, who were harder to trace
once the record system developed by the Women Police had been abandoned
after the integration of the men's and women's forces.[52]

Into the 1980s and 1990s children's homes and local authority child welfare were seen as often ineffective and at times abusive. Inequality of income
in Britain rose faster than in almost all industrialised countries and the removal
of state benefit entitlement for those between 16 and 19 and reducing it for
the under 25s also served to increase homelessness, low wages and marginality. Youth unemployment was growing faster than that for adults and criminal
and semi-criminal activities including working informally, begging, drug dealing and prostitution tended to be the resultant survival tactics. Brown and
Barrett suggest that in the 1990s there were around 5000 young people working in prostitution in Britain at any one time, 4:1 girls to boys – a rising
figure, but lower than in other European countries such as France and far lower
than Thailand. Today the sex trade has increasingly global dimensions and has
extended into cyberspace. Trafficking, sexual tourism and internet 'grooming'
have become (post)modern ways of sexually exploiting vulnerable or marginal
women and children.[53]

Women, fertility control and criminalisation

If historically prostitution has been a response of (marginal) young women to
very constrained social and economic opportunities, the fact remains that very
many other women did address such constraints without selling sex. Nevertheless, their sexuality could still bring working women into the reach of the
criminal law.

A second key continuity has been that both single and many married women
had very good reasons to control their fertility. For the greater part of the period
we are discussing, pregnancy was often difficult to be sure about in its early
stages. Poor nutrition and health problems made menstruation a more uncertain phenomenon.[54] Cases of infanticide also show weight gain being explained
as 'dropsy' or even a birth or miscarriage as some sort of 'flux'. The bodily

signs were sufficiently ambiguous to encourage different interpretations for women who (often desperately) did not want to find themselves pregnant.[55] The surest sign of pregnancy was 'quickening' – foetal movement *in utero*. Commonly, 'preventative' measures taken before quickening were seen as reasonable and well into the nineteenth century the law punished early abortion more lightly.

In the Early Modern period fertility was controlled at the level of local populations by patterns of late marriage.[56] Sexual relations could commence on (formal or informal) betrothal and community pressures helped steer young couples into marriage if a child was conceived. Of course such mechanisms worked better in small, settled communities and by the mid-eighteenth century at least, where towns were growing faster, migration was increasing, or 'put-out' industry was providing young women with an independent cash wage, illegitimacy rates increased. Young women textile workers in some communities had a little more autonomy and were able to bear and raise illegitimate children, particularly where the help of family was available. However, inevitably young men had far better chances to escape or at least minimise the consequences of conception before marriage if they wanted to. By the Victorian period, when domestic service of all types was the largest occupational sector for women and girls, the pregnant, live-in, single servant was in a dire position. Although some servants, especially if they were working in an artisan household where the class difference between themselves and their employer was not so very great (the more so where the father of the child was a male member of the household) might obtain some support. More often pregnant single servants were dismissed 'without a character', making further employment difficult to obtain even if they could make arrangements for the care of their babies.

It is not surprising therefore that from the seventeenth to the nineteenth century, infanticide cases most commonly involved single women often in (domestic) service. Most of these young women kept their pregnancies a secret, misinterpreting or ignoring the bodily changes. Even in the often crowded living conditions, people who saw them daily and shared bedrooms or even beds could deny in court that they knew that the woman was pregnant or even that she had given birth. The abjection and impossibility of motherhood in such living and working conditions made not knowing a sensible option, though some witnesses admitted to suspicions. Most infanticidal mothers delivered their babies alone and either killed them shortly afterwards or left them to die. A servant's box (about the only private space she had), under the bed, or the privy were the most common places where infant bodies were found. Having (frequently) denied or concealed their pregnancies, labour was most often described as pain and illness and the baby's body was dealt with as with other bodily waste products. Infanticides could certainly involve violence, and babies were sometimes stabbed, strangled or smothered. Infanticide tended to be the action of isolated women. Even more than prostitution, infanticide was a response born out of vulnerability and marginality.[57] Sarah Cooper, a single mother aged 38, was already supporting two illegitimate children out of a very low and uncertain income, and was reported to be a good mother to them. In 1847 a third baby was found in the privy. As Cooper stated, she simply could see no way of supporting the new baby.[58] Married women who killed somewhat older children were sometimes in a better economic position, but depressive mental states are also a recurrent feature of this kind of case. Polk's work on the late twentieth century shows that young children who are murdered are most likely to be killed by their parents, particularly mothers. Most parents who kill their children feel themselves in an impossibly constrained social and material situation, and explain their actions as saving their children from the continued pains of living. Many such killers also commit suicide.[59]

The mid-nineteenth century saw a moral panic over infanticide, particularly in the huge and fast-growing metropolis. These anxieties broadly coincided with the concerns about prostitution and venereal disease. The alarmist literature on infanticide described the urban landscape littered with the corpses of dead babies:

> bundles are left lying about the streets, which people will not touch, lest the too familiar object – a dead body – should be revealed, perchance with a pitch plaster over its mouth, or a woman's garter around its throat. Thus, too, the metropolitan canal boats are impeded, as they are tracked along by the number of drowned infants with which they come in contact, and the land is becoming defiled by the blood of her innocents.[60]

This panic had not a little to do with agitation by the then developing medical profession for official appointments as coroners. Campaigners such as Thomas Wakeley, founding editor of *The Lancet* (1823 until his death in 1861) and sometime Middlesex coroner, insisted that medical expertise was necessary to discern cause of death, most crucially in the case of infants purportedly still-born but perhaps murdered. Edward Lankester, Wakeley's successor as coroner in Middlesex, also believed in the infanticide epidemic and estimated (on little hard evidence) that 12,000 London women had murdered their babies – a figure that was thereafter regularly reported in the pamphlet literature but bears little relationship to the cases of infanticide tried. Although the cases that came to court cannot be assumed to account for anything like all the cases which occurred, Arnot discovered an average of around only ten cases per year of infanticide at the Central Criminal Court between 1840 and 1879 as well as 306 cases of concealment of birth across this period.[61] The contradictory perceptions of the infanticidal mother as both victim and social threat meant that courts also were reluctant to respond with heavy sentences.

A small number of cases of new-born murder continue to occur, even given many women's comparatively greater autonomy and wage-earning capacity in recent decades, as well as the significantly reduced stigma of illegitimacy. In patterns strikingly similar to eighteenth- and nineteenth-century cases, a very few women do conceal or deny their pregnancy, give birth alone, kill their babies or allow them to die and by either not disposing of the body or doing so where it is likely to be found, are soon detected. Poverty, particularly considered in relative terms, had hardly been eliminated by the late twentieth century and, as we have argued, the young, single, unemployed became an increasingly vulnerable group in the 1980s and 1990s. Nevertheless the isolation and desperation that give rise to infanticide seem to have become rather differently configured by recent times.[62]

The law on infanticide

In the mid-seventeenth century, infanticide was covered by some especially severe statute law. The Act to Prevent the Destroying and Murthering of Bastard Children (1624) not only created a separate capital crime in the killing of newborn illegitimate infants by their mother, but also uniquely shifted the burden of proof from the prosecution to the defence. Although there were some differences of interpretation over time, where an illegitimate child was found dead and the mother had attempted to conceal the birth or had not summoned help in labour, it was presumed in law that she had murdered it.[63] Little regard was paid by the law to the possibility of still birth. The infanticide law was not always used in cases of neonaticide: some single women, married women and men were tried for homicide of newborns. Across the middle of the seventeenth century there was a high conviction rate, though from the outset of our period juries were increasingly reluctant to convict. Francus found 20 convictions in the 28 London cases she identified between 1673 and 1692. Sharpe notes a marked increase in indictments in Cheshire after 1650 but these were all either acquitted or discharged by the late seventeenth century.[64] Hoffer and Hull found a marked decline in conviction rates from the beginning of the eighteenth century and Malcolmson sees the 1624 statute as substantially falling into disuse amongst Staffordshire and Old Bailey cases by the reign of George II.[65]

Accused women were likely to make the defence that they had prepared for the birth by assembling baby linen, or that they had told other people they were pregnant. Clearly such defences were less plausible if demonstrable violence had been used. Francus argues that the demeanour of the accused woman in court was perhaps even more crucial. She found that not only defiance but also intelligent rationality displayed, for example, in cross-examining witnesses, substantially increased the chances of conviction and thus of hanging. The infanticidal mother, perceived as particularly threatening in the mid-seventeenth century and requiring curb by stringent statute, seemed as cultures of sensibility developed by 1800 more of a victim, debilitated by the excess of her sexuality – as long, that is, as her conduct and behaviour accorded to that role.[66]

By the turn of the nineteenth century, the 1624 statute appeared outdated and undeniably inefficient. It was replaced in Lord Ellenborough's 1803 Act against Wounding and Maiming, which also shifted the law on abortion (see below). This was a portmanteau statute intended to bring the criminal law of England and Ireland into line following the Act of Union in 1800 which also marked the beginning of a longer term Victorian programme of systematising and extending the law on interpersonal violence.[67] Ellenborough removed the anomalous burden of proving innocence of infanticide from the defence and required that the prosecution provide evidence of guilt. Since clear evidence was particularly hard to obtain for infanticide (an act characteristically carried out in secret) the chances of conviction reduced. However, the 1803 Act also created the new offence of concealment of birth, punishable by up to two years in prison, to cover cases where the evidence was not strong enough for an infanticide conviction. The 1828 Offences Against the Person Act extended the charge of concealment to married women and the comprehensive 1861 Offences Against the Person Act made concealment by a person other than the mother a crime. Concealment charges were used in the majority of cases of neonaticide in the nineteenth century,[68] and concealment charges were more likely to be found than those of infanticide.[69] Acquittals could still be secured against the evidence. In 1852, even when neighbours had heard a baby cry after it had been put into the privy and seen its mother throw a brick down after it, the 22-year old mother was convicted only of concealment. Sentences for concealment in the nineteenth century were not severe, despite the acute moral panics over infanticide in the 1850s and 1860s. Only 8 per cent of those found guilty in Higginbotham's sample received prison sentences of over six months. 14.5 per cent were released immediately and 35.5 per cent were sentenced for one–three weeks.[70]

From the later nineteenth century the development of psychological and psychiatric explanations of behaviour meant increasing acceptance of the idea of post-partum insanity. The 1922 Infanticide Act made provision for a mother's possible psychological dysfunction up to a year after the birth of a child, and reduced sentences for infanticide accordingly, to up to two years imprisonment. Such provisions clearly established the infanticidal mother as victim before the law, but firmly located her sexually induced instability in the psyche. This provision is perhaps the more notable, since the law was behind the times in its interpretation of psychological knowledge, which had by the interwar period moved on from such blanket formulations. The Infanticide Act of 1938, still on the statute book, makes use of the notion of 'lactational insanity'.[71]

Other ways out: risks and stigma

The social disruptions of demographic and urban growth that accompanied industrialisation may well have increased the incidence of infanticide as more economically marginal and socially vulnerable women found themselves with babies they could not keep. Many other women so situated did manage to find, albeit pretty difficult and problematic, ways out of the situation. The first Foundling Hospital taking in infants and children whose parent(s) could not afford to keep them was founded in London in 1754.[72] It took in both legitimate and illegitimate 'foundlings' but its places were few and even when other provincial foundling hospitals were established in the nineteenth century, the impact they made on the social problems of impoverishment, childcare and working women were necessarily slight. Single mothers who needed to work might secure childcare from family or friends or from neighbours who would mind children for a fee. There were also deals done where the baby was handed over for a one-off payment on the tacit assumption it would not survive to trouble its mother much longer. Such arrangements need to be understood in the context of very high infant mortality rates until the end of the nineteenth century, reaching 55 per cent in some urban areas and even higher for illegitimate children.[73] In the 1870s a public outcry at the very high mortality rate of infants in some larger 'baby farming' operations made clear that some at least expended only nominal care on the babies and in one notorious case in 1870 involving a baby farm in Brixton, Margaret Waters and Sarah Ellis were successfully prosecuted.[74] The case led to the establishment of a Select Committee on Infant Life Protection (1870). The Infant Life Protection Act 1872 imposed some regulation of child-minders, but also made conditions difficult for other working-class women who efficiently and in good faith looked after other people's babies.

Into the twentieth century child welfare became a developing field of state action which augmented the existing philanthropic institutions, and institutionalisation and adoption became the fate of most illegitimate children. By this point, unmarried motherhood was highly stigmatised, and although babies had better material chances of survival than in earlier centuries and many found secure and affectionate adoptive families, the emotional and social costs of illegitimacy could be very high. Consequently, until the availability of oral contraception and changing public opinion on single parenthood in the last 50 years, pregnant unmarried women were placed in very difficult circumstances unless they had supportive and/or affluent kin or friendship networks. Although married women were obviously in a better position to bear and raise children, and at all periods children were a desired and valued part of marriage, nevertheless there were many good social and material reasons for women to want to limit and control their fertility. The rate of population growth, which had been rising since the eighteenth century, slowed in the second half of the 1800s and by the interwar period, smaller families had become the norm amongst all classes. This trend began amongst the middle classes and also selectively in communities with more paid work opportunities for women.[75] Fewer children, more labour-intensive childcare practices and the desire to provide a better material start for each child combined with the pattern amongst many middle-class women in particular to combine motherhood with prolonged education and either a career or other activity. This demographic shift was achieved mostly by limiting fertility within marriage. Long periods of breast feeding, restricting penetrative sex or *coitus interruptus* were all relevant but hardly foolproof methods.[76]

Removing obstructions

There is evidence that women have attempted to end unwanted pregnancies throughout the three and a half centuries we are discussing. Chemical abortifacients were known and used in the seventeenth century. Early Modern women in small communities sometimes sought to avoid stigma, preserve their position as servants, or retain their place in familial and local support networks.[77] With the widening market availability of diachylon lead-based compounds by the later 1800s, the practice seems to have become more widespread. Although hard evidence of incidence is elusive for such a concealed and illegal practice, by the first half of the twentieth century, sexually active working women, both married and single, seem to have tried to control their fertility through a range of measures from vaginal douching, through chemical abortifacients to instrumental abortion.[78] Particularly in early pregnancy such practices could be understood as 'removing obstructions' or 'keeping regular'. Barrier contraception in the form of the condom was available from the mid-eighteenth century but was principally seen as a protection against venereal disease, and as such was associated with men's casual or paid-for sexual encounters. Husbands, or sexual partners who were (or seemed to be) promising marriage could prove unreliable users of contraception.

Working women sought to control their reproduction above all for socio-economic reasons. More detailed survey data becomes available from the later nineteenth and early twentieth centuries. The limitations of cramped living space were acute for many. There is evidence of married women carefully balancing up the cost of another child against their rent (housing costs were the largest outgoing of the household budget). Health provided other pressing reasons. Repeated childbirth had profound long-term health consequences for married women whose nutrition was poor, whose workload was heavy and whose access to (expensive) medical treatment was extremely limited.[79] Other women feared childbirth – justifiably, since maternal mortality remained high into the interwar period even after infant mortality rates had declined. Still others feared their husband's anger at another pregnancy. Single women often had reasons to do with paid work – either the impossibility of earning a living sufficient to keep a child or the fear of losing their employment if they were found to be pregnant.[80] The history of abortion, like that of infanticide and prostitution, is therefore marked by key class issues. More affluent women could pay for safe(r) medical abortions in the nineteenth and twentieth centuries. At earlier periods they could also more easily martial the money necessary to pay for private lying-in and informal adoption of illegitimate children. Reproduction and its management posed far greater risks to health as well as the risks of criminalisation to poor women and was a significant way in which poverty as well as crime was gendered.

The law on abortion

In the Early Modern period, though the prevailing common law was unclear, there seems to have been a perception both in the courts and in social practice that measures taken before 'quickening' (the foetal movement *in utero* that for most women conclusively indicated pregnancy) were more acceptable than during late pregnancy.

The first statute law proscribing abortion was Lord Ellenborough's Act of 1803 which also reformed the law on infanticide (see above). The 1803 Act definitively and for the first time constituted abortion before quickening as a crime punishable by transportation or the pillory. Abortion in later pregnancy became a capital offence, though the use of instruments was included only after further legislation in 1828. The death penalty for abortion was perceived as harsh at a period when questions were being raised about the widespread use of capital punishment in English law. In 1837 abortion was made a non-capital felony throughout pregnancy. The Offences Against the Person Act of 1861 also made it a felony for a woman to procure her own abortion. Anyone who provided her with the means to do so also committed a crime. This remained the situation in statute law until the Abortion Act of 1967. However, between the wars and in the face of an active campaign to reform the law, some key case law shifted the situation. For example, Dr Aleck Bourne aborted an adolescent girl, pregnant following a rape, with the intention to set up a test case and was acquitted. Such precedents established the position where a reputable, qualified doctor could be immune from prosecution and rely on his (or her) medical judgement where maternal health (widely defined) was at risk from a pregnancy.[81]

Several attempts to reform the statute law on abortion in the 1950s and the early 1960s failed until a changing climate of political opinion enabled a private member's bill to succeed as the 1967 Abortion Act. Whilst not repealing the provisions of the 1861 Offences Against the Person Act, it enabled medical abortion to be carried out where two doctors agreed that (a) continuing the pregnancy would pose greater risks to the mother's physical or mental heath than would the abortion; or (b) that the foetus was damaged. In many ways, therefore, the 1967 Act consolidated and clarified the position that had evolved through case law – that the decision to abort should lie with medical opinion – but widened the range of factors that justified abortion in two key ways. Firstly, psychiatric opinion as to the effect of pregnancy on the mother's mental health and, secondly, a social dimension that allowed the mother's 'actual or reasonably foreseeable environment' to be taken into account.[82] A 1996 amendment reduced the time permissible for an abortion to 24 weeks gestation.

Although this was innovatory and liberal legislation in 1967, by 2000 other Western countries (Austria, Belgium, Denmark, France, Germany, Greece, Italy, the Netherlands and the USA) had enacted far more liberal laws which left the decision on termination to the mother alone in the early weeks of pregnancy.[83] The debate continues as to the moral and social efficacy of abortion, with the grounds of concern shifting towards younger girls and migrants as well as issues around genetic research. The issue of abortion as crime *per se*, and the criminalisation of women seeking to end a pregnancy and the 'back-street' abortionists who 'helped' them, was largely settled in 1967 (at the same historical juncture where oral contraception gave women far more control over contraception). Early scares about medical tourism and the exploitation of vulnerable women by the private sector fairly soon evaporated.[84] Although access to abortion can be problematic, particularly for young or otherwise vulnerable women, and doctors and health services can be adept at deploying a range of delaying tactics, the growing number of UK abortions into the 1990s and beyond testified to the popularity and comparative effectiveness of the legislation.[85]

Conclusion

Overall, therefore, there have been historical continuities in women's practices to control fertility – some of it criminal behaviour. Their efforts involved a range of practices from avoiding penetrative intercourse (while not necessarily rejecting other kinds of sexual activity) or protracting lactation after childbirth, to post-coital douching and ingested abortifacients, to instrumental abortion. In some measure, infanticide can also be placed at the most desperate end of such a continuum. Furthermore, the legal frameworks that criminalised abortion and infanticide changed over time, were applied with changing and uneven severity, and responded to particular historical moments of moral panic when the abortionist, the baby farmer or the infanticidal mother were demonised.

Comparably, prostitution demonstrates long-term sociohistorical continuities as a resource-gaining strategy by marginal and vulnerable young women whose access to familial or other support networks was limited. The sale of sex, however, has had key symbolic resonance, periodically signifying social disorder and even breakdown, while understandings of the irrepressibility of masculine sexuality (and the acceptance of casual sex in male leisure practices) have meant that prostitution has often been tolerated and regulated rather than eradicated. Criminalising sex-for-cash *per se* has never been contemplated, even though vocal groups, from the Societies for the Reformation of Manners in the late seventeenth century to the National Vigilance Associations of the late nineteenth, have energetically tried to suppress prostitution. Policing prostitution has therefore frequently relied on laws around obstruction and soliciting that are about the policing of public urban space. Most notably in the middle of the nineteenth century, discourses of public health permitted new levels of discipline over prostitutes and women taken to be such.

The manifest tensions and fluctuations between representing women found guilty of criminal offences touching on their sexuality (from soliciting to infanticide) as victims or as social threats have been a key feature of historically shifting regimes of law and policing such offences. Such uncertainties seem to have arisen out of the fact that much of such offending has arisen out of the broad historical continuities of disadvantage for working women that cannot be tackled within prevailing class and gender unequal social order.

5
Women, Social Protest and Political Activism

Over three centuries women have been involved in much political activism that was within the law. Here we explore the interface between (political) protest and the criminal law, asking how, over time, this boundary has been inflected when the protesters that the law confronted were women. We can distinguish two kinds of protest at this interface. Firstly, some protests have called on customary or informal codes of legitimacy, or have exploited loopholes in the law, but the state (either local or central) has invoked the criminal (or civil) law to control protesters. Secondly, some protesters have deliberately protested by defying the rule of law, usually through acts of violence, so as to draw attention to their cause or to coerce the state to accede to their demands. For the purposes of this discussion, we can think of such actions as 'political crimes', committed deliberately to challenge the state to respond through the criminal justice process. The violence involved has extended from the minor property damage committed by Early Modern grain rioters to the arson and bombing carried out by militant suffragettes. Our focus here is on women protesters, and we have already argued in Chapter 3 that criminal justice interaction with women's violence has been inflected by gender power in complex ways. Though both kinds of protest have been committed by women and men, there have been particular resonances when women have taken protest action that put them outside the law.

Historians as well as historical actors have differed in their interpretations of violent – or forceful – political protest. Feminist historians, unsurprisingly, often write sympathetically of women who have encountered the sanctions of the criminal law because they were acting in protest against the (patriarchal) state. Our discussion therefore often addresses actions at the boundaries of crime, and also raises some quite difficult questions about the nature of political protest in relation to the law. When and how does forceful political protest shade into criminal violence? Where have women protesters deliberately defied the criminal law and where have they acted constitutionally? Has the criminal justice process been differentially applied to protesters who were women? The answers to such questions have been variable and historically situated.

Women's gender identities have always had an effect on their protest. Sometimes this can be discerned in the issues or the methods of protest and often in the interactions between protesters and the criminal justice system and public opinion. Nevertheless, women's gender identities have not always been foregrounded in their protest. Sometimes they acted primarily as workers, or as members of a political movement, or as adults responsible for providing for their households. On other occasions women have protested explicitly as women, using their gender identity as a key aspect of the protest, and not only when they took up issues directly about women's rights and status. The possibilities and constraints on women as protesters have depended on the nature of the prevailing gender order as well as on the wider political and social context.

Subsistence Riots

Riots over the price and availability of food, especially grain, flour, or bread, were part of community politics in the eighteenth and early nineteenth centuries. Such riots disturbed public order, but took place at the boundaries of crime and the criminal law, amounting to contests between differing notions of legitimacy and social order. Women frequently led or joined the disturbance; some riots consisted entirely of women. Crowds would assemble in the market when bread prices were (they thought) too high or around wagons shipping grain elsewhere. Sometimes mills or grain stores would be targeted. Although instances of greater violence are known, often the riot involved the seizure of the bread, flour or grain and its distribution among the rioters for what was considered a fair price. Sometimes larger protests involved processions and the display of potent symbols – a loaf held on a pike and draped in funereal black or streaked with red to symbolise blood. The authorities (often local magistrates) had few resources to control such riots and to a certain extent accepted that ensuring the availability of food was part of the responsibilities of governance. In E. P. Thompson's phrase, there existed a 'moral economy' in which the ritual of the food riot opened a limited cultural and political space for the negotiation of subsistence entitlements within local, mostly urban, communities. When riots were large, widespread or particularly violent, magistrates made use of local militias or sometimes regular regiments to restore order. Organised police forces were not available before the second third of the nineteenth century in some towns and from the 1860s in the counties. Magistrates were often restricted to reading the Riot Act and the retrospective action of the law against the most visible rioters. Although those involved in smaller riots often avoided severe punishment, both women and men could pay heavy penalties where the threat to public order was thought significant.[1]

As we have argued, Early Modern conceptions of gender emphasised women's unruliness. Thompson and others have suggested that these stereotypes and the rioters' assumption that women would be treated more leniently by the law combined with women's household responsibilities to make the subsistence riot a particularly female form of social protest. However, this view has now been modified.[2] It was certainly true that women were involved in food riots, and in a significant minority of cases led them. In Colchester, Essex, in July 1789 a grain wagon was stopped and Mary Langley, a labourer's wife, led around 20 people who aimed to stop the wagon and sell the grain.[3] In 1795, in Carlisle, 'a band of women accompanied by a vast number of boys paraded the streets'. They seized grain stored at a merchant's house and held it in the public hall until 'a committee could be formed for the purpose of regulating the price etc.'.[4] The same year in the nail-making area of the Black Country, nailers Hannah Phillips and Rebecca Oatley led a crowd into a weaver's house and took away two flitches of bacon.[5] By contrast women were recorded less frequently in other contemporary kinds of riot. John Bohstedt found that between 1790 and 1810 women were specifically mentioned in 77 press accounts of 240 food riots compared to 8 of 134 military recruiting riots, brawls or mutinies. His sample of 617 riots overall includes those with 50 or more people.[6] There is some indication that in more minor disturbances, the range of women's participation may have been wider. In a further example from Colchester, in 1779 'a number of people mostly women and children' had stopped a recruiting corporal of the marines escorting a new recruit and, in a side street, 'by force rescued the said recruit and got him into the house of the Widow Langton where the door was immediately shut and bolted.'[7]

Women food rioters appeared more often in small or medium-sized towns and/or in areas (such as the Black Country or the textile towns of eighteenth-century East Anglia) where many working households were heavily dependent on manufacturing work that was 'put out' by merchants and completed by workers in their own homes where women and children were key earners. Women often rioted alongside men because both shared the responsibility for maintaining their household economies. The differentiation of gender roles which, by the first half of the twentieth century, had created food shopping and the management of household consumption as a normatively feminine activity, was not applicable to earlier periods. Bohstedt further argues that in the developing industrial towns, the most relevant kind of social protest became that around labour disputes, where men were most often the rioters. Women remained involved in at least some food riots, but these were an increasingly redundant form of protest. The development of industrial capitalism had ruptured the limited consensus of the moral economy and food riots consequently lost their political leverage.[8] The implications of this argument are that women became marginalised as protesters as well as in other ways in a public sphere that was increasingly defined as masculine. This is an argument that requires some qualification. To the extent that this transition occurred, it was a complex and differentiated process.[9] Women were involved in the last major wave of protests of agricultural workers, the Captain Swing riots of 1830. These widespread but largely peaceable protests combined grievances about subsistence with those about wages, under-employment and the introduction of threshing machinery. Friendly societies, ostensibly sick benefit and social clubs, were in the early nineteenth century often thinly veiled guises for labour associations (trades unions) which were banned under the Combination Acts until 1827. Whilst the majority were men's associations, there were also numbers of female Friendly Societies. Bohstedt comments that in areas such as the textile region of Lancashire, there were both more food riots involving women and also strong membership of female friendly societies.[10] We shall further explore popular politics and labour disputes below. Firstly, we should take note of one area where women continued to risk legal repercussions well into the nineteenth century over a different customary practice to do with subsistence.

In agricultural communities and in rural areas surrounding small to medium-sized towns it was an established practice that the women and children of labouring households gleaned (gathered) the spilt grain left in the fields after harvest. The history of labour relations in the countryside broadly prefigures that of manufactures. The development of the market and the pressures to increase agricultural output meant that capitalist relations of production came to shape rural society in the later eighteenth century. This meant that over time, weekly waged or casual labour replaced annual hiring of farm servants and also that agricultural land became increasingly commoditised and privatised. Access to land and the exercise of common rights to firewood, grazing, fruit and nuts and other items that were an important part of the household economy of agricultural labouring families were restricted in many areas. It is estimated that gleaned grain could provide around 10 per cent of a household's annual income. A common law judgement of 1788 stated that gleaning required the permission of the farmer. However, Peter King's research on Essex petty sessions records demonstrates that despite this formal legal prohibition, in practice gleaning continued. It was not only farmers who prosecuted the gleaners; until the mid-nineteenth century women continued to prosecute farmers who tried to remove them from the fields for assault. One Essex widow in 1785, told a farmer 'she had as much right to glean as he had'.[11]

The survival of petty sessions records is patchy, yet it seems clear that the courts were reluctant to use the houses of correction against gleaners or to refer the matters to higher courts. On the other hand, farmers could find the courts decidedly unsympathetic. Technical legal difficulties hampered farmers who wanted to end gleaning but more tellingly, magistrates continued to give an ear to local 'customary law'. Hence the criminalisation of gleaning was uneven and ambiguous. Perhaps even more to the point, gleaning indirectly helped keep down the poor rates. The majority of women who appeared in gleaning cases were married. Gleaning was part of household provision that was specifically women's and children's work. Consequently, where the criminal law came into play this affected far more women than men, not only as defendants but crucially also as prosecutors.[12] If the food riot, and women's role within it, was losing effectiveness as means of social protest, women gleaners continued to defy authority and exploit the ambiguous application of the law. It is also perhaps significant that gleaning involved comparatively low-level infringements of legality and was consequently not perceived as socially threatening.

There is a further way in which gender inflected the ritual conduct of riot and popular disorder – through rioters' manipulation of gender symbolism. On occasion, when men rioted they dressed as women. Men who broke down turnpike tollgates in the Welsh 'Rebecca' riots frequently wore women's clothes and blackened their faces. It was earlier thought that in this way they were appropriating a particular feminine discourse about household subsistence, or hoping for the judicial leniency that might attach to women.[13] However, more recently historians' growing understanding of the cultural and symbolic role of gender has led to a rather different analysis. As we have suggested, dominant constructions of women protesters frequently drew on gendered stereotypes of unruly and disorderly women. Men rioters cross-dressed in part as a disguise but also because this gesture drew on the symbolism of social inversion, adding to their protest additional elements of critique and the mockery of authority. There are many ways in which the crowd in the early industrial period was marked by gender instabilities and confusions.[14]

Women's involvement in rural protest reduced in England during the nineteenth century. However, looking across the British Isles as a whole, these chronologies need some revision. Robertson argues that in Scotland the crofting (small farming) economy that had resulted from eighteenth-century land clearances gave women ongoing responsibilities for providing for their households through holding and working the land while men were away at sea, fishing. Consequently women were prominent as rioters in later land clearances as recently as around the First World War.[15]

In the industrialised economy of the later nineteenth and twentieth centuries women's activism around consumption shifted for the most part into the area of legality. The co-operative movement, and the Women's Co-Operative Guild in particular, became a locus for women to lobby around issues arising out of their domestic role in working-class households; for example, state maternity benefits. Karen Hunt has traced interwar socialist women's politics of consumption, though Matthew Hilton argues that the political pressure that women could exert as consumers had become a conservative practice by the later twentieth century.[16]

Women and political radicalism

The uneven transition from the riot to the strike as the quintessential form of working-class protest is a well-studied historical theme since it is one thread in the historical processes of class formation in the first half of the nineteenth century. Alongside subsistence protest and labour disputes, sections of the working classes took up the cause of the parliamentary franchise along with middle- and a few upper-class reformers. This popular radical politics, which had both constitutional and insurrectionary elements, was threatening to the state, particularly following the outbreak of war with revolutionary France in 1793. In 1794 the government suspended *Habeas corpus*[17] and unsuccessfully tried a group of London political radicals for high treason. Further legislation on sedition and treason following in 1795. Public protest for political reform was therefore potentially within the scope of very severe criminal laws.

Under the unreformed system, votes in parliamentary elections were strictly a matter of property and were thus unevenly distributed amongst the male population. Some working men could vote in towns that held a borough charter; some such constituencies had electorates of several thousand freemen. In the county constituencies a vote depended on the ownership of property worth more than 40 shillings annual rental. Many of the urban middle classes were not voters. Although the first statute that specifically excluded women from voting was the Reform Act of 1832, it was understood that the franchise was a masculine prerogative. Although some brands of early socialism did envisage a franchise that included all adults, the loose popular radical coalition amongst those who could position themselves as the unenfranchised 'useful classes' campaigned for a universal (or at least wider) adult male franchise. Women were amongst those actively campaigning on this issue and at moments had particularly high visibility. The popular radical platform assumed that an extension of the franchise would produce parliaments which would pass measures to alleviate the economic difficulties that many working people were experiencing in the highly volatile industrialising economy – difficulties which, as subsistence riots demonstrate, were of direct political interest to both women and men.[18]

Space does not allow us to explore women's involvement in popular radicalism in detail. Rather we will consider one singularly important historical moment, the Peterloo Massacre of August 1819 in Manchester. In the textile areas women often earned wages as well as managing their households. Unsurprisingly, they counted themselves as members of the 'useful' classes. Many women had been present at the 1817 Manchester Rally which saw off the 'Blanketeers' march of working men to petition parliament.[19] Feared as a potential insurrection, the march had been quickly stopped and no marchers got south of Macclesfield. Several specifically female reform societies were formed in summer 1819 alongside the male societies in the Manchester region. At a Blackburn rally in June 1819 the new female society committee, wearing green favours in their hats, mounted the platform and presented a hand-sewn cap of liberty to the Reform Society chairman. The Manchester Female Society acquired 1000 members in its first week. Female reform societies underlined the decorum as well as the constitutional stance of their members, not least to counter charges of 'indelicacy' for their public actions. They promoted universal *male* suffrage but they did so in forceful terms. The Union Female Society of Royton's flag bore the legend 'Let Us Die Like Men and Not Be Sold Like Slaves.' The mass rally planned for 16 August in St Peter's Fields was to be addressed by Henry 'Orator' Hunt, the radical MP; 50,000–60,000 men, women and children marched from the surrounding towns with flags and banners, and something of a carnival atmosphere prevailed.[20] True, the men had been practicing military drill on the moors in the previous weeks and they marched into Manchester bearing black flags that proclaimed such sentiments as 'Liberty or Death'. However, at Henry Hunt's injunction, the 16 August meeting was intended as entirely peaceable. The men were to march unarmed and the very visible placing of the women emphasised the non-violent intent.[21] Generally marching together and apart from men and children, mostly dressed in white, the high profile of committed women reformers emphasised the respectability of the reform movement. The leaders of the Female Reform Societies were placed either on the speakers' platform with their banners or sat nearby in Hunt's open carriage.

The Manchester magistracy took a different view of the proceedings. They had been prompted repeatedly by central government to deal firmly with the reform movement. Persuaded by the military mien of the male delegates, they feared that this massive rally could herald an insurrection. They had troops on hand; in the forefront, a regiment of volunteer Yeomen Cavalry comprising mostly Manchester men who could afford to own and maintain a horse. These were seconded by a force of around 200 volunteer Special Constables with truncheons – also local employers and shopkeepers. There were also around

375 mounted hussars and over 400 infantry from regular regiments. The magistrates moved to break the demonstration and arrest Hunt, and then the yeomen cavalry charged into the crowd with drawn sabres that had been specially sharpened for the occasion. A second charge by the hussars began a stampede in which demonstrators were run down by the horses and cut with sabres. Special constables bludgeoned the demonstrators with their truncheons. The banners and caps of liberty, key symbols of the movement, were captured and those holding them were frequently cut or beaten. Some of the injuries were inflicted hours later and a mile or so away from St Peter's Fields: 654 people were injured, 11 were killed that day and 6 others later died of their injuries. Of the 654 injured nearly half were wounded by sabres and other weapons, the balance were trampled or crushed: 168 of the wounded and four of the dead were women; in other words around one in three of the women present compared to one in eight of men.[22] Opinions have differed as to how far confusion and incompetence can explain the levels of fatality and injury, though recently historians have convincingly demonstrated that the authorities and the military were pretty much set on inflicting violence on the crowd which, true to Hunt's orders, offered no (or very little) resistance.

The Peterloo Massacre was a formative event in the history both of parliamentary reform and of emergent class relations in England, and Bush's findings of the high visibility of women at the demonstration and the markedly higher proportion of women who were injured situates women reformers at the centre of this key historical moment; 110 women were directly injured by the military or the police compared to 44 who were hurt through crowd pressure. Overall 'the retribution exacted by the police and the military fell more heavily upon women than upon men.' No chivalry or leniency to women operated at Peterloo. The women had been placed at centre stage of the rally; even these respectably presented femininities were especially threatening. Women protesters at Peterloo were not only subjected to the chaotic retribution of the Yeomanry, some were also singled out for serious criminal charges. Six women were arrested following Peterloo. Two were originally remanded along with Henry Hunt on a charge of high treason, though neither Elizabeth Gaunt nor Sarah Hargreaves, a leader of the Manchester female reformers, were in fact brought to trial.[23]

Michael Bush sees Peterloo as a landmark event in women's participation in working-class politics. In the northern districts in particular mass protests in the mid-1830s arose from attempts to impose the harsher provisions of the New Poor Law. This broke up working-class families, since poor relief for the able-bodied was only to be available in the gender-segregated workhouses. The 1832 Reform Act enfranchised many of the urban middle classes, but not the working class. The Chartist Movement of the late 1830s and 1840s gained mass support from working people across the country for a People's Charter whose core demand, predicated on a gender-differentiated model of working-class domesticity, was universal male suffrage. The Chartists retained the popular radical view that political representation would provide the leverage to raise wages and defend the household economy. Women chartists, like the women reformers at Peterloo, worked towards a parliamentary vote for their menfolk and preserved female respectability through a militant domesticity that (more or less) kept within the law. Chartism combined moral and physical force platforms, and it was men who defied the rule of law and drilled with pikes on the moors.

From popular radicalism to labour politics

Anna Clark explains why women were marginalised from social protest and organised labour politics in the decades following the Napoleonic wars by situating gender at the centre of her analysis of class formation.[24] Clark describes how a crisis in working-class gender relations was produced out of the stresses in social relations induced by industrial change, economic hardship and the differential opportunities for women, men and children in wage earning. Political radicalism had to appeal to the different perspectives of working women and men, as well as challenging dominant perceptions that working people lived disorderly social and sexual lives. Out of this dilemma were forged politicised gender identities – the manly, independent (breadwinner) artisan and the female household manager. These distinct, yet complementary roles defended working-class domesticity but also reinforced women's subjection to male authority at home and concealed domestic violence – an area where criminal sanctions have historically been limited and uneven. Clark argues that, despite the comparative gender inclusion of textile areas where women were a large section of the workforce, misogynist artisan culture organised in clubs and associations outside the home had a greater role in shaping labour politics. Using respectable working-class domesticity as a platform for political mobilisation highlighted the male wage as the key political and economic factor. Political struggles around the breadwinner wage became the business of men. The 1840s campaigns for a Ten Hours Bill that would limit working hours and over the Factories Acts saw a labour politics which constituted both women and children as subsidiary workers. Under these conditions, working women had good reasons for positioning themselves politically as household managers and therefore for being absent from social protest around labour questions that were at the margins of legality. Nevertheless, in so doing they lost ground in terms of both their political representation and their status as wage earners. Moreover, male workers became on occasion pitted against employers' attempts to substitute the cheaper labour of women and children. Mary Fletcher, speaking in 1853 to striking Lancashire textile workers, held it 'a disgrace to an Englishman [...] to allow his wife to go out to work'.[25] By the 1860s social protest about the conditions of labour had become a central element in the politics of class relations and was conducted for the most part by men organised in trades unions.

From the 1850s there developed different kinds of political activism which brought women into the public gaze and sometimes to the margins of the criminal law. A women's movement, originating in the middle classes, directly argued for women's claim to the vote. The suffrage campaign became militant in the early twentieth century and its challenges to the rule of law will be discussed at length in the next section. Before doing so, some mention of other contemporary issues is necessary. Women came into public view as activists and protesters through the philanthropic and other social action of (mostly) middle-class women which sometimes involved highly contentious political issues. As a middle-class woman controversially campaigning for the rights of prostitute women and the repeal of the Contagious Diseases Acts in the 1870s, Josephine Butler emphasised her role as that of an 'English mother'; she argued that the legal/judicial system was guilty of the criminal assault of women as a result of the introduction of forced internal examinations of women suspected of prostitution.[26]

As well as the suffrage, the women's movement also took up issues of women's education and employment, campaigning by constitutional means, and contributed to the growth of labour organisations in the mature industrial economy that had become established by the later nineteenth century. The first trade organisation specifically for women workers was the Women's Protective and Provident league founded in 1874, and by the closing decades of the nineteenth century there had been some attempts by 'malestream' trades unionism to organise workers classified as semi- or unskilled amongst whom were many women. There were some notable victories, as in 1888 when the young women workers at Bryant and May's match factories in the East End of London won improvements in their working conditions.[27] The 'Match Girls' had help organising their strike from Annie Besant, a committed socialist and campaigner for birth control. Besant had stood trial with Charles Bradlaugh in 1877 for publishing birth control information. Women's involvement in labour protest at this period, particularly where they were visible on the streets in large numbers, such as during the Bryant and May strike, defied the convention that such public action compromised women's respectability. The press presented the Match Girls as reluctant strikers manipulated by socialist activists.[28] To gain their tactical objectives, and to be recognised as workers with legitimate grievances, women strikers tended to avoid falling foul of the law. Much the same could be said of those women struggling for entry to the professions or into higher education, or indeed for those women activists in the movement for women's suffrage. They had to counter representations of themselves as unfeminine and unruly for seeking to enter what were then male preserves and so tended to emphasise orderly, respectable femininity in their self presentation.

Suffrage

The 1832 Reform Act and the 1835 Municipal Corporations Act were the first statutes to stipulate specifically that only men could vote. The campaign for women's suffrage originated during the lead up to the 1861 Reform Act which enfranchised men of the urban middle classes. The writings of J. S. Mill and Harriet Taylor had laid out utilitarian grounds for women's suffrage and in the 1860s a small but active constituency of middle-class women (and men) were developing the movement for women's rights. Mill was elected to parliament in 1865 on a pro-women's suffrage platform. Activist women such as Barbara Leigh-Smith Bodichon and Bessie Parkes – the so-called Langham Place set – took up issues such as dress reform and labour questions as well as the vote. Manchester was another centre for the women's movement, where activists included Lydia Becker. The National Society for Women's Suffrage was founded in 1872. By the 1890s the suffrage movement had a widespread membership, especially in major cities and across the north of England. In 1897 societies united as the National Union of Women's Suffrage Societies led by Millicent Fawcett. The NUWSS is generally described as constitutionalist; despite their lobbying and public demonstrations, the approach was gradualist and empha-sised the social responsibility with which women could be expected to use a parliamentary vote. By 1903, when no material progress had been made, a section of the suffrage movement sought more radical means to advance the cause. A group in Manchester around Emmeline Pankhurst and her elder daughters Christabel and Sylvia formed the Women's Social and Political Union (WSPU). The WSPU was led and funded by a small group, in particular Emmeline and Christabel Pankhurst, and on more than one occasion members were ejected for querying this leadership. Emmeline Pankhurst was a long-term political activist in Manchester, the wealthy widow of a lawyer. Although the Pankhursts presented themselves as conventionally feminine and eminently mid-dle class, they were prepared to use politically forceful methods. From 1905 the WSPU began a militant campaign, disrupting public meetings and using other forms of civil disobedience such as a tax strike. In 1908 the WSPU began to target public property, smashing shop windows and damaging public buildings and artworks. In 1914 Mary Richardson slashed Velasquez' painting of Venus in the National Gallery. The glass case containing the crown jewels in the Tower of London was smashed. In 1913 the WSPU began a campaign of arson and bombing, which ended only with the outbreak of the First World War. The Representation of the People Act of 1918 gave the vote to women over 30 who met the property qualification, largely in recognition of the service given during the war, and in 1928 all women over 21 were enfranchised on the same terms as men.[29]

The suffrage movement is now a well-researched aspect of women's his-tory. Historiographical opinion on suffrage militancy is divided, both about the effectiveness of militancy as a political strategy, and the degree of, as well as the interpretation of the criminality that was involved.[30] The ultimate goal of women's suffrage campaigns was for inclusion into the state, through the vote. They were liberal feminists who opposed the structural inequality of patriarchal law rather than the legitimacy of the law *per se*. In the following chapter we will see how women's rights activists were also campaigning to become part of the criminal justice system, as police, magistrates and lawyers. Our discussion here considers only the interface of militant suffrage protest and the criminal law, asking how suffragettes used often violent action to defy the rule of law and indeed how the criminal justice process found them problematic to deal with, not least because they saw arrest, trial and imprisonment as very potent locations to continue their protest.

Major demonstrations such as storming the House of Commons or the attempt to petition the King at Buckingham Palace, as well as smaller incidents where, for example, suffragettes chained themselves to railings, led to arrests for public order offences. However, it was with the escalation of the WSPU militant campaign that women deliberately set out to break the criminal law. The first windows broken by WSPU activists were those of 10 Downing Street, smashed in 1908 by Edith New and Mary Lee to protest at a six-week sentence passed on Emmeline Pankhurst. This may have been an impromptu response, but the violent campaign was rapidly adopted by the Pankhursts as WSPU policy. In October 1912 Mrs Pankhurst asked:

> those of you who can express your militancy by going to the House of Commons and refusing to leave [...] do so. [...] Those of you [...] who can break windows – break them. Those of you who can still further attack the secret idol of property [...] do so.[31]

1912 saw very visible uses of (criminal) violence including a five-day campaign damaging letter boxes in London and other large towns and breaking windows in West End shops. Mrs Pankhurst declared 'guerrilla warfare' in January 1913 when a suffrage bill had been defeated in the House of Commons.[32] A number of women's historians, sympathetic to the suffrage movement, have viewed WSPU violence as a reaction to the imprisonment and forced-feeding of hunger-striking suffragettes (something we discuss below). Sandra Stanley Holton argues that WSPU violence was governed by a 'moral philosophy' which attacked property whilst it respected human life – in contrast to the damage to life caused (as Mrs Pankhurst put it) by 'men in their warfare'.[33] Nevertheless the WSPU (in effect Emmeline and Christabel Pankhurst) also positioned their cause as warfare, a position which offered 'warfare' as a refutation of implied 'criminality'. The WSPU Seventh Annual Report (1913) argued:

> That private citizens should be affected is inevitable, for this is war, and in all wars it is the private citizen who suffers most. In the Women's war for the vote, the private citizen cannot complain of suffering the pains and penalties of warfare because there is nobody who can plead innocence and irresponsibility where the question of Votes for Women is concerned.[34]

There were indeed some lives lost and others endangered. For example, a fire set in a large stables in Bradford in June 1913 killed both men and horses. One suffragette was killed directly as a result of protest action. Emily Wilding Davison stepped out onto the racecourse and grabbed the reins of the King's horse during the 1913 Epsom Derby in an attempt to stop the race, but was trampled and died of head injuries.[35]

Bearman has uncovered a significantly higher number of bombing and arson attacks than had previously been assumed; in total there were 337 incidents between January 1913 and the end of the campaign in August 1914. These caused damage to a probable estimated value of between £1 and £2 million.[36] The incidence of violence fluctuated with the progress of the suffrage cause, but this was an organised and continuous campaign. The temporal and geographical patterning of these attacks, when read together with WSPU documentary sources, shows a certain level of local initiative co-ordinated and funded by a central committee. Many of the attacks were carried out or organised by women on the WSPU payroll, or receiving a retainer from the organisation, some of whom travelled widely throughout the United Kingdom (including Ireland) and violent incidents followed their itineraries. Bearman argues that the choice of comparatively 'soft' targets for bombs and fire-setting was shaped by tactical preferences rather than by moral philosophies of the protection of human life. It seems likely that there was an interplay between political ideals and practicalities. WSPU attacks also targeted those who had acted to impede the organisation's goals. The attacks in Ulster in 1913 followed the refusal of the Ulster Volunteer Force leader, Sir Edward Carson, to undertake that if Ireland gained independence it would allow women the vote. Four members of the WSPU set fires in the Theatre Royal Dublin as the audience were leaving a performance (and were reimbursed 17s 6d expenses by the organisation). On a more local scale, the church at Bradshall, Derbyshire, was burned after the rector had opposed an outdoor suffrage meeting.[37]

Historians are divided over the effects of WSPU violence. Women's historians tend to argue that even though the WSPU voluntarily ended its campaign at the outbreak of the First World War without achieving the vote, it was the prospect of renewed violence that helped prompt the enfranchisement of women over 30 in 1918. Others see the violence as having been a positive disincentive to governments. Such historians see NUWSS constitutionalist tactics as more persuasive and emphasise the changed post-war political situation and the government's realisation that women would be likely to vote Conservative. Whatever its final political effect, WSPU violence is central to our discussion here, as a key example of women directly engaging in violence to protest against what they perceived as a tyrannical and obdurate (male) government and who were consequently subjected to the mechanisms of criminal justice. The Pankhursts were highly charismatic leaders, and emphasised their female, middle-class respectability.[38] However, unlike the constitutionalists, militant suffragettes refused to interpret femininity as requiring pacific, nurturing behaviour. Militant suffragettes developed a deep emotional as well as political attachment to 'the cause', and were prepared to commit acts of violence, to break the law and to risk not only the pains of imprisonment but the undermining of their respectability in order to pursue the goal of votes for women. Such women were markedly different from the offenders that contemporary women's prisons normally dealt with. Indeed, militant suffragettes used imprisonment to further their campaign. For the prison authorities and the government, suffragette prisoners became a particularly problematic group of offenders.

Cat and mouse

Over the course of the militant campaign, around 1000 suffragettes served prison sentences. Convicted suffragettes found themselves in the gloomy world of early twentieth-century women's prisons (Chapter 7). Their belief that they were political prisoners coloured their experiences across a diversity of age and class. The image of the young, middle-class suffragette prisoner may dominate popular representations (including those of the suffragettes themselves), but those imprisoned included older women, married women, and working-class women as well as those in poor health or with disabilities. Within prisons, suffragettes established supportive networks, associated whenever possible even to the extent of round games, fancy dress and amateur theatricals.[39]

Suffragettes often pitied the disadvantaged lives that had brought other women into prison, but these perceptions were forged across a recognition of distance and difference. Sylvia Pankhurst described the prisoners sent to scrub the floor of the hospital cell she occupied when recovering from forcible feeding as 'old women; pale women; a bright young girl who smiled at me whenever she raised her eyes from the floor; a poor ugly, creature without a nose, awful to look at'.[40] Suffragettes also had contradictory reactions to women prison staff. Theoretically, they were campaigning for the rights of womankind in general but sympathetic relations with women warders were barely possible, since the warders were imposing the prison regime that suffragettes protested against. This was especially true when women warders assisted with forcible feeding. Some suffrage memoirs describe warders as 'monsters'. There were allegations of assault by women warders, and clearly the physical coercion that was a routine part of prison discipline was shocking to imprisoned suffragettes. Mrs Pankhurst herself was disciplined for abusing and striking a warder, though she contested much of the allegation.[41] When Lady Constance Lytton took on the dress of a working-class woman and was arrested as 'Jane Warton', she proved that working-class women were treated worse in prison than those of higher social class. Prison warders and in particular the prison matron, nevertheless, had great formal and informal power over all suffragette prisoners, destabilising the class privileges of those who were better off.

The presence of so many (often middle- or even upper-class) suffragettes in prison did much to prompt changes in the prison rules for women in 1910. Rule 243a permitted approved 'ameliorations [...] in respect of the wearing of prison clothing, bathing, hair-curling, cleaning of cells, employment, exercise, books, and otherwise'. Not only did suffragettes often eat better than other offenders, since food hampers were provided by families and sympathisers, they were also distinguished by dress. Miss Allen, a well-off suffragette, attended prison exercise wearing a hat and lemon kid gloves.[42] Rule 243a did not convey the legal status of political prisoner, even though the suffragettes represented it as such – the government had long resisted acknowledging that category. Although Rule 243a amounted to a *de facto* recognition within the penal system of different conditions for prisoners 'of good character' who were not guilty of 'dishonesty, cruelty, indecency or grave violence', as Alyson Brown points out, since it conveyed privileges that could be withdrawn for misconduct, 'if anything [it] may have rested more power in official hands than before.'[43] Prison was the 'baptismal experience' of many committed suffragettes. Numbers of them resisted prison regimes by breaking windows and damaging the few objects in their cells, refusing to obey the rules and, most politically telling, by going on hunger strike. During the course of the campaign, Mrs Pankhurst was imprisoned and went on hunger strike 11 times.

So deep was the conviction of imprisoned suffragettes, they were prepared to go to great lengths and understood that their physical suffering had great political effect. Annie Kenney declared that 'we are prepared to die.' She also argued that suffragettes knew that 'if one woman dies in prison, those women who do not approve of militancy today will come out to be militant tomorrow.' Hunger strikes produced a grave problem for the prison authorities, since the political consequences of the death of a hunger-striking suffragette were almost unthinkable. Consequently, they resorted to a measure that had been used (without any great notice of the pains it was inflicting) on mentally ill patients, that of forcible feeding. Mrs Pankhurst challenged this decision at law arguing that she was not mentally ill, but lost the case on the grounds that forcible feeding was necessary to preserve life.[44] Hunger-striking suffragettes were force fed, sometimes with a cup but often through a tube inserted into a nostril and on occasion via the rectum. These procedures caused much pain, bruising and injury particularly when, as was often the case, the prisoner resisted. The sense of powerlessness and the indignity involved was, as Sylvia Pankhurst recalled, almost as bad as the physical pain.[45] Imprisoned suffragettes strategically used their bodies and their physical suffering as a means of furthering their political cause. This was recognised within their movement and by the government. As the Permanent Undersecretary at the Home Office wrote to the Prime Minister, Gladstone, in 1909 'anything is better than having one of these foolish women die during, or kill herself after, the forcible feeding.'[46] The outcome of these deliberations was the Temporary Discharge for Ill Health Act of 1913, more expressively known as the Cat and Mouse Act. This allowed the discharge of prisoners on licence on grounds of poor health, subject to re-arrest on expiry of the licence. Suffragette publicity argued that the Liberal government cat was playing with the suffragette mouse, rather than torturing her to death in one go. As Alyson Brown comments, the suffragettes defied the judicial process 'by interrupting the link between crime and punishment'. Despite WSPU propaganda, and the grave health consequences for some suffragettes, numbers of them did serve less than their original sentences because of their resistance to prison regimes particularly through the hunger strike.

From suffrage to Greenham

Some militant suffragettes, not least Sylvia Pankhurst, later became left-wing political activists. Women's suffrage was, however, far from being a left-wing movement. Some militant suffragettes joined Oswald Moseley's British Union of Fascists in the 1930s.[47] If militant suffragettes are a key example of women actively challenging the criminal justice system for political goals of women's rights, the BUF is important to our discussion in a different way. It was a mass political movement with around 20 per cent female membership and where women had a prominent role, which deployed violence and hence lawbreaking as a key political strategy.[48] Moseley saw women as a crucial part of his organisation.[49] BUF women's units held outdoor political meetings and members were trained in ju-jitsu. Women were allocated the very visible duties of stewarding at BUF rallies, and the ju-jitsu training was preparation for this since violence was expected at such events. As a result some BUF women ended in court both as witnesses and as defendants in assault cases.[50] Others broke the law in other ways in the interests of the fascist cause. During the Second World

War, BUF sympathies remained with the fascist regimes in Germany and Italy. Miss Nora Briscoe, a civil servant and BUF member, served five years penal servitude for taking official documents from the Ministry of Supply; 747 BUF members, women and men, were interned during the war as a threat to national security.[51] Twentieth century modernity included modes of femininity which incorporated citizenship and public action. For a few years in the 1930s the BUF attracted widespread support. Its populist, patriotic style not only incorporated a visible role for women and acknowledged (a version of) women's rights, but also incorporated public violence and law-breaking into its approved models of femininity.

Following the Second World War and the use of nuclear weapons in its closing months, nuclear disarmament became a new area where mass protest, and encounters with the law on public order involved women and men. With the 1960s, anti-establishment youth protest movements took up an overlapping collection of issues, in particular the Vietnam war. The movement in the United Kingdom was informed by an awareness of black civil rights protests in America. Anti-war demonstrations, in particular those at the American Embassy in Grosvenor Square (1968) involved both women and men and made tactical use of crowd violence. This generally libertarian climate also touched on environmentalist issues, and was framed by a youth culture of music festivals, illegal drug use and 'sexual liberation'. Young women, finding that 'sexual liberation' and political awareness still benefited men rather than themselves, heightened their political sensitivity to gender issues and developed the Women's Liberation movement – now generally known as Second Wave Feminism. Radical feminists used the political tactics of the demonstration, the sit-in and other kinds of civil disruption to further their cause, such as disrupting the Miss World beauty contest.[52] The agendas set, and the (qualified) gains made by feminist activists in the 1960s and 1970s in many ways form the backdrop of the closing case study in this chapter, the Greenham Common Women's Peace Protest.[53]

Greenham Common Peace Protest

In the early 1980s there was a re-escalation in the nuclear arms race. A decision was taken to deploy US cruise missiles in Europe including the United Kingdom, using RAF bases. There was a corresponding resurgence in the activities of CND and the formation of many other anti-nuclear campaign groups. In August 1981, 'Women for Life on Earth' marched from Cardiff along with men and children to RAF Greenham Common in Berkshire. Their written protest underlined their fears 'for the future of all our children and [...] of the living world'. Against the expectations of the authorities they decided to stay, and set up camp immediately outside the perimeter wire fence. The Greenham peace protest was from the outset framed as a women's issue and in February 1982 the protesters decided that the camp would be women only. This was a controversial decision at the time (and subsequently) which ensured that Greenham's 'unique dynamic [...] (amongst peace groups) [...] was a demand for disarmament yoked to an analysis of patriarchy'. Echoing Mrs Pankhurst's condemnation of 'men in their warfare', nuclear arms were positioned as the products of patriarchal states, whereas women were better able to argue and demonstrate for peace. The protest came to involve several hundred thousand women over its 13 years. Roseneil comments that it was the 'most visible manifestation of women's politics in Britain in the 1980s'.[54] The continuous presence of women in the camp was periodically augmented by massive demonstrations, predominately by women, but sometimes with men in supporting roles. The camp became a focus for women from all around Britain and elsewhere, and for the media. At the height of the protest the original camp at Yellow Gate had been supplemented by camps at all the other gates.

Greenham Women used non-violent direct action which defied both criminal and civil laws to disrupt the running of the base. They blockaded the base for the first time in March 1982 and 34 were arrested. The following August a group of women broke into the base and occupied a sentry box. The first major demonstration, in December 1982 aimed to 'Embrace the Base'. Women protesters encircled the nine-mile perimeter, and decorated the fence with photographs, writings, toys, balloons, peace symbols and myriad other objects. The following day 2000 women blockaded the base and police used 'considerable force' to eject them. On New Year's Day 1983 44 women scaled the perimeter fence and sang and danced on the top of one of the silos.[55] The following Easter women and men joined into a 14-mile human chain that linked Greenham Common with Aldermaston and the Burgfield Ordnance factory. In October 1983, having revised their views on non-violence to permit cutting the fence, another large women-only demonstration cut down four miles of the perimeter and thus rendered themselves liable to charges of criminal damage. Missiles were deployed at Greenham in November 1983 and the following month some 50,000 women encircled the base, using mirrors to reflect back the militaristic images of wire, concrete and weapons. The creative use of symbolism, imagery and the performative, as well as writing, poetry, speech and song were a deliberate tactic. Greenham women politicised their gender identity; the protest emphasised women's maternalist concerns for peace and for the environment and some commentators have found this both biologically essentialist and even anti-feminist.[56] The experience of protest proved transformative for many, both in terms of wider issues like nuclear disarmament and gender and sexual politics. The experience of political and social action without men and opposed to the masculinities attached to the military, political and criminal justice establishments, radicalised protesters' feminism. Heterosexuality came to seem increasingly problematic for many and lesbian sexuality became common. Roseneil argues that Greenham was 'a crucible for the construction of lesbian identities', a term she uses to express far more than sexuality, embracing both social and political identity.[57] Clothing (boots, overalls, trousers, often brightly coloured) best adapted for outdoor camp living also expressed a 'queer politics' around (political) lesbian identity. Some women adopted deliberately challenging behaviours, such as openly displaying same-sex affection or mocking heterosexual masculinities. Chapter 7 will argue that the cutting of hair or even shaving heads was a stigmatising punishment for women in Victorian prisons or in convict factories in Australia. Militant suffrage campaigners in the early twentieth century were, we have seen, careful to maintain respectable and 'ladylike' appearance. In contrast, Greenham women cut or dyed their hair or shaved their heads as an assertive performance of political and sexual identity.

The gender and sexual identities of Greenham protestors were placed at the forefront of their relations with the media, the public and the different arms of the state that they confronted (the military, the criminal justice system, the local authority). Journalists were always keen to interview Greenham women but inevitably their words were heavily mediated by media fascination with their daily lives, their sexuality, their appearance, their (purported) abandonment of their family responsibilities. Particularly in the early stages of the protest, the dominant image was that of the concerned heterosexual mother protesting to save her children from a future nuclear holocaust. However, as the campaign of non-violent direct action got underway, media discourse emphasised dirt, depravity and deviant sexuality, as well as criminal 'deviance'. Greenham women conducted their protest less through words but crucially through the performative deployment of their bodies, assertively gendered as female, in ways which exceeded the suffragette emphasis on protest through bodily suffering. At one point the base was blockaded by naked women who had smeared their bodies with ash, deliberately confronting the gender sensibilities of the police who donned protective clothing before removing the women.[58] The media expressed the affront of the dominant gender order by constructing those bodies as deviant. The transgressive bodies of Greenham women were subjected to both official and unofficial punishment. The camp became a target for violence and harassment by local men. One woman was killed by a USAF vehicle in 1989.[59] Repeated eviction attempts were legally complicated by the original status of the campsite as common land and the women's removal to land owned by the Ministry of Transport.[60] Two women charged with contravention of newly formulated by-laws argued in court that the laws were *ultra vires* (outside the power of the government to make) because they contravened the rights of common that prevailed over Greenham Common land. Although judgement was made for the women at the Crown Court the decision was reversed on appeal and only in 1990 did the House of Lords finally settle the matter in favour of the Greenham Women.[61]

The criminal law was readily used to charge women for activities arising from non-violent direct action. However, as Alison Young points out, very often the criminal justice system exercised discretion in choosing to prosecute Greenham Women for comparatively minor offences considering that it could have brought more serious charges such as breaches of the Official Secrets Act. This might at first sight seem an example of judicial leniency. However, the means that the women employed in their protest, as well as the magistrates' awareness that imprisoned Greenham women used their sentence as a means to continue their protest, also made lighter sentencing an expedient option for the courts. For example, women found reading and writing on classified documents in the air traffic control tower (December 1983) were in the first instance charged with burglary. However, to avoid their electing a jury trial at Crown Court (with the resultant additional publicity that would involve), the charges were reduced to criminal damage. The carnivalesque, irreverent form of the demonstrations extended into arrest, court appearances and prison. Greenham Women made articulate and impassioned political statements in court, they also sang, wept and shouted from the dock. When some of the women were imprisoned in Holloway, in February 1983 six other Greenham women climbed *into* the prison to demonstrate their solidarity.[62] Apparent leniency was also punctuated by comparatively punitive uses of the criminal law. Following the October 1983 demonstration when stretches of the perimeter fence were cut down, around 300 women were arrested and individually charged with criminal damage 'not exceeding £200'. All these were fined at the magistrates' court. However, two women selected apparently at random were charged with criminal damage to the whole value of the fence destroyed (several thousand pounds). The case went to the Crown Court and they were sentenced to 12 months imprisonment.[63]

Greenham Women repeatedly confronted the law through articulate arguments in defence. In November 1982, feminist lawyers representing Greenham Women argued that the deployment of cruise missiles contravened the obligations of both Britain and the United States under the Genocide Act of 1969. A number of prestigious (male) witnesses including the historian and peace activist E. P. Thompson and the Bishop of Salisbury argued that the women's action was designed to *keep* the peace that was jeopardised by the threat of nuclear war. Despite the problematics of a feminist protest relying on male, authoritative expert witnesses (in later trials women expert witnesses were called on) the trial certainly afforded a good deal of media publicity for the peace action.[64] Greenham women also made bold use of international law in bringing an action against the US Government in the Federal Court in New York to prevent the deployment of cruise missiles in Europe. Although unsuccessful at law, the case succeeded in widening the protest and forging links between the Greenham women and other peace groups in Europe.

Roseneil assesses Greenham as a key moment in the British women's movement. It was both empowered and limited by its stance as a women-only protest. As Helen Poulsen points out, more recently trans-gender politics has challenged the male/female dichotomy through which the Greenham philosophy was articulated.[65] It remained substantially a movement of white women, and there was a period of bitter struggle between established Greenham women and black feminist groups in 1987.[66] Nevertheless Greenham remains a landmark in the history of social protest. Like the women of the WSPU, Greenham Women deliberately broke the law and made tactical use of gender stereotypes to confront the criminal justice system. Indeed, they went further, they mobilised the creative, capable and often lesbian female body (as well as the suffering female body) as a means of protest and politicised their identities as women in issues that were far wider than those of women's rights.

Conclusion

This chapter has provided a brief and necessarily selective overview of the history of women's political activism in relation to the law. We have not, for example, explored the distinct and complex historical, legal and political dynamics of women's involvement in the cause of Irish nationalism, where they have carried out a range of actions liable to criminal sanction, both violent and non-violent, including direct combat.[67] However, our discussion has indicated some broad shifts that are aligned to the historical development of modernity (and arguably post-modernity). Early Modern subsistence protest used a rich performative discourse of riot in which women had a recognised role. Such protests comprised forceful negotiation with the law, which, while it was not lenient with women protesters in major incidents, did recognise some obligation to ensure working people's subsistence. The development of industrialisation shifted the key item of contention from the price and availability of foodstuffs to the cash wage, and these concerns were linked to the issue of the parliamentary vote. At key moments when this movement appeared insurrectionary, the authorities could be highly repressive. At Peterloo (1819) women were very visible protesters and were targeted for the violence of the yeomanry. Women's activism in defence of their household economies was subsumed into popular radicalism, culminating in Chartism at mid-century, and generally focused on obtaining universal male suffrage. This political platform envisaged differentiated (and unequal) gender roles, which saw women's marginalisation and concomitant withdrawal from (especially illegal) protest action by the second half of the century. The women's movement, originating with middle-class women around the 1860s, took in issues of employment and education and claimed 'sisterhood' between women, though this was always mediated by the maternalist authority of middle-class women. Much of the women's movement was constitutionalist. Women's suffrage was the dominant issue by the 1900s and middle class-led militant suffragettes challenged the government and the criminal justice system through public protest to the extent of organised violence. Imprisonment itself became an important site of protest through non-compliance with prison discipline, the hunger strike and the authorities' responses of forcible feeding and release on licence. No other area of the contemporary women's movement challenged the criminal law so directly. Women were not entirely absent from nineteenth-century strikes, and were sometimes key participants.

Political uses of violence and illegality re-emerged in the interwar period on the political right as numbers of women, some of them ex-suffragettes, joined the BUF – an organisation controlled by men but which accorded women a visible role and applauded their violence. Women were involved in the anti-nuclear movement as well as youth and peace protests in the 1960s. Radical feminists not only developed a (to an extent) essentialist politicisation of gender identity, feminists on occasion challenged the law as a means of protest. Second Wave Feminist ideas and tactics directly informed the theory and practice of women's protest at the Greenham Common Peace Camp, which openly challenged the criminal (and civil) law, formed a woman-centred politics that was about women's capabilities for action, and addressed wide issues of global concern such as warfare and environmental harm. Compared to the suffragettes, Greenham women were more limited in their uses of physical violence and more creative in how they used their bodies as well as their words to make their protest.

6
Women in Control?

Women's inequality before the law and hence within the criminal justice system itself was a central focal point of feminist campaigning for much of the nineteenth and twentieth centuries. Arguing for votes for women in 1851, Harriet Taylor and John Stuart Mill depicted women's political subordination as inseparable from their lack of legal status: 'women, whenever tried, are tried by male judges and a male jury'.[1] A series of educated women who were active in professional and philanthropic work used their public prominence to call for women's increased presence in the courts and in policing. Elizabeth Blackwell, the first English woman to qualify as a doctor, argued in 1881 that there was a need for a small number of 'superior women' to take up 'positions of power and authority' in 'the police organisation' to work specifically with female offenders.[2] As Chapter 1 has shown, women participated in the courts as complainants and witnesses across the Early Modern and modern periods. Yet, until 1919 women were unable to practice as lawyers, or to act as judges, magistrates or jurors. During the nineteenth century it became customary to clear the room of all female observers when cases of rape or indecent assault were tried; it was argued that this was necessary to protect their modesty.

This chapter is concerned with women's direct involvement in criminal justice as professionals, experts and officials, but also as movers and shakers, who combined private resources and access to social networks with significant organizational and rhetorical skills to effect change within the system. It charts women's pioneering activity but also offers an analysis of the ways in which ideas about gender shaped these contributions. It asks to what extent women in varying positions of influence, authority and control have sought or achieved the creation of alternative ethical frameworks. Did women who assumed positions of authority within the criminal justice system reinforce conventional gender and class stereotypes or did they challenge them? Nineteenth-century feminists made use of a powerful set of arguments that emphasized *both* the need for equal rights *and* recognition of the unique qualities associated with womanhood. This chapter will show that the argument about gender difference was ultimately double-edged; whilst it created an important space in which women could develop a 'special sphere of usefulness' distinct from masculine traditions and cultures, notions of gender difference ultimately served to circumscribe their activity.

Midwives, matrons and medical men

The exclusion of women from an official capacity within courts of law can be viewed as a nineteenth-century phenomenon. There is some evidence that in the manorial courts of medieval England women held legal jurisdiction over serfs and tenants.[3] During the Early Modern period women had been called to give testimony in court as 'watchers' and 'searchers' in witchcraft allegations. Married women, widows and, in some cases, midwives were asked to determine whether marks on the body (often on the genitalia or 'secret parts') were teats through which a witch suckled her 'imps' or 'familiars'. The practice was well-established by the 1580s and it featured strongly in the trials associated with Matthew Hopkins in Essex, Suffolk and Norfolk in 1645.[4] Sleep-deprivation was also used by Hopkins as a strategy to extort confessions or other evidence; those accused of witchcraft were carefully watched during this time, sometimes by other women, to see whether they invoked the devil or summoned their familiars. The close involvement of women, as watchers and searchers as well as formal accusers, has been viewed by historian James Sharpe as clear evidence of women's agency and authority in the courtroom. Clive Holmes has suggested, however, that their role should not be overstated. Leading men in the community often instigated the legal process and women were simply called upon as 'ancillaries' to provide additional evidence in support of an allegation.[5]

Moreover, women's 'specialist' role in the courtroom in witchcraft trials was gender-related, linked to an older precedent. From at least the thirteenth century onwards the English courts had made use of married women's knowledge of reproduction and the body by asking them to sit on special purpose juries, usually described as a 'jury of matrons'. Female jurors did not require specific standing as midwives, although the term 'matron' denoted maturity and good reputation. Common experience of marriage and childbirth was deemed sufficient and the 'jury of matrons' was used for matters in which it was deemed inappropriate for male jurors to inspect female bodies. The 'jury of matrons' was mainly used to determine pregnancy, indicated by 'quickening' or the movement of the child within the womb. In civil cases this was sometimes linked to matters of inheritance (ascertaining, for example, whether a widow was pregnant by her late husband) or non-consummation of marriage (ascertaining proof of virginity). In the criminal courts, women convicted of capital offences might receive a stay of execution and sometimes a pardon if they could successfully 'plead the belly'. In the early eighteenth century it was common for female defendants sentenced to death to plead the belly. Increasingly, however, the 'jury of matrons' was represented in popular literature as incompetent or corrupt as well as complicit with female defendants. Its use had significantly declined by the 1760s.[6] With the advent of new bodies of male medical practitioners, including specialists in gynaecology as well as medical jurisprudence (forensic medicine), the jury of matrons was further discredited and eroded. Doctors were increasingly called to identify the foetal heartbeat using the stethoscope and 'quickening' was rejected as an indicator of the moment that a child took life. Medical experts argued 'it is high time that this absurd trial by a jury of matrons were done away with'.[7] There is no evidence of its official use after 1879, although references to the use of female 'searchers', particularly in cases of rape or indecent assault, were occasionally made.[8]

The development of scientific technology had created the new role of 'expert'. Nevertheless, the professionalisation strategies used by the emerging medical elite ensured that this expertise was consolidated in male hands. As in the case of law (which similarly acquired formalization and status as a profession in the late eighteenth century), the opportunity to qualify as a practitioner and to join prestigious professional associations was closed to women on grounds of sex.[9] With the development of the 'new police' after 1829, male 'police surgeons' were appointed not merely to attend to the health of police officers but to examine victims of assault as part of crime investigation. As a result of persistent and vociferous campaigning, women were permitted to qualify as physicians in Britain from 1865 onwards. Yet their numbers remained small (less than 0.1 per cent of all GPs in 1914) and they were rarely used in the courts to provide expert testimony.[10] In 1904 Dr Marion Elford acted as a medical witness in a case of statutory rape (involving a girl under the age of consent) tried at the Lincoln Assizes; commenting on the case later, she referred to the incongruous procedure whereby all women (except herself as expert witness) were asked to leave the court because of its indelicacy.[11] It was not until 1927 that Nesta Wells took up a position as the first woman police surgeon in Britain, employed by the City of Manchester Police on a part-time basis specifically to examine women and child victims of assault and to offer expert testimony relating to these cases in the courtroom.[12]

Middle-class women, philanthropy and the public sphere

Middle-class women's engagement with nineteenth-century criminal and civil justice took two related forms. Firstly, their lack of legal status became a central campaigning plank for the early women's movement. Secondly, as a result of growing involvement in philanthropy and voluntary social work, they voiced concerns about the treatment of women and children (predominantly of lower social class) as convicts within the prison regime and the courts. These two areas of activity came together most explicitly in the work of Josephine Butler who, in opposing the Contagious Diseases (CD) Acts in the 1870s, argued that the brutal treatment of working-class women suspected of prostitution was symptomatic of all women's lack of equal rights.

At the beginning of the nineteenth century, the doctrine of '*feme covert*' could be used to deny a married woman legal status, the ability to control personal property, the right of custody over her children, and the ability to request a divorce.[13] The Parliamentary Reform Act of 1832, which gave the vote to 'male persons' who paid rates of £10 or more a year, assumed that a woman's interests were represented by those of her husband. In 1836 Caroline Norton, whose husband had refused access to her three sons, began to lobby Parliament for women's custody rights. The 1839 Infants and Child Custody Act was a partial and piecemeal response (women who had committed adultery were not recognised), but it was lauded by Harriet Martineau as 'the first blow struck at the oppression of English legislation in relation to women'.[14]

From the 1850s onwards activists, such as Barbara Bodichon and the Langham Place Circle, focused on married women's lack of property rights, arguing that women, through the act of marriage, passed 'from freedom into the condition of a slave'.[15] The Married Women's Property Act of 1882 finally recognised that husband and wife were discrete entities. Yet some of the assumptions that underpinned *feme covert* lingered on. Despite the mid-nineteenth-century campaigns of Frances Power Cobbe, who highlighted the incidence of marital cruelty (including sexual assault), the rape of married women by their husbands, condoned in terms of men's conjugal rights, was not criminalised until 1991.

Thus the demand for votes for women, which emerged in the nineteenth century and culminated in the militant suffragette campaigns of the Edwardian period, was accompanied by broader concerns about the need to improve women's legal status. Indeed, the lack of clarity regarding women's position was exposed in 1868 when rate-paying members of the National Society for Women's Suffrage tried to register as voters in Manchester. When their claims were rejected, they took the matter to the courts (the case of *Chorlton v. Lings*). Lord Brougham's Act of 1859 had attempted to clear up one anomaly regarding women's culpability, stating that 'in all Acts words importing the masculine gender shall be deemed and taken to include females unless the contrary [...] is expressly provided'.[16] However, in *Chorlton v. Lings*, the judge ruled that 'man' did, indeed, mean 'member of the male sex' as a result of custom and practice. The common law tradition that women were not 'persons' was also used to exclude women from public office and from the legal profession.

Despite their lack of formal recognition, middle-class women were assuming a highly visible presence within a public sphere as they participated in debate over women's legal status. This was paralleled by significant involvement in philanthropy and voluntary social work. From 1816 onwards Elizabeth Fry worked to improve the conditions of women prisoners in Newgate, persuading the prison authorities to replace male supervision with matrons and female turnkeys. Education, religious instruction and training for future employment were designed to reform women prisoners, a notable shift from an older assumption that convicts were social misfits to be punished. Fry's 'lady visitors' sought to befriend prisoners and to elevate their spiritual and moral aspirations through conversation and example. In 1821 she formed the British Ladies' Society for Promoting the Reformation of Female Prisoners, the first national women's organisation in the country and an important precedent for the women's movement more generally. Penal reformer Mary Carpenter campaigned for the reform of young offenders in special institutions separate from adult prisons. She founded two juvenile reformatories in her home town of Bristol: Kingswood (for boys) in 1852 and Red Lodge (for girls) in 1854. Although initially reluctant to associate herself with the lobby for women's rights, she went on to join Josephine Butler's campaign against the CD Acts and became involved in women's suffrage just before her death in 1877.

The work of activists such as Fry, Butler and Carpenter, has been analysed by historians Annemieke van Drenth and Francisca de Haan through the concept of 'caring power'. Van Drenth and de Haan argue that women's philanthropic work must be understood in terms of a religious commitment that involved humanitarian compassion, sympathy and a duty of care towards others. They view this form of power as a 'productive' process, suggesting that it enabled middle-class women to influence those less fortunate than themselves, empowering both groups to change their own lives.[17] 'Caring power' was not an exclusively female preserve, since its operation was apparent across the work of male and female social reformers. Indeed, its primary exponents were associated with forms of evangelical religious belief (Quakerism in the case of Fry, Unitarianism in the case of Carpenter and Butler) that advocated more egalitarian and democratic roles (spiritual and social) for female members of the congregation. However, women's involvement in caring roles gained wider acceptance because it could be viewed as an extension of their nurturing roles as wives and mothers within the private domestic sphere.

Women's philanthropic intentions can be understood in terms of a desire to rescue or save the unfortunate out of genuine religious commitment; but it is also important to examine how class position affected perception and outlook. Fry aimed to persuade women prisoners to abandon the popular pursuits of drinking, card games and gambling in favour of Bible study, needlework and knitting. Although she stressed that the women with whom she worked did so of their own volition, it is difficult to argue that their choices were anything other than extremely limited. This is not to deny their agency, but to recognise that nineteenth-century relationships between women were shaped by class as well as patriarchy. Through her Red Lodge reformatory in Bristol, Mary Carpenter sought to instil in her youthful female charges patterns of self-discipline and industriousness that were deemed appropriate for their class position. Her friend, the feminist campaigner Frances Power Cobbe, undoubtedly carried out extremely significant work in exposing the problem of domestic violence and the ways in which it went unrecognized within the criminal justice system. Yet she ultimately reinforced class prejudice when she argued that it was rarely of a serious nature amongst the upper and middle classes: 'The dangerous wife-beater belongs almost exclusively to the artisan and labouring classes [. . .].' In the industrial north, so she claimed, women of the manufacturing classes were often 'unwomanly, slatternly, coarse, foul-mouthed – sometimes loose of behaviour, sometimes madly addicted to drink', an exacerbating factor in incidents of wife-beating.[18] In their attempt to protect working-class women from violence, to save them from prostitution or to rehabilitate them from criminality, this 'pioneering' group tended to represent middle-class standards and values as superior in opposition to a brutalised 'other'. It can be argued that, in depicting the women that they worked with as 'poor creatures' or 'poor outcasts' to be pitied, they offered a kindness and sympathy that also objectified. The recasting of 'deviant' women as 'victims' to be saved – rather than social 'threats' to be locked up – still avoided the issue of personal autonomy.

Historians who focus on the rhetoric of 'saving' emphasise the ways in which language itself serves to construct social action. Power is negotiated and distributed through the labels and categories that are selected. However, a 'realist' analysis would suggest that Fry, Carpenter, Cobbe and Butler were extremely radical in the context of the gender politics of the nineteenth century, that they effected actual changes in women's lives, leading to substantial material and physical improvement, and that they were skilled communicators who mustered whatever arguments were available to support a greater cause.[19] Thus Butler made use of her shifting identity as an 'English' patriot, as a respectable 'Lady' and as a wise and caring 'Mother' to appeal to different constituent parts of the nation.[20] Given that Victorian moral propriety demanded that 'ladies' should not talk about improper matters such as prostitution and sexuality, Butler recognized the rhetorical and strategic importance of stressing her own position of middle-class matronly respectability.

There has been a tendency to contrast the work of paid (often male) professionals with that of voluntary (female) 'amateurs', whose approach is assumed to be unskilled and uninformed. Such a distinction emerged during the nineteenth century as part of a male-led professionalisation strategy, and it was used at the time to criticise the activities of Fry and others.[21] However, recent work within the area of women's history has made use of collective biography or 'prosopography' to demonstrate that women campaigners and activists of the nineteenth century were highly organised, highly informed and highly efficient. Whilst not officially admitted to professional bodies, they made use of informal social networks to develop campaigning tactics and to pool knowledge. Despite the lack of formal training, women such as Fry, Carpenter and Butler developed considerable expertise through research into social problems, through experience in running social welfare initiatives and through the practice of activism.[22]

To what extent can we view those women who campaigned for changes in the law and in the criminal justice system in the nineteenth century as 'feminist'? Whilst it is important to acknowledge that the term was not used at the time, the question is important analytically. Women's historians have tended to argue that the term involves two components: first, an assertion of women's 'autonomy' or 'self-determination'; second, a sustained critique of 'male supremacy'.[23] There are many examples of nineteenth-century activists who asserted the first, but not the second. Fry argued for women's involvement in social reform and for the need to improve the lives of ordinary women (such as women prisoners), but she fell short of criticising gender imbalances in the system. There were also those who viewed women's contributions as delimited by gender. In arguing that there was a natural sympathy 'for woman to woman', the 'lady' prison visitors of the early nineteenth century assumed that women had a special role to perform in working with their own sex.[24]

Elizabeth Blackwell called for women to take up positions of authority within policing in the 1880s in order to fulfil a gender-specific function:

> I know that policemen themselves often dread more to arrest a half-drunken woman than a man, and that it requires more than one man to overpower the maniac who, with tooth and nail, and the fury of drink, fights more like a demon than a human being. I know that such wretched outcasts rage in their cells like wild beasts, filling the air with shrieks and blasphemy that make the blood run cold. Nevertheless, wherever a wretched woman must be brought, there a true

woman's influence should also be brought. When the drink is gone, and only the bruised disfigured womanhood remains, then the higher influence may exert itself, by its respect for the womanhood which is still there.[25]

Blackwell was arguing for the appointment of a small number of women from superior social backgrounds rather than the introduction of 'ordinary women' to policing, which she argued would be 'out of the question and extremely mischievous'. She emphasised the spiritual nobility and high moral virtue of 'a true woman' who would redeem those who had lost their intrinsically feminine qualities. Blackwell opposed the CD Acts on the grounds that they encouraged immorality in condoning prostitution, but she believed both men and women should learn to exercise restraint. She called on rescue workers to 'plead earnestly and affectionately with the prostitute to leave her vile trade' but to 'do nothing to raise the condition of prostitutes as such, any more than you would try to improve the condition of thieves as thieves'.[26] Whilst Blackwell and Fry were important contributors to the development of a women's movement in that they expanded women's involvement in the public sphere, it may be difficult to argue that their interventions were specifically 'feminist'.

For a clearly stated critique of gender inequality it is necessary to turn to the writings of Josephine Butler. Butler scathingly attacked the CD Acts – which sought to control the spread of venereal disease by permitting the detention and forced medical examination of women who were suspected of being prostitutes – by arguing that it was in fact the law that had reduced ordinary women to 'the character of wild beasts'. The CD Acts were contrary to English justice and liberty and they directly impinged on the rights of all women as a group, since any woman, technically, could come under suspicion. Butler directly referred to 'the unequal standard in morality' which meant that 'we never hear of a young woman that "*she* is only sowing her wild oats"'.[27] She refused to condemn women who chose to continue with prostitution, recognising that poverty was often a significant factor.

The campaign against the CD Acts acted as an umbrella movement for a broad constituency of viewpoints, including those such as Elizabeth Wolstenholme Elmy, who believed that women as well as men should achieve sexual fulfilment. Others argued for 'social purity' or sexual restraint in both men and women, and many viewed women as spiritually and morally superior to men. Respectable women, it was argued, had a special mission to save their fallen sisters and lead them to a path of righteousness. The expansion of the social purity movement in the 1880s led to the growth of 'rescue' work, which involved 'saving' young working-class women before they fell into prostitution, offering them shelter and religious instruction, and training them to take up 'respectable' work as domestic servants. Campaigners who worked to raise the age of consent for girls continued the work of Cobbe and Butler in demonstrating that what we might now call 'sexual abuse' was condoned by the law.

Thus, despite women's exclusion from the legal professions and official positions within the criminal justice system, they were nonetheless able to exert considerable pressure as lobbyists and campaigners. The net effect was that a considerable feminist assault on the inequalities of the system had been sustained by the early years of the twentieth century. This was taken forward in the new century by the activities of suffrage activists. Anger about men's sexual exploitation of women and about the sexual double standard fed into the suffragette slogan of 1913 'Votes for Women! Chastity for Men!'.[28] The suffrage movement was not a one-issue campaign. The Women's Freedom League ran a vociferous campaign in the pages of its journal *The Vote*, exposing cases in which men had received lenient sentences for assaulting women or children. They called for the appointment of women magistrates, women jurors and women police officers to remedy the gender bias. Within this rhetoric, ideas about women's equality continued to be combined with a sense of women's 'special' role that was linked to ideas about gender difference.

Women as criminal justice professionals: the 1919 Act and its effect

In 1918 women were given the parliamentary vote for the first time (provided they were ratepayers or the wives of ratepayers and over 30 years of age). Of equal significance, however, was the Sex Disqualification (Removal) Act of 1919, which stated that sex or marital status could no longer be used to disqualify a person from holding public office or from admittance to the professions. In the wake of the act, Nancy Astor was the first woman MP to take her seat in the House of Commons. The act paved the way for the appointment of women as lawyers, magistrates and jurors; it also added impetus to campaigns for the employment of women police officers. To what extent, then, did it make a difference? Further, did women officials and professionals develop different approaches when they were admitted to previously masculine spheres? This section of the chapter will compare the activities of women as lawyers, police officers and magistrates in turn, assessing the ways in which ideas about equality and gender difference informed their working lives.

Women were employed in solicitors' and barristers' offices in significant numbers from the 1880s onwards, but their roles were restricted to clerical support as secretaries and typists.[29] They had begun to undertake a legal education with the setting up of women's higher education colleges. Eliza Orme was the first woman to be awarded a degree in law (the LLB) in 1888 after studying at Bedford College, University of London. Although Orme went on to develop a successful conveyancing business, the Law Society refused to recognise women because of their lack of legal status, effectively excluding them from the profession. Those who defended the profession as a male bastion also argued that women, as emotional beings, could not make rational and objective judgments.[30] The 1919 Act removed women's sex as a legal impediment to the practice of law and Carrie Morrison became the first women to be admitted to the Law Society in 1922, soon followed by Maud Crofts and Mary Sykes. Significantly, however, the change in the law was not met by cultural changes within the profession. Appointment and advancement were heavily dependent upon what has come to be known as 'old-boy networks', the fraternity provided by educational ties (including public school links) and gentlemen's clubs. The Law Society's headquarters continued to exclude women from its coffee room in the 1950s, indicating women's social and cultural marginalisation within the profession despite their formal admittance.[31] Crofts, who was the daughter of a barrister, became a partner with her brother and husband and established her own base of clients who were supportive of women's professionalism. In many other practices, however, there was a reluctance to take women on as partners because it was assumed it would not be welcomed by existing clients, decisions being justified on business grounds.

By the 1940s women constituted barely 3 per cent of the legal profession and this had risen to just under 10 per cent by 1971. Although their participation has increased to nearly a third in recent years, women tend to be concentrated in the lower echelons of the profession as solicitors rather than as barristers or as judges.[32] Women's rare appointment to higher posts has attracted controversy. When Sybil Campbell was appointed as the first professional woman judge in Britain in 1945 (as stipendiary magistrate at Tower Bridge Police Court, London), complaints were made on technical grounds because she had not practiced as a lawyer for the preceding seven years (she had, instead, been employed as a civil servant advising on black marketeering). She was carefully watched by critics, who went on to accuse her (in highly gendered language) of being a 'fiendish vixen [...full of] vindictiveness to the unfortunates', although the sentences she imposed were not significantly different from her male contemporaries.[33] Across the century, women solicitors have been sidelined into specific areas that have been viewed as 'softer': wills, probate, conveyancing and family law, often with female clients.[34] The passive absorption or assimilation of women into the male-dominated legal profession in small numbers has meant that they have not, as a group, been able to challenge dominant cultures and practices. Unlike medicine, in which female practitioners formed an active Medical Women's Federation in the early twentieth century, women solicitors did not deliberately construct their own networks, lobby on professional matters as a distinct group, or develop an occupational identity linked to gender.[35]

A rather different model emerged within policing, in which women were partially segregated into 'Policewomen's Departments', as 'a force within a force', with a clearly gendered identity as female officers.[36] In the nineteenth century the wives of policemen had often carried out unpaid or hidden work, supervising female prisoners. During the First World War women had patrolled public spaces, again in a voluntary capacity, aiming to protect 'vulnerable' women and children from the dangers of street life but also to prevent sexual encounters between servicemen and 'amateur prostitutes' (young women in their teens and twenties) which, it was thought, would lead to the spread of venereal disease. A small number of 'policewomen' were also appointed to supervise female munitions work (although not attached to the police service as such), effectively acting as women 'in control' of other women. Thus overtly feminist agendas were, from these early days, combined with strategies of moral regulation in which women sought to control the behaviour of others of their own sex.[37] Moreover, women's role in policing was linked to a 'separate sphere of usefulness' that pigeon-holed them as experts in matters relating to women and children.[38] Indeed, arguments about gender difference shaped their entry into policing (unlike law, where an equal right to qualify and practice had been asserted). Although Edith Smith had been given powers of arrest as a woman officer in Grantham in 1915, the piecemeal appointment of women as attested officers only made headway after 1919. Vociferous campaigns for the appointment of women police (as well as women police surgeons) were orchestrated by the National Council of Women and other women's organisations, with the full support of the first women MPs. Labour MP Ellen Wilkinson maintained that women constables 'have a special job to do, work that it is undesirable that any man should be called upon to undertake [...] the many difficult cases arising out of offences committed by and on women and children'.[39] The number of women employed in British policing increased slowly from only 282 in 1940, to 418 in 1945 and to 4000 in 1966 (still less that 5 per cent of the overall establishment). Yet they formed a critical mass of officers who, particularly in the larger cities in Britain, developed a distinct occupational identity.

Pioneering women police officers such as Dorothy Peto (head of the Women Police Branch of the Metropolitan Police from 1930 to 1946) and Barbara Denis de Vitré (employed as a policewoman in Sheffield in 1928 before moving to posts in Cairo, Leicester and Kent) carved out a significant operational role for women in relation to, firstly, child protection, and secondly, indecent assault cases involving female and child victims. This was assisted by legislation such as the 1933 Children and Young Persons Act, which stated that any female child or young person who was 'detained, being conveyed or waiting' at a police station must be under the care of a woman.[40] Women police officers developed styles of record-keeping and family intervention that imitated modern social casework. A small number of women were employed within Criminal Investigations Departments (CIDs) for the specific purposes of taking statements from victims of rape and sexual assault. This was a role carried out by Lilian Wyles in the Met and by Mildred White in Birmingham; both developed substantial expertise as statement-takers and were involved in the training of women officers in these specialist areas. Unlike male officers, the rank and file of whom viewed the university-educated with distrust, pioneer policewomen sought to shape policing into a highly trained profession although, ultimately, they were unsuccessful in attracting graduate recruits.

It can be argued that women's association with emotional or caring work shaped the profile of their activities in policing. They were painfully aware of the existence of child sexual abuse as well as of the need for some form of aftercare after an allegation had been made, although their pioneering efforts would be judged woefully inadequate in terms of current practice. During the interwar years Wyles ensured that a clean supply of clothes was available for child victims following medical examination. She accompanied children in the courtroom when called as witnesses, claiming that she had reprimanded a defence barrister after one trial for adopting a highly aggressive style of questioning.[41] She also liaised closely with voluntary social workers if temporary accommodation or counselling was viewed as appropriate. In relation to rape cases involving adults, women officers also developed a more sympathetic style of questioning. They were, however, constrained by the law and by wider cultural assumption about gender and sexuality. Thus Mildred White told a conference of policewomen

in 1937 that rape in adult women was 'very much rarer than is sometimes sup-
posed; in twenty years I have only known three cases in which a conviction
was secured'.[42] That juries were reluctant to convict was seen as indicative that
few rape cases were genuine rather than as a result of a situation in which the
dice were loaded against rape complainants. Cases that might now be labelled
as 'date rape', were assumed by both male and female officers to have involved
women's consent. Arguably the changes they were able to make were superfi-
cial, although they led to some improvement in the treatment of female and
child victims before they came before the courts.

In the post-war period senior policewomen negotiated with male bosses
to expand the remit of policewomen's work despite the continued use of the
rhetoric of women's specialism. In this they can be seen as working strategically
towards women's 'autonomy' in terms of career and work satisfaction. They
rarely, however, offered a feminist critique of the criminal justice system or of
the institutions of policing. Rather, they tended to uphold the system because of
their position as law enforcers. The existence of Policewomen's Departments,
along with separate structures of pay, conditions and promotions, meant that
the masculine culture of policing was rarely challenged. In the early 1970s, as
a result of the Equal Pay Act and the Sex Discrimination Act, women officers
were formally integrated with policemen on the same terms. Cases of sexual
harassment and discrimination (unheard of in the old days of the Policewomen's
Departments) came to light as women battled for a new form of recognition –
as police officers.

Thus women's passive absorption into the legal profession can be contrasted with their highly gendered role and identity within policing until
the 1970s which meant that the problem of assimilation was not dealt with
until much later. Both occupations continued to be male-dominated across
the twentieth century. A third example, that of the voluntary magistracy, can
be viewed as a much clearer success story in terms of women's advancement. Historian Anne Logan has argued that the 1919 Sex Disqualification
(Removal) Act made a real and substantial difference, not only in terms of
women's numerical appointment to the bench as magistrates, but also in terms
of women's contribution to the modernization and professionalisation of the
magistrate's role.[43]

The property qualification for voluntary magistrates (also known as Justices
of the Peace) in petty sessions courts had been abolished in 1906 and, whilst
appointment was clearly a marker of status within a community, it had come to
be viewed as 'the poor man's knighthood'. Yet the first women magistrates to
be appointed in December 1919 were elite women, including Mrs Humphrey
Ward, Lady Crewe, Lady Londonderry, Gertrude Tuckwell, Elizabeth Haldane,
Beatrice Webb and Margaret Lloyd George (selected across the Labour, Liberal
and Conservative political spectrum). In 1920 a further 172 women were nom-
inated, again from the upper and middle classes, many of whom were members
of campaigning women's organisations. They were joined by a number of
working-class women. In 1938 the Women's Co-Operative Guild stated that
137 of its members were magistrates. Even in the 1940s, however, women
magistrates tended to be younger as well as of higher social class than their

male colleagues. Their numbers were significant. By 1947 nearly a quarter of all magistrates were women, rising to 40 per cent by the 1980s.[44]

Once appointed to the bench, women magistrates did much to oppose older custom and practice based on gendered assumptions about female modesty. Mrs Scott, a JP in the north-west of England, a member of the Women's Co-operative Guild and a former felt-hat worker, described such a moment in her published autobiography. She had been instructed by the Chief Constable that she might leave the Bench if she did not want to hear a case involving an allegation of male 'indecency' towards another man: 'I was vexed and I said, Mrs Scott does not *like* to hear unpleasant cases, but I was appointed a magistrate to hear all cases and I consider it my duty to take the unpleasant ones along with the others [...] I told him that if I had heard of a woman magistrate leaving the bench I should not consider her fit to fill the position [...].'[45] In this case she was adamant that gender difference should not impact on the duties of the magistrate, which should make no distinction of sex.

Women magistrates came to be closely associated with the juvenile court; from the 1930s onwards the Home Office advised that juvenile justice benches should, wherever possible, include at least one women. This was, as in the case of women police officers, a result of 'social maternalist' assumptions that women were, by nature, better suited to understanding and working with children. To some extent, then, it meant that women magistrates were pushed into a particular niche. Like women police officers, they came to construct their juvenile justice role as a 'specialism' about which they garnered knowledge and expertise. In Birmingham in 1924, Mrs Cadbury took a lead in establishing a Child Guidance Clinic linked to the juvenile court, whilst women's organisations such as the National Council of Women encouraged women magistrates to promote the use of psychological reports within the juvenile courts. Significantly, however, these ideas were extended further through the key roles that women played in the wider national Magistrates' Association, which they helped to constitute as a 'professionalised' body (the term 'professional' is used here to indicate the development of training and expertise even though magistrates were technically 'unpaid'). Women attended conferences in large numbers and performed prominent roles as officers of the Magistrates Association; far from being ghettoised, they played a central role in the modernisation of policies, practices and procedures. As Logan has argued, although not all women JPs were opposed to corporal punishment, forms of probation and child guidance were given 'prominent support by leading women JPs'. Thus women magistrates were at the forefront of debates regarding the use of ' "scientific" rehabilitative treatment' in relation to offending behaviour.[46]

Women's professional practices

Along with these specific examples, the twentieth century has seen the employment of women in new occupational roles as probation officers and psychologists, as well as the expansion and professionalisation of existing roles as supervisory staff in penal institutions (including prisons). This final section of the chapter will consider the ways in which women interacted with their (usually female) charges, examining techniques of persuasion and control, and assessing the ways in which they constructed and negotiated their identities as women 'in authority'. Given the subjective nature of this type of enquiry, women's life-writing – including autobiography, memoirs, diaries and other forms of personal testimony – provides an extremely useful body of primary source material. Whilst diaries may record the microscopic detail of everyday life, they are also of historical value in the light that they shed on personal perceptions, encounters and experiences. Autobiographical texts written after the event may lack this immediacy. Because they are inflected by the passing of time they enable a reflection that is retrospective. They are not a direct 'window' onto experience; but they do tell us as much about the present identity of a writer, about the ways in which that identity has been constituted through past events, and the ways in which the individual has made sense of these through language. They are, thus, particularly useful in assessing ways in which some women came to terms with the complexity of their position 'in authority'.

Dating back to the First World War, the diary of Gabrielle West presents an extremely revealing account of one woman's experiences as a policewoman in the munitions factories, where she was employed to regulate and supervise the female workforce. As West's diary shows, an authoritative status could not be assumed, but had to be won as involving a position of respect. Authority is neither a mantle that is donned along with a uniform or job title nor can it be reduced to coercive force, although this may be used on occasion. It suggests legitimacy, acceptance and the ability to influence and persuade. West's diary makes it clear that this was not achieved by all policewomen. She describes her arrival at Pembrey munitions factory in South Wales, where she was sent with her colleague Miss Buckfitt ('Buckie'):

> The previous sub inspector had only one sergeant and three constables under her and they managed to make themselves most heavily detested by the girls, with the result that for a policewoman to so much as show herself was a signal for all the girls to shout rude remarks [...] One of our duties here is to get the girls out of the dining halls and back to the sheds at the proper time. When Buckie and I and the three constables first attempted this they merely hooted and booed at us, and when we tried to insist, they all went on strike and assembled on a sand hill and announced that they would down [with water] the first constable who came near them. However, Buckie and I marched boldly in amongst them much to their amazement and commenced to hold forth. Bye and bye one or two cried out to the others to 'shut up, they've got a bit of pluck anyhow' and after 1½ hours of argument and entreaty they went back. They have never been quite so naughty since.[47]

The tactics and resistances of the 'policed' are revealed here as, indeed, are the strategies used by West and Buckie to assert their control. A relationship of trust was further established, according to West's diary, when the policewomen calmly assisted the panicking and the injured following an explosion. They also used their position of authority to press for improvements to the poor toilet facilities which won them further support from the workers. Within a month of their arrival at Pembrey, West recorded that 'the girls really do seem to almost adore us. Every time we go into the dining rooms to call them out to work we are presented with sweets, oranges, cakes, flowers and all kinds of things'.[48] Their position 'in control' was also negotiated through class difference. From confident middle-class backgrounds, the policewomen believed that many of the munitions workers would become 'as meek as little lambs' as a result of persuasive 'oratory'.

The careful balancing of tact and firmness in order to win authority is also apparent in the autobiographical discussions of work in approved schools written by Helen Richardson and 'Jane Sparrow' (a pseudonym). Sparrow's account of life at a specialist farm school ('Downcroft') in the mid-twentieth century, in which attempts were made to reform girls' behaviour by engaging them in agricultural work, was allegedly based on the diaries she kept at the time of her employment as a residential teacher. She contrasted the unstructured regime of headmistress 'Miss Gracey', whose laxity led to patterns of absconding as well as riot, with the authoritarian style of 'Miss Strang', whose bullying tactics undermined the confidence of staff and girls alike by 'terrifying' them 'into submission'.[49] Sparrow's discussion reveals the need to establish a 'benign authority' that was based on respect for both staff and inmates. She wrote that 'the girls show a great need to see the Head as a specially good person, as a kind of ideal mother on a grand scale'.[50] Whilst Sparrow ultimately left Downcroft, disillusioned with residential care and what it might achieve, she continued to work within social work, retraining as a psychotherapist. Her testimony suggests that, as a residential worker, she had in fact successfully and skilfully built up a position of 'benign authority' despite her concerns as to whether she was temperamentally suited. Helen Richardson had worked at the Shaw Classifying School, Cheshire, in the 1950s as a residential teacher (gaining promotion to the role of Deputy and then Head). Upon marriage she returned as an educational psychologist. Like Sparrow, she suggested that patience, humour and a certain type of passivity (rather than temper) were required to maintain a controlled environment and to diffuse potentially conflictual situations. The ability to be 'cheerful and affectionate', 'calm', 'firm' and to demonstrate 'warmth' and 'reassurance' were all vital disciplinary tactics. For Richardson, this was a specifically feminine style, which was not necessarily understood by male commentators.[51]

Women's occupational roles in relation to criminal justice straddled models that stemmed from law enforcement (policing), education (work in approved schools) and social work (the probation service). Arguably, however, the term 'benign authority' can be used to describe the intentionality behind the formation of these professional relationships by the mid-twentieth century. Like the assumptions that lay behind Victorian evangelical attempts to reform convict women, it explicitly positioned 'care' and 'control' as mutually constitutive categories. Disciplinary structures and frameworks were seen as constitutive of the well-adjusted individual in the years before 1960; those in authority were to provide positive role models for their charges.

Personal testimonies (diaries and memoirs) are indicative of the close social proximity, sense of community and shared culture that women in positions of authority shared with their charges. However, women's responsibility for responding to and resolving conflict created stresses and anxieties that required a range of coping mechanisms. Sparrow conveys the difficulties that emerged under the 'Gracey' regime when staff had to confront a series of riots over a 11-month period:

> Few if any of us considered leaving during this time, partly because we never visualized it continuing so long, also we seemed as committed as the girls though in a different way. It is hard to convey that we remained on fairly good terms with the girls throughout, and that this was only interrupted, not lost, by small or large upheavals [...] Also we grew closer as a team – we simply could not afford to bicker among ourselves, nor did we meet enough socially to irritate each other.[52]

The pecking order within the regime, with an ineffectual and then a harassing Head, created further tensions in which the interests of girls and rank-and-file staff were sometimes aligned and sometimes opposed. For Richardson, too, the experience of residential work was draining, leading to tiredness and fatigue.[53] Humour was, however, a very important coping mechanism that welded together the camaraderie of teamwork and acted as a further diffuser of anxiety and conflict.

A final coping mechanism lay in the careful balancing of empathy on the one hand, and processes of distancing on the other, which created distinctions between 'us' and 'them' as objects of scrutiny and analysis. West's diary of 1916 conveys a strict sense of social stratification. It begins by complaining about elite women engaged as volunteers in the war effort who had only the slightest knowledge of the most basic domestic skills as a result of their sheltered background.[54] In her description of working-class women, she resorted to regional stereotypes. The 'rough, regular, cockney' might became 'Billingsgate gone mad' when roused, whilst women from the Swansea docks, mining villages of the Rhondda and Welsh hill farms were distinguished as distinct 'types', although all 'very rough'.[55] West's image of herself seems to be one of assured, sensible respectability; ideas about duty, competency and proficiency are suggestive of an incipient professional identity. The language of social distinction is also apparent in the memoirs produced by other women officers as they gained admittance to the police service. Reflecting on her work during the Second World War, Lilian Wyles depicted herself as engaged in struggle with 'difficult', 'tough' and 'reckless' adolescent girls who ran away from home to consort with soldiers. In opposition, she portrayed the 'helping hand' of the policewoman as based on attributes of 'common sense, tolerance, patience' and 'charity' as well as 'efficiency'.[56] Policewomen were increasingly drawn from the lower middle and 'respectable' working class by the mid-twentieth century; as, indeed, were other professions as grammar school and then university education became attainable for high-achieving working-class girls. As Joan Lock's memoirs show, social stereotypes that were circulating within a wider police culture – in which 'problem' groups were labelled as 'nutters' or (in the case of prostitutes) as 'toms' and 'tarts' – had been absorbed into women's culture by this point.[57]

Within penal or reform institutions and in probation work, social typologies similarly served to demarcate the supervised from the professional.

Helen Richardson's comments were obviously shaped by her employment within a Classifying School, which, as its name suggests, was concerned with diagnosing, assessing and labelling. Girls were grouped into a number of 'types' including 'normal', 'abnormal' or 'dull'.[58] Whilst she was at pains to reject Lombroso's suggestions that there was a specifically 'criminal type', she nevertheless elided discussions of girls' physiognomy with their personality, singling out one girl in particular who had a 'strangely old shrewd expression' for discussion.[59] Conventional identifiers of feminine beauty or their lack – whether an absconder was 'a pretty girl' or 'a bit odd-looking' – were forwarded to policewomen who would undertake subsequent searches.[60] Marjory Todd, who worked as a probation officer in London in the 1950s, was aware that her university education as well as the status attached to her work had separated her from the working class into which she had been born:

> Social work, any kind of social work – I've been thinking this on and off for years – is bound to imply some measure of superiority, blended, perhaps with guilt. Aware of the follies and disasters of the unsuccessful, one feels, that somehow, one can provide a remedy. At one level this is surely arrogance, though it may be an arrogance which is disguised, sicklied over with humility. The concept of 'we' and 'they' is the bone structure of much vocational impulse.[61]

Todd used these personal reflections as a warning against smugness and self-righteousness. Arguably it was her ability to cross classes that had sparked this recognition. Her comments were far removed from the assumptions of Victorian 'lady visitors' that their natural superiority would prompt imitation in others. For Todd, 'superiority' was acquired as 'different standards of taste, wider horizons, [and] better powers of reasoning' created social divisions.[62]

Arguably, women's identity as criminal justice practitioners was fractured when the mechanism of social distancing was challenged and they lost a clear sense of their professional legitimacy. Sparrow, who ultimately lost faith in the approved school system, had found her initial assumptions challenged by the work: 'Della asked if she could ask a question: "What is it that makes people like you and Miss Herrison ruin your lives to help people like us?" I, taken aback, said something fairly incoherent, "Well, for one thing we don't ruin our lives, we've been very happy with you – I don't know that we have helped, you've helped us [...]".'[63] Similarly Joan Lock, who decided to leave policing after only a few years' service, ends one of her chapters with the comment, 'Whose side am I on anyway?'. She found undercover observations relating to illegal drinking particularly difficult: 'If we got to know and like the proprietor and/or customers we felt absolute heels sneaking around telling lies and later "shopping" them [...].'[64] Loss of confidence was not necessarily exclusive to women as practitioners. It was, however, experienced in gendered terms given the historic association between women and caring roles, and given the highly gendered language of 'respectability' and 'recklessness' that was used to distinguish self and 'other'.

Many of the personal testimonies produced by women professionals in the mid-twentieth century point to the high sense of duty and vocation that structured their working lives. Having grown up at the end of the Victorian era and entered professional life just after the First World War, Lilian Wyles described her generation as fired by 'energy, courage, hard work and self sacrifice'.[65] In occupations such as teaching, social work and policing, a formal marriage bar was in place for women in England and Wales until the 1940s. Even after this, the demands of work in residential institutions or of shift work within policing left little space or opportunity for leisure or private life, and it was assumed that women would leave on marriage to live with their husbands. Undoubtedly the sense of duty served to link women in to a shared sense of community; but it could also be experienced in terms of sacrifice as it acted as a form of enforced spinsterdom. For some women, single status undoubtedly offered personal autonomy and admittance to a community of other like-minded women; for others, it was a compromise rather than an active choice.

There is undoubtedly a sense of heroism that informed the personal reflections of this first generation of women 'pioneers' – such as West and Wyles – who moved into occupations such as policing during and after the First World War. To a large degree their commitment and self-determination was a prerequisite if they were to carve out occupational roles for themselves as figures of authority in a man's world. It is noticeable that a later generation of practitioners, often from less solidly middle-class backgrounds – exemplified here in the writings of Lock, Sparrow and Todd – had become increasingly aware of the limitations within the system in its attempt to do 'good', more hesitant in their relationship to 'authority', and more critically aware of the role of class and status in shaping social action. Marjory Todd, who had hoped to 'do the best for [...] young lives' felt let down by a system that failed to offer the support that she viewed as necessary for her clients: 'once I had begun to feel constricted by the limits of my powers to help others, once I had acknowledged inadequacies of my own, I felt bound to be the one to break it off [...].'[66] The optimism, belief in progress and simple faith in the power to help others that had shaped the work of pioneers such as Fry, Carpenter, Butler, and then Wyles was replaced with a more measured recognition of the limitations of 'caring power'.

Conclusion

This chapter has examined the ways in which arguments about both gender equality and gender difference were used by pioneering women to create roles for themselves as experts within the criminal justice and legal system: firstly, in a voluntary capacity and, subsequently, through admittance to paid posts. Structural and legal restrictions on their agency were removed, but continuities remained in terms of cultural and social determinants. In the case of law, the appointment of women in very small numbers had little impact on the profession, where masculinist assumptions and standards remained the norm. Within policing, women fought hard to develop a specialist role; despite initial opposition, arguments about gendered specialism were accepted since women's work could be positioned as 'soft' and not, therefore 'proper' police work. Thus, ideas about gender difference continued to inform the practices of policing, social work (including probation) and institutional care given that 'respectable' femininity acted as a benchmark for professional identity. The idea of 'benign authority', based on a social maternalism that incorporated ideas about class superiority as well as gender, can be identified as a dominant paradigm within women's contribution to criminal justice and welfare systems from the nineteenth century through to 1960. As autobiographies suggest, however, there were tensions within this model that were increasingly apparent in the years after the Second World War. This sense of anomie was of course broken in the 1980s as the feminist movement once again focused on gender inequalities within the criminal justice and welfare systems, highlighting in particular the social prevalence of sexual abuse and the poor treatment of rape victims as targets for campaigning action.

7

Women and Punishment

Placing women offenders in the foreground complicates the established trends and chronologies in the history of punishment. Historians are in broad agreement about how the punishment of the criminal offender has changed over time, though their explanations of this transition differ. Early Modern social order was hierarchical and the punishment of criminal offenders confirmed and reflected social status. The most punishable bodies were not infrequently those of the poor. Punishment was orientated towards the body of the criminal; its purpose was to punish through pain or shame. For serious offences, punishment aimed to exile the criminal from the social order, either permanently through capital punishment or for long periods through transportation to the Americas. In contrast, by the later nineteenth century, penal regimes relied most heavily on incarceration or, from the twentieth century, through other means of curtailing the freedom of the offender, such as probation or subsequently, 'tagging' or community service. The emphasis of modern penal policy has shifted between viewing imprisonment as punishment, as deterrence and/or as encouraging rehabilitation.[1] However, across these broad shifts, there have been important continuities in the technologies and ideologies of punishment when applied to women offenders.

This chapter reviews the changing uses of different modes of punishment over time, and revisits recent feminist arguments that women offenders have been doubly punished by penal regimes; firstly, for the social offence of their criminal acts, and secondly, for the transgressions against the home-centred submissiveness and passivity that the dominant gender order has required of respectable femininity (Chapter 1). The historical experience of women in the penal system, as well as the meanings and impact of regimes of punishment when applied to them, has differed from that of men. Penal regimes have punished both women and men in gendered ways and although there has been apparent lenience towards women in some respects, on closer examination the picture is more complex. Women were held to be far more controlled by their sexuality than men and this produced two (contradictory) assumptions about their criminality. Female sexuality was assumed to produce unruly and deviant behaviour, especially in working-class women. It was also thought to make women morally weaker by nature and therefore less responsible for their actions. The punishment of women criminal offenders has had recurrent similarity with that of women in semi-penal institutions such as reformatories. Closer surveillance and discipline has often been thought appropriate for women, either to contain their sexually derived and gender-specific unruliness or to achieve rehabilitation. There has been no straightforward linear chronology in such approaches over the three centuries we are considering. Change, as in other aspects of women's history, has been uneven and sometimes reversible.

Women have always been a minority of criminal offenders under punishment, very often being treated as anomalous in systems designed for male offenders. The history of women and punishment challenges and revises both whiggish approaches, which perceive increased humanitarianism in penal measures as part of the growth of the modern liberal state, and those approaches (generally inspired by Foucault) which see the development of modern society from the later eighteenth century as accompanied by increasingly pervasive disciplinary techniques (designed to reduce offenders to the docile bodies required by capitalist industrial production). For Foucault, the prison became emblematic of the proliferation of 'micro-technologies' of discipline and surveillance throughout society as a whole.[2] Feminist theory has argued that women offenders have been subordinated in hierarchies of gender as well as power differentials that also apply to men, such as class or race. The rehabilitative objectives of modern punishment in progressive, whiggish interpretations take on a different meaning for women, whose status as full citizens of the modern liberal state has been questioned.[3] Further, continuities in the close discipline and surveillance applied to women offenders modify Foucault's ideas about the essential modernity of disciplinary power.

Corporal and capital punishment

In the Early Modern period corporal punishment (the pillory, stocks or whipping) was, along with fines, the predominant mode of punishment for minor offences. Execution and transportation were the chief sentences for felonies. All these measures were applied to women and men offenders. However, corporal and capital punishment took on different meaning when inflicted on feminine, reproductive bodies. Both men and women were whipped in public for theft early in the eighteenth century, though within a few decades women were whipped away from the general gaze. In Colchester, Essex, for example, in January 1764 Quarter Sessions, for the theft of a brass kettle, James Green was ordered to be whipped in public on market day when the town would be crowded, whereas Mary Blake who had stolen a brass boiler was whipped in private.[4] Arguably, changing ideas about sexuality and an increasing cultural emphasis on sexual difference by the early nineteenth century made the spectacle of female bodies undergoing public physical punishment more worrying.[5] The visible punishment of female bodies could have disturbingly erotic overtones which contradicted the deterrent and moralising effect that public punishment was intended to have. Defiant transgressive women were an abomination incapable of penitence – weaker and pathetic women seemed not to deserve their punishment. Corporal punishment of women was therefore displaced to the confines of prisons or to the penal colonies of Australia, where from the 1820s punishments were also only administered to women confined in 'factories'.

Figure 7.1 Death sentences at the Old Bailey, 1674–1799: number of women compared to all cases
Source: OBP.

Not least because the criminal justice system served to filter out many women accused of felonies, far fewer women than men have been sentenced to capital punishment since the seventeenth century. Women were a small proportion of those condemned to death at the Old Bailey (see Figure 7.1).

As Gatrell points out, only four of the 59 people executed in London between 1827 and 1830 were women, all for murder.[6] The broad trends in capital punishment from the late seventeenth century to the mid-twentieth century are well known. Although there was an increase in capital statutes in the later 1600s, especially for property crime, the number of indictments had dropped and the rate of execution consequently also declined, remaining low until the second half of the eighteenth century when many new capital statutes were passed. From 1770 to 1830, over 200 offences were liable to capital punishment, including burglary, forgery and counterfeiting.[7] Though hanging the bodies of some executed felons in chains (both male and female) was an established deterrent, the eighteenth century introduced the sentence of hanging followed by medical dissection. This sentence was passed on 11 women in 9 Old Bailey cases (around 6 per cent of cases where death sentences were passed) between 1750 and 1774. By this period the purpose of criminal justice was less to restore consensual social order and more to discipline individuals who had transgressed the social hierarchies that the institutions of the law embodied.[8] Nevertheless, many felons sentenced to death were reprieved through an extensive system of mercy.

Pardons were regularly granted to both men and women on application by patrons such as clergy or local gentry. Benefit of clergy, a legal fiction whereby anyone able to read (or memorise) a standard text was reprieved, saved many. It had been extended to women during the later seventeenth century. Although its use was restricted in 1706 and many of the newer criminal statutes were exempt from clergy, it remained on the statute book until the 1820s.[9] Some eighteenth-century men escaped the gallows by accepting enlistment into the army.[10] Women could save their lives by pleading the belly – declaring they were pregnant.[11] In theory the sentence could be carried out once they had given birth, but in practice most women who successfully claimed 'benefit of the womb' were transported, imprisoned or escaped without further punishment. Over 25 per cent of the 463 women who were sentenced to death at the Old Bailey pleaded the belly between 1674 and 1699, and 38 per cent from 1700 to 1724, though a much smaller proportion did so later. Only three of the 155 women given capital sentences between 1825 and 1834 pleaded the belly. Processes of remission were therefore also gendered. Sharpe estimates that in the mid-eighteenth century normally only around 10 per cent of those condemned to death at any Assize were executed. Emsley's figures for the later eighteenth and early nineteenth centuries show between 9 and 15 per cent of those condemned for property crime were executed, but usually well over 50 per cent of those sentenced for violent sexual offences.[12] The impression is that at this period it was the socially marginal, who could find no one to intercede for them or those who had committed crimes of extreme violence, who were most likely to hang. This was an arbitrary and seemingly non-rational system of justice, argued reformers, but the combination of terror and mercy was in the interests of the ruling class and other players in the criminal justice process including prosecutors.

The procedures of public execution – the long ride to the gallows through noisy crowds already wearing one's rope and sitting on one's coffin, the opportunity for last words and speeches of pathos or bravado, the attentions of the clergyman and the urging to repentance – was in form the same for both men and women, old and young. The condemned's last hours and moments varied, however, given both their individual character and the crowd response. Women who had killed children generally had a rough reception. Both men and women who had committed reprehensible acts were jeered and pelted. Others were seen to their deaths like heroes or martyrs. The conditions that produced such differences were inevitably inflected by gender; 'dying game' was a 'masculine cult'. Women who were defiant or resolute on the gallows tended to be represented as 'hard' or unfeminine. The acceptable female stance was to be penitent and tearful.[13] Published Newgate Calendars and broadsides reproduced (or made up) appropriately gendered penitential last words and narrated the death of the condemned. 19-year-old Elizabeth Osborne, sentenced to hanging and dissection, had cut her stepmother's throat because the old lady had refused permission to Elizabeth to marry. A broadside published after her execution in Hereford recorded her gallows speech in which she offered herself as an example to the crowd 'not to suffer your passions to work too forcibly on your minds, which has been the cause of the melancholy situation in which I am now placed [. . .] good people, pray for me, O pray for me'.[14] Although with appropriate modesty she did not elaborate, the passion for revenge against her stepmother clearly originated in her sexual passion for her lover.

The gendered nature of capital punishment can be further considered through the example of petty treason. High treason was a crime directly against the state and the eighteenth-century penalty for men was hanging, drawing and quartering, though such extreme punishments were rare. Petty treason was held to be more serious than simple murder. Between 1351 and 1826 the stipulated penalty for women was burning at the stake. Most women so sentenced were strangled as the fire was set, which mitigated some physical suffering but it is questionable how much it alleviated the terror of the victim. No women were burned after 1790. Petty treason involved an apparently incongruous collection of offences: the murder of a husband by his wife, the murder of a master by his servant, and lastly coining or passing forged currency. For different reasons, exemplary sentences for petty treason were didactic measures as well as subjecting specific women to cruel punishment.

A husband who killed his wife has only ever been guilty of murder at worst and in many instances the offence was defined as manslaughter.[15] Some feminist scholars have used this example to demonstrate the crude patriarchalism of the Early Modern state. However, the collection of offences involved indicates greater complexity. All these offences caused a disturbing dislocation of the social order. Women were subordinated to husbands, as servants were to masters. The fact that husband-killing was ideologically positioned as so serious underlines how women's sexual status framed their moral identities – and that the social order was hierarchically gendered. Nevertheless, more women were sentenced at the Old Bailey for coining than husband murder (Figure 7.2). The

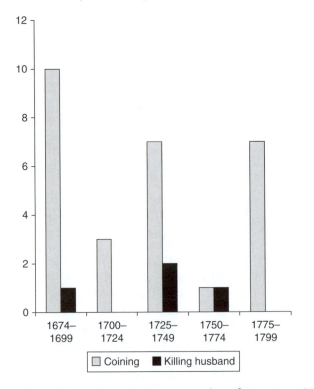

Figure 7.2 Death by burning for petty treason: number of women sentenced at the Old Bailey, 1674–1790
Source: OBP.

state was very sensitive about the coinage in a period when specie was short and coining and forging were destabilising the currency. Most of those involved in coining were poor people, taking a heavy risk to provide much-needed subsistence. Coining was often a 'household enterprise' and 46 per cent of those tried at the Old Bailey between 1694 and 1749 were women. Although the full rigour of the law was set aside in many cases, some women faced a ghastly death for practices that were an extension of daily subsistence and were not infrequently condoned in local communities.[16]

By the 1800s it was clear that severe sentences did not reduce crime. Population was growing fast during the early stages of industrialisation and standards of living for many working people were worsening.[17] Gatrell argues that the system simply broke down as the numbers convicted rose to far more than the established mechanisms for dispatching them could cope with. Remission became so common that hanging the remaining few appeared both arbitrary and vindictive. The risk of riot from the large crowds that assembled at public executions was worrying to the state. The reactions of the women in the crowds were often commented upon with disapproval. Transportation to Australia was providing an alternative penal measure and prison reformers were advocating penitentiary sentences to combine punishment with rehabilitation.[18] Young, attractive, female bodies subjected to the violence of the gallows provided material for romantic narratives in favour of the restriction of public hanging. Condemned women who could display demure, submissive femininity could be represented as victims, even though they were criminals. A clear contrast remained between such victims and those women whose crimes made them seem not only unfeminine but monstrous. Esther Hibner was hanged at Newgate in 1829 for starving a child to death in the workhouse. She was 'assailed by a loud volley of yells from the people, particularly from the females of which the crowd was in great measure composed'.[19] Huge crowds attended the public hanging of Marie Manning and her husband in 1849, for a callous murder with mercenary objectives. The streets were packed for over 24 hours and numbers of people were injured by the press of the crowd. An atmosphere of black carnival prevailed; bonfires were lit, there was much drinking, fire crackers and 'Maria Manning peppermints' were on sale. She died in a black satin dress and was so unpopular that the fabric became unfashionable for some time after.[20]

By the 1840s capital punishment was effectively restricted to treason and murder, a situation confirmed by the Offences Against the Person Act of 1861. From 1868 executions were carried out inside prisons. Technical improvements such as the mechanical drop made a speedy death more likely, though not invariable. Capital punishment was used selectively. Wiener argues that men who killed, and in particular those that killed their wives, were increasingly likely to hang, whereas the most disquieting murderous stereotype had previously been a female killer.[21] Nevertheless little sympathy was extended to women such as baby farmers hanged for the murder of infants that they had taken money to care for, such as Margaret Waters in 1870.[22] However as Chapter 3 has argued, women subjected to violent domestic relationships who eventually killed violent partners were also likely to hang unless they could show the proper feminine demeanours.

The first half of the twentieth century saw the combination of a strongly rehabilitative tendency in penal policy and very low murder rates. The mechanisms of post-sentence appeal and reprieve by the Home Secretary meant that between 1900 and 1949, 40.3 per cent of convicted male murderers and as much as 90.8 per cent of sentenced women avoided the gallows, though there were around 13 executions each year.[23] The apparent bias towards the reprieve of women conceals the active processes of evaluation of sentenced women's performance of femininity as well as of their violence. As Ballinger argues:

> Of the 15 women who were hung between 1900 and 1955 five had been prostitutes at some point, 2 had abortions, 7 had illegitimate children, 6 had affairs while still married, 5 had lived with men who were not their husbands, 6 had children who were in care or not living with them, 3 were separated from their husbands, 5 had affairs with men several years their junior, 6 were described as promiscuous or over sexed, 7 had previous criminal records, 4 were described as heavy drinkers.[24]

The last woman to be hanged in Britain was Ruth Ellis in 1955, at whose trial an argument of diminished responsibility on the grounds of her feminine instability was argued unsuccessfully. However, it was also the execution of men of less mental capacity, such as Derek Bentley and Timothy Evans, which swayed parliamentary opinion on the repeal of capital punishment. The 1957 Homicide Act created a classification of non-capital murder on the grounds of diminished responsibility and capital punishment for murder ended in 1965.[25]

Transportation

Transportation became the predominant sentence for property crime in the eighteenth century, accounting for around 60 per cent of disposals according to Beattie's calculations.[26] English and Welsh courts sent around 50,000 convicted prisoners to the American colonies between 1718 when the Transportation Act regularised the practice and 1776 when the American War of Independence closed that route.[27] The colonies had a shortage of labour and used different types of unfree labour to bridge that gap, including slaves, indentured labourers and convicts. After a decade when male convicts sentenced to transportation were incarcerated in the 'hulks' – dis-masted ships in the River Thames – and employed on government labour, penal colonies were set up in New South Wales. What in Australian history has come to be known as the First Fleet reached Botany Bay in 1788. The First Fleet included 196 female convicts and though at first the rate of transportation of women was comparatively low (only 4200 had arrived by 1820) numbers increased rapidly thereafter.[28] When transportation to Australia ended in 1868, 132,308 men and 24,960 women convicts had been sent there.[29]

Transportation was fully part of the British penal system.[30] There were exchanges of policy and ideas. Transportation facilitated the transfer from capital sentencing to incarceration for many property offences and modifies the history of women's imprisonment. Women convicts were perceived as particularly disorderly in both English prisons and Australian penal settlements. Australia was the location of experiments in penology; some practices were used in England and some (in particular assignment of women convicts for domestic labour in private homes) were not. Penal regimes applied to aboriginal Australians were even more punitive than those experienced by transportees. Transportation was a highly gendered process. Dominant perceptions of women convicts frequently characterised them as especially deviant, sexually transgressive and difficult to control. In 1842, the superintendent of the Hobart women's factory was attracted by a noise, and watching through the window of one of the wards observed several women:

> dancing perfectly naked, and making obscene attitudes towards each other, they were also singing and shouting and making use of most disgusting language. [...] the disgusting attitudes towards each other were in imitation of men and women together.[31]

All these women were sentenced to confinement, five of them to 12 months hard labour. Perceptions of their disorderly sexuality affected the ways that women convicts were managed and regulated. The shaving of women's heads until the 1830s and subsequently cutting off their hair as a punishment struck at a key symbol of female attractiveness, and some women rescued their cut hair to make wigs.[32] Such penal practices made for differential constraints and opportunities for female as opposed to male convicts, experiences which varied further according to the date of transportation and the place they lived and worked.

The early penal settlements until 1813 were comparatively open and loosely managed. Potentially, women's opportunities for agency were greater than they later became and numbers of them acquired property, independence or social mobility. Sexuality could be a component of complex social, affective and economic relationships. Mary Reiby was a convict whose social mobility and eventual respectability was such that her image now appears on modern Australian banknotes. After arriving in Sydney in 1792 Mary was assigned as a domestic servant to a military officer's household and later married a ship-owner, continuing the shipping line after his death, taking on a range of philanthropic work and becoming one of the elite social group in Sydney.[33] Some assigned servants married their masters.[34] Long- or short-term sexual relationships could earn the money needed for rent or result in women's acquisition of houses and property.[35]

However, loosely regulated penal regimes in a society where men were the great majority left women convicts extremely vulnerable to violence and sexual exploitation. Assignment was a lottery which could lead to a more materially comfortable life, sometimes to social mobility, the opportunity to trade, to find husbands or sexual partners. Other placings could be abusive, lonely or violent.[36] An 1812 Select Committee on Transportation, using the recurrent leitmotif of sexual fall, commented that 'Women convicts had been indiscriminately given to such of the inhabitants as demanded them, and were in general received rather as prostitutes than as servants, and so far from being induced to reform themselves, the disgraceful manner in which they were disposed of operated as an encouragement to general depravity of manners.' From this year women convicts were assigned only to married couples.

From the 1820s more women were transported direct to Van Diemen's Land (Tasmania) and direct transportation of women to New South Wales ended in 1840. During the 1840s women convicts were arriving at VDL at a rate of 667 per year compared with 223 from 1826–40 and 74 per year from 1820–25. Reforms of 1814 had increased the regulation of both men and women convicts and coincided with the arrival of many further settlers and the emergence of a social elite.[37] For women, the reformed penal regime meant either assignment on domestic service or forced labour confined in the female factories. Factories served as nominally secure places of confinement before or between assignments, as the location for secondary punishment for convict women who transgressed against penal discipline, as houses of industry and as lying-in hospitals. Women were thus subjected to closer discipline than male convicts, whose work assignments were often in groups and with less direct supervision.

The ideas of Elizabeth Fry, the English prison reformer, had been influential in the 1820s. Factory inmates in Van Diemen's Land experienced enforced separation, silence rules and a finer system of classification of convicts. New regulations from 1845 required the constant employment of inmates, more regular religious instruction and extensive medical supervision, though these were not fully effective.[38] Female factories proved problematic places to enforce such regimes because of their unsuitable architecture and multiple functions. A third 'crime class' for secondary offenders was meant to be distinguished by dress, cropped hair and a poorer diet, though in practice such distinctions became blurred. In the older factories there were often insufficient punishment cells. At Ross Factory tiny (4×6ft) dark punishment cells were built, with stone walls and beaten earth floors around 18 inches below the level of the doorway. There were also some radical departures in prison architecture; the Launceston Factory for women (1832) adopted the radical panoptical plan being advocated by Benthamite reformers in England (see below) a decade before the construction of Pentonville prison in London (1842) and 15 years before penitentiary principles were built into the male convict prison in Port Arthur (VDL) in 1847.[39]

Women resisted the penal regimes in the factories by disobedience, trafficking goods and letters, insubordination and laziness. Convicts who had some money could obtain a variety of food, tea, sugar, tobacco and alcohol. The trade was organised by turnkeys (women prisoners of the first class). Sexual and economic trade were linked. Homosexuality was heavily punished and was consequently a profoundly resistant element in women's subcultures and a confrontational rejection of dominant femininities. Notwithstanding the predatory nature of some women's homosexual practices, such relationships cemented strong social bonds between confined women that provided protection from male overseers, turnkeys and other female prisoners, as well as access to black market goods. If individual acts of insubordination were constitutive of resistant identities for women convicts, they were subsumed into the system of punishments and rewards on which the factory penal regime depended. Collective resistance through riot and rebellion posed more serious problems of containment and discipline, and were met with force. At Paramatta in 1827 women on punishment, whose food rations had been reduced, broke out of the factory and went into the town stealing food. They were controlled only by armed soldiers. At Launceston Female house of correction in 1841 a riot which aimed to rescue one woman from the punishment cells was triggered by the rage of her sexual partner. This disturbance required 50 male convicts enrolled as special constables and armed with crowbars and sledgehammers to defeat.[40]

Despite the limited success of reformed penal regimes in Australia, by the middle of the nineteenth century women convicts were subjected to increased periods of incarceration under more heavily controlling and infantilising regimes, intended to produce docile feminine subjects who could safely be released into the labour or marriage markets of settler society. Penal regimes for women convicts mirrored the silent and separate systems which at that period had been adopted only in the few convict penitentiaries in England, and – as we will argue below – were as yet not the experience of the majority of offenders in the local prisons.[41]

Incarceration

Local houses of correction had from the sixteenth century used incarceration and (nominally) productive labour to correct the misbehaviour of a great variety of minor criminals and other deviants. Originally designed to control problems of vagrancy, the houses of correction were very much prisons for the 'servant class'.[42] However, until their incorporation into the Union Workhouses of the New Poor Law after 1834, their uses had proliferated and their inmates came to include men who left their families chargeable to the Poor Law, sellers of gin under the 1736 Gin Act, as well as women criminals serving penal sentences. Houses of correction had a role in disciplining women's sexuality; from 1610 'lewd' women bearing a chargeable bastard could be confined there for a year as could other 'disorderly' women, especially during the Societies for the Reformation of Manners' campaigns against prostitution (1690s–1730s).[43] However, short stays in a house of correction were also part of the survival tactics of the poor.[44] The Master of the Colchester house of correction provided clothes and claimed to have been 'Nurse and Doctor' to one sick and destitute woman.[45] Poverty was hardly an experience confined to women, nevertheless their lower earning power, comparatively restricted employment opportunities and the hazards of female reproduction from bastard-bearing to the sale of sex, meant that poor women were always vulnerable to stays in a house of correction. Especially in London, the eighteenth century saw some optimistic new departures in philanthropy, such as the Foundling Hospital (for children whose parents could not support them), lying-in charities and the Magdalen Hospital for the redemption of (a very few) prostitutes (Chapter 4). Around the mid-eighteenth century these charities had comparatively benevolent regimes. However, confinement and close supervision were characteristic. London lying-in hospitals, for example, were keen to prevent women from swearing, drinking and playing cards.[46] Historians of eighteenth-century philanthropy have also detected more closely disciplinary regimes, and growing cultures of blame for women's sexual transgressions from the later eighteenth-century.[47] The history of the disciplinary incarceration of women across the transition to modern society seems therefore to be marked by a greater degree of overlap between the regimes of penal and semi-penal institutions. A developing 'economy of criminal justice' overlapped with an 'economy of welfare' involving both public and private, penal and charitable institutions.[48]

Aside from the houses of correction, Early Modern gaols had no reformative nor corrective intentions. Their sole purpose was to confine people awaiting trial or punishment, or small debtors pending a court appearance or until their debts were discharged. Prison was nevertheless a painful and unpleasant experience for most who suffered it. Prison keepers commonly ran the gaols as money-making concerns. Wealthier prisoners purchased material comfort; the poor had a far rougher time of it. There were charges for accommodation, often for food and fees or fines on admission or before discharge. Prisons contained people acquitted in court, but unable to pay the gaoler's fee for their release. For much of the time prisoners mixed freely. There were separate women's quarters, but in Newgate at around 1700 men could gain admission for a sixpenny fee to the gaoler. After all, women on a capital charge had an interest in becoming pregnant so they could plead their bellies. Unsurprisingly drinking, gambling, extortion and sexual activity characterised prison life. Conditions were squalid and insanitary. Gaol fever or typhus dispatched many more prisoners than the gallows. In 1750 an outbreak of gaol fever killed 43 officials including judges and jurors at the Old Bailey.[49]

Observers often commented that women were the most unruly and disruptive prisoners. One Newgate convict's memoir of 1707 claimed that 'the Licentiousness of the Women [...] is so detestable that it is an unpardonable Crime to describe their lewdness.'[50] Women were thought to be especially vulnerable to corruption and to be made dangerous through prison experience. In 1816 Elizabeth Fry found not only the filth but also 'the furious manner and expressions of the women towards each other and the abandoned wickedness, which everything bespoke, [...] quite indescribable'. As she later reported to the Parliamentary Select Committee of 1822, 'we were witnesses to the dreadful proceedings that went forward on the female side of the prison; the begging, swearing, gaming, fighting, singing, dancing, dressing up in men's clothes.'[51] These comments are separated by over 100 years and come from highly divergent viewpoints. However, the concatenation of dirt, disorder, unbridled and deviant sexuality whether because of an excess of female licentiousness or by usurping the dress (and perhaps the social and sexual initiatives) of men is shared by both observers. What we seem to be seeing here, in descriptions that mirror those of women convicts in Australia, is a view that recalcitrant and resistant behaviour arose less from the conditions of imprisonment and more from the sexually founded, corrupted natures of women prisoners.

Fry was one of several vocal prison reformers at this period who often based their thinking on the influential *De Delitti et delle Pene* by the Italian Beccaria (first translated into English in 1767). John Howard's *State of the Prisons in England and Wales* (1777) is generally acknowledged as the key English text. Howard insisted on the separation and classification of prisoners; young and old, male and female, debtor and felon. Gender segregation was important within a co-ordinated system of classification which recognised different kinds of distinctions.[52] The common ground amongst reformers was that prisons should be ordered as well as secure places of punishment, and secondly, that penal regimes should not only punish offenders but also render them penitent and reformed. The philosopher Jeremy Bentham translated these intentions into an architectural scheme for the ideal 'penitentiary', organised spatially so that prisoners were both segregated and kept under constant surveillance. Elizabeth Fry's methods with the women in Newgate were, however, based on religious instruction, cleaner and more orderly material conditions, needlework and the personal influence of middle-class lady reformers such as herself. She held that women were better reformed through education and association. In 1817 Fry founded an informal school in Newgate for women prisoners and their children which proved an early success. The prisoners were supervised by a newly appointed matron and chose monitors from amongst their number to assist her. Their material environment improved and their behaviour became more closely aligned to dominant models of respectable femininity. The women were schooled in their new demeanour like children, and female sexuality was curbed through modesty, discipline, religion and work. Their needlework was sold to the Australian penal colonies and the profits used at Fry's discretion for 'small extra indulgences' for the women. Fry's Association for the Improvement of the Female Prisoners in Newgate aimed to 'form in them, as much as possible, those habits of order, sobriety and industry, which may render them docile and peaceable while in prison, and respectable when they leave it'.[53]

Fry became a celebrity and an expert on women's incarceration, consulted both in England and Australia. Largely through her evidence, the 1823 Gaols Act included a provision that women prisoners should be under the control of women gaolers. Her ideas followed the penitential impulses of her contemporaries – she was an advocate of cutting the hair of recalcitrant prisoners – but her arguments that women should be imprisoned entirely separately from men on a different classification system were never adopted.[54]

The first half of the nineteenth century saw the construction of flagship penitentiaries – none of them precisely to Bentham's design, which proved too expensive. Nevertheless the new convict prisons at Millbank (1816) and at Pentonville (1842) in London, and elsewhere[55] took something from the architecture and a good deal from the regimes proposed by prison reformers. In 1877 there were 13 penitentiaries to accommodate convicted felons compared to 113 local prisons. The latter were controlled by local magistrates and normally held prisoners on shorter sentences. Legislation of 1823, 1835 and 1839 extended the separate system to local prisons, though such provisions were not always strictly enforced. Prison regimes were intended to produce rehabilitation by isolating prisoners – compelling silence and prohibiting or controlling association. Prison regimes included controlled conditions of physical deprivation (a hard bed and a scant diet), enforced work (much of it entirely pointless through devices such as the treadmill or handcrank) and exposure to religious exhortation. Inmates were classified by offence, offending history, stage and type of sentence, and even basic comforts became privileges to be earned through compliance. Male convicts had to wear masks so that they could not recognise each other, though this practice was soon found ineffective and abandoned. At first the penitentiaries saw frequent protests. Women convicts in Millbank rioted in the chapel over the poor food in 1818. In mid-nineteenth-century Millbank women prisoners were still able to form relationships with male prisoners and male warders. Dobash and colleagues found that women convicts in Millbank were more frequently punished for disciplinary offences inside prison in the 1860s and argued that 'penal regimes for women were being enforced in a more rigorous manner than those established for men'. This finding is accurate for the Millbank women convicts during the ending of transportation, though it cannot safely be generalised throughout the Victorian prison population. Certainly the extent of self-harm amongst men at Dartmoor convict prison at the same period indicates the rigours of the regime imposed there.[56]

Women remained a small proportion of the prison population – around a quarter of those in local prisons in the second half of the nineteenth century.[57] In 1901 the daily average prison population of sentenced and unsentenced prisoners was 14,459 male and 2976 female.[58] Women prisoners were a 'special category' in a prison system designed for men, by men. In some respects the penal regime was modified for women, who were not subjected to the tougher physical punishments for disciplinary offences such as whipping or the treadmill (from the 1840s).[59] Women could have their babies in prison for the first 12 months, a practice which made the rules of silence impossible to enforce.[60] They were often allowed more association, though some commentators argued that women would be further corrupted by association with other prisoners. Others worried that women were more likely than men to suffer mental and physical effects from prolonged solitude.[61] Overall nineteenth-century 'reformed' prisons reduced the risk of sexual assault or exploitation at the price of a dismal penal regime. Forsythe argues that, given the poor material and social backgrounds of many women in local prisons and the comparatively benevolent regimes that could operate before the nationalisation of prisons in 1877, women offenders cannot be said to have had a worse experience than their male counterparts.[62] Evidence to the 1895 Select Committee still claimed that prison could be a refuge for disadvantaged women, but also underlined how separation from children and family made imprisonment harder for many women than for men.[63]

Overall, the incarceration of women criminal offenders needs to be considered in the context both of the gendered and classed disadvantages that brought women into prison in the first place and the wider range of semi-penal institutions which subjected women to very similar regimes without their having committed a criminal offence. As Jane Long argued from her study of Northumberland, women were at greater risk of poverty, and poor women were less likely to have the ordered, domestic and sexual relationships that would position them as 'deserving'. Within the workhouses of the post-1834 New Poor Law, 'the experiences of the female poor were structured more explicitly by regimes of control and surveillance.' They experienced gender segregation, uniform, regulation braided hair under a mob cap, and their social and sexual conduct was monitored. Elizabeth Anderson was twice accused of having sexual relationships with male inmates. Both times the men simply left the workhouse, whilst she was locked in a strong-room on a bread and water diet.[64] The disciplinary strategies applied under the 1860s Contagious Diseases Acts and also the punitive regimes in reformatories for 'fallen women' (involving confinement, religion, regulation dress, domestic work and separation from homes and families) were similarly intended to produce penitent and deferential femininities (Chapter 4).

By the 1860s, the rehabilitative goals of penal incarceration had manifestly not materialised and transportation was being phased out. With Edward DuCane's 1863 appointment as Director of Convict Prisons and as chair of the Prison Commissioners in 1869, and especially after both convict and local prisons came under central government control in 1877, punishment became the main objective of penal policy. As well as the loss of liberty, the tough prison regime was itself a means of punishment. Sentencing options for judges and magistrates were more limited given the end of transportation and the restriction in capital punishment. Corporal punishment was reserved as secondary punishment within the prison and administered away from the public and the judicial gaze. The oppressiveness of prison life increased from the 1880s, for both men and women. Some sense of the bleak regime is conveyed in the memoirs of English suffragettes imprisoned between 1908 and 1914 (Chapter 5). Initial reception involved a perfunctory medical examination (by male doctors), strip searching and an obligatory bath taken in unhygienic conditions and with little privacy. Prisoners were then given ill-fitting, uncomfortable and often dirty prison dress. The practice of cutting prisoners' hair persisted until 1932.[65] Cells were bare, unheated, airless and badly lit. For the first four weeks prisoners were locked in for most of the day. Association was very strictly controlled and the food was limited and unpalatable. Wardresses mostly maintained detachment and distance.[66]

Despite some policy intentions to the contrary, the comparatively few women prisoners did their time in small groups. They tended to be serving shorter sentences which reduced their access to education, work or other opportunities. Short sentences meant that the staged classification of prisoners, which bought progressive rewards were not so readily available to women. Lacking such incentives some argued that 'difficult' women were particularly hard to control. Nevertheless, there is some evidence of positive relationships between prisoners and staff. The matron at Strangeways told the Gladstone Committee in 1895 that her informal approach to discipline was surprisingly effective. She explained, 'I feel they like me. They trust me, and would be sorry to offend me.'[67]

At this period crime rates were declining and professional perceptions focused on 'habitual', recidivist offenders who were an increasing proportion of the prison population. Many women recidivists were in prison for drunkenness or drink-related pilfering or disorder. As minor property crime declined, the 'habitual' women who were a very visible minority of prisoners appeared to exemplify the point that women's weaker natures made them particularly susceptible to social and mental depravity. The Prison Commissioners' figures for 1894 claimed that 22.8 per cent of women prisoners were drunkards compared to 8.4 per cent of men. Most women doing time for drunkenness were very poor and were imprisoned because they could not afford their fines. They were often in poor health and immured in an alcoholic's lifestyle which returned them to prison within weeks, days or even hours of release. Irish, Scottish and Welsh migrants were disproportionately represented amongst women recidivists – presumably not through any particular cultural propensity for drink and disorder but because of their greater social and economic marginality.[68]

Habitual Drunkards Acts were passed in 1872 and 1879 which allowed for the establishment of institutions to cure drunkenness, and Inebriates Acts of 1888 and 1898 enabled involuntary long-term incarceration of repeat offenders. Around 80 per cent of admissions were women. In fact few such institutions were built and the initiative failed, mostly because 'by the time women reached the state of chronic alcoholism which secured their admission to reformatories, many were barely susceptible to moral influence and some were so mentally impaired as to be incurable.'[69] Nevertheless, Zedner interprets these moves as a medicalisation of (female) recidivism which laid the ground for the subsequent identification of the 'feeble minded' as a key group amongst recidivist offenders. Zedner argues that 'feeble-mindedness' was a generic category that came to account for failures of both penal and welfare institutions. The assumption that 'feeble-minded' women were more likely to require incarcerating than feeble-minded men was linked to the recurrent assumptions about female weakness together with new fears about the health of the nation. Eugenics and its more extreme form, Social Darwinism, blamed poor public health and the perceived physical enfeeblement caused by urban degeneration for jeopardising the imperial destiny of the British race. For a short period, it was the prolific reproduction of feeble-minded women that was assumed to be at the root of the problem.[70] The 1913 Mental Deficiency Act worked with ill defined concepts which blurred the distinctions between mental illness, crime and immorality. A category of 'moral insanity' could justify the incarceration of women who had illegitimate children. Although the 1913 Act was soon superseded by new research which countered the worst fears of the social costs of 'feeble mindedness', the blurring of distinctions between mental illness and criminal offending, and of the responses in terms of both penal and welfare measures, operated over a far longer period. Incarceration, close discipline, training in respectable femininity and, for a while during the 1930s, sterilisation were the suggested solutions. Arguably such new thinking meant a particular focus on women and juveniles in penal and welfare institutions over the following 50 years.

By 1900 DuCane's punitive penal regimes seemed increasingly outdated – a realisation focused by the Royal Commission of 1895. Even though the institutional cultures within prisons and therefore the experience of the inmates very often proved resistant to change, a new generation of voices advocated penal reform and a focus on the offender rather than the crime. The 1907 Probation Act avoided custodial sentences, but enabled extended surveillance through the 'befriending' of a probation officer. Juvenile offenders were a priority; borstals supplemented the earlier industrial and reform schools in 1908 and under the Children's Acts (1908, 1933) these measures interlaced with the new powers for the 'care and protection' of children, both those defined as 'at risk' and those who had offended. The implications of this for the control of teenage girls whose precocious sexuality was positioned as deviance is discussed in Chapter 8. More sentencing options became available, especially in the lower courts which by then were disposing of a much larger proportion of offences. The language that explained petty criminal recidivism was now informed by the developing disciplines of psychiatry and psychology. The social causes of offending were generally addressed through the family and home background of juvenile offenders, which brought parents and in particular mothers into the range of the disciplinary gaze.

Cecil Leeson's study of probation was published in 1914, a year after the Mental Deficiency Act of 1913 and only six years after the 1907 Probation Act, when the acceptance of probation officers was by no means universal. For Leeson the effectiveness of probation depended on a prior assessment of the 'character and environment' of the offender. In 'the case of a boy, aged 10, arrested for theft', a first offender and a 'tractable lad' and thus superficially suitable for probation, Leeson argues that a probation enquiry into the home environment of this (imaginary?) offender was crucial. The boy's (drunken) father had departed. Mother and four children lived in two small rooms. She worked in a restaurant, but (said the boy's school teacher) also supplemented her earnings through prostitution together with another woman who shared the lodgings. For Leeson, to make a probation order in this case would 'itself be little short of a crime'. The priority was to remove the boy from the immoral home environment for which his mother was to blame.[71]

A growth in state welfare from the early twentieth century meant a pro- liferation of institutions and a hybridity between penal and welfare regimes; something which had particular resonances for women inmates. Nevertheless, the activities of privately-run institutions was always limited by resource con- straints and by internal policies. Pamela Dale's study of mental health care identifies differences between the ideologically and eugenically inflected ways institutions discussed the issues and the practical attention paid to the individual problems of the people they dealt with. Penal-welfare was, she argues, char- acterised by diversification rather than a common carceral experience; mental institutions were not necessarily the last resort after penal and other strate- gies had failed. She finds that the Royal Western Counties Institution (RWCI) resisted taking mentally defective criminal offenders and preferred to work with 'bad boys' and 'wayward girls' – client groups where there was a greater chance of success.[72] Inevitably, these strategies were gendered. Given that there was a demand for domestic labour in the area, training was given to female patients which often enabled their early discharge on licence subject to the supervision of lady social workers.[73]

By the interwar period crime and committal rates were very low and the emphasis was to find appropriate treatment or training for different categories of offender. In 1930 women were only 11 per cent of the local prison popula- tion and there were only 60 women convicts compared to 2000 males.[74] Apart from women serving short sentences or on remand in small, segregated groups at regional local prisons,[75] most women prisoners were housed at Aylesbury or at Holloway[76] in uncomfortable and generally poorly maintained Victorian institutions. Because women prisoners have been few, the women's estate has frequently lacked the facilities possible for male prisoners.[77] The material conditions of men's prisons were not that much better, but they were often able to serve their sentences nearer home.

By the 1930s, progressive opinion on prison reform favoured rehabilitative training in a non-secure setting for first offenders. Columns of men or boys literally marched out of closed institutions and built their own open camps in the countryside, staying under canvas the meantime. Wakefield prison had its own camp from 1933. 'Work in the woods clearing or cultivating the land' was understood to be rehabilitative, inculcating, it appears, normative and conformist brands of masculinity.[78] Such models were not considered appropriate for women and girls for whom domestic training was preferred.[79]

By 1937 the Prison Commissioners had plans for an open women's prison in the countryside, 'organised on a cottage-home system' as well as a girl's borstal, but the war delayed their implementation.[80] It took till late 1946 for the opening of the open girls' borstal at East Sutton Park, Kent. Askham Grange open prison first admitted adult women prisoners in January 1947. Askham Grange offered its inmates a nine-month programme of training in housekeeping, laundry and cookery. Askham was located not in the rugged moors or forest, but in a picturesque village in the Vale of York. Women at Askham were not to be accommodated in self-built huts but in a late-Victorian mansion, complete with ballroom. Askham Grange was born into Beveridge's post-war world of austerity combined with faith in reconstruction through planning, welfare and social improvement.[81] The ethos of the institution was marked by a combination of thrift, self-sufficiency and progress, self-discipline and cheerfulness, although prisoners' memoirs show that discipline, goodwill and compliance were not always as perfect as the Governors' reports represented.[82]

Because of the nine-month training period, Askham did not accommodate prisoners on very short sentences. Only prisoners 'suitable for training' were admitted; 'free from infectious disease, and both mentally and physically fit'.[83] Such criteria were maintained through the exclusion of 5–10 per cent of women in each of the first three years, as 'unsuitable for training' through 'mental or physical defects'.[84] The prison may have been open, but the Governor and her staff were vigilant in maintaining boundaries between Askham and the rest of the prison system. During the first year the average age on reception was 33.5 years and 65 per cent were described as 'housewives',[85] though of course this doubtless disguised women's casual or intermittent wage earning. Askham successfully restricted the intake of very young women.[86] Consequently, the early prison population was selected strongly from women in their late twenties and older, whose offence could often be linked to the strains of working-class family and community life during the war or in immediate post-war austerity. On release, a large proportion of prisoners were 'discharged to their own homes'.[87] Askham inmates were selected from those most likely to find relevance in its domestic training programme and, unhampered (we are told) by severe physical or psychological problems, had a reasonable chance of successful normalisation within the prison regime.

Although Askham Grange and RWCI were positioned very differently in the complex of penal-welfare institutions of the period, they both achieved success through limiting their intake to cases likely to be successful, they both worked with an ethos of engaged interest in the individual problems and situations of their inmates and they both rehabilitated women inmates through training in domestic work and the inculcation of respectable femininities.

From the Second World War crime rates rose. In 1960 the prison population consisted of 26,198 males and 901 females. Across the professional distance kept between staff and prisoners, some positive and supportive relationships are documented, as well as some romantic ones. In the 1960s women's prisons were administered by a comparatively small group of professionals and civil servants amongst whom psychological explanations of women's offending were dominant. Short sentences for drunkenness still accounted for many of the inmates. Xenia Field compared Holloway prison in the 1960s to a girls' school. The prisoners, she said, 'are not dangerous; they are a pathetic group of inadequate, often mentally subnormal people'.[88] Criminological explanations of women offenders emphasised abnormality as a characteristic of the whole prison population. This is not to deny that men's prisons were also concerned to discipline deviant masculinities, and that the criminological literature offered psychological explanations for male 'habitual offenders', nevertheless criminal behaviour in general was (and is) far more congruent with dominant constructions of masculinity than of femininity.

Despite the apparently limited potential of many female recidivists, women's prisons still aimed for rehabilitation, and still prioritised the development of respectable domestic femininity as evidence of reform. Domesticity and femininity have been marks of recovery even of women patients detained under the 1959 Mental Health Act for treatment 'under conditions of special security on account of their dangerous, violent or criminal propensities'. Over the twentieth century the notion of inculcating domesticity has meant a concentration on laundry work both to occupy prisoners and to provide income (or at least to minimise costs). In 1963 of 632 women prisoners deemed fit to work, 55 per cent were employed as cooks, bakers, laundry workers or cleaners compared to 28 per cent (of 21,080) male prisoners.[89] Heavy work in often poorly equipped laundries served neither to cultivate the skills of bourgeois domesticity that the cheery regime at Askham Grange aimed at, nor to develop other more employment-related skills in prisoners.

The discursive shift from moral to psychological explanations of offending which highlighted women prisoners' inadequacies also emphasised medical intervention. Violence remained incipient within the women's prison, particularly amongst young offenders, and medication was a frequent response. Tranquilisers and sleep-inducing drugs were in frequent and heavy use. The Prison Medical Service has been the agent of the state rather than that of the prisoner that consults it, and medical services available to prisoners have remained poor. Joan Henry wrote that the prisoners in 1950s Holloway 'all looked unkempt, with straggly hair and shiny faces; and they all had the incurious expressions of sleep-walkers'. In 1975 one prisoner wrote: 'You lived in your own little world surrounded by medication. [...] Its like you had a blanket over your head. You do things like you put food in your mouth and you'd forget to chew it [...].' The line between criminality and mental illness preoccupied the governor and staff of Holloway prison reporting to the 1975 Butler Committee: 'There are very few mentally ill women in Holloway, but, there are many who may be considered "mentally abnormal" [...] in that there is a great deviance from sociological and psychological norms.'[90] Such views informed the design of the new Holloway prison implemented at a period when the penal system as a whole was coming to emphasise containment over rehabilitation. This therapeutic intention was subverted by the practicalities of attempting to construct the new Holloway whilst the old was in occupation. This led to delays and spiralling expense. The architecture of the new build was in direct contrast to the radial Victorian prison; its small informal spaces and poor sight lines were not amenable to surveillance, and in fact resulted in increased discipline on prisoners. Holloway still attracted a poor Inspectors Report in 1995.

During the 1970s penal policy again took a more retributive turn, as did the internal (and informal) practices in women's prisons; there is evidence of beatings and physical coercion of prisoners in the 1980s. Defiance and disruption were not uncommon in twentieth-century women's prisons. In modern populations discipline has been more intrusive in women's prisons than for men. Levels of self-harm and suicide attempts are also markedly higher for women in prison, though concerns about suicide have more frequently been expressed for young (male) offenders. The continued use of psychotropic drugs in late twentieth-century women's prisons, even whilst therapeutic rationales were questioned, emphasises the control function of medication. Women in prison received over 145,000 doses of anti-depressants, sedatives and tranquillisers between January 1984 and March 1985, though these broad figures cover much local variation in practice.[91]

Alana Barton finds key continuities between the regime of a modern probation hostel, Vernon Lodge, and Victorian semi-penal institutions for women. This hostel had originated as a nineteenth-century reformatory. The discourses and processes through which women were labelled as 'deviant' and needing institutionalisation for the purpose of 'normalisation' were remarkably persistent over time, as was the 'dominant, hegemonic discourse constructed around idealised images of femininity'.[92] Although perceived by staff and the institution to be empowering for hostel residents, activities and educational initiatives at Vernon Lodge remained embedded in a total regime in which heavy surveillance and monitoring produced disempowerment and infantilisation. Furthermore, penal policy at the beginning of the twenty-first century maintained its commitment to psychological programmes aimed at changing women's perceptions of their (usually disadvantaged) social situation, rather than considering wider social welfare measures that might alleviate some of these disadvantages.[93]

Modern women have experienced prison differently from men for several reasons. Firstly, because they are part of a differently structured prison population. Secondly, because there are comparatively so few female prisoners, the system suffers from organisational problems which combine both overcrowding and a lack of facilities compared to men's prisons. Most women prisoners spend a good deal of their time inside at long distances from their homes, which makes visiting particularly difficult. Also, women prisoners are moved from one establishment to another much more frequently than men to serve different stages of their sentence, either because they are difficult to manage or because of overcrowding. Consequently, imprisonment is a more solitary and isolating experience for women. This bears on them particularly heavily, because, unlike men, women retain their outside family responsibilities whilst in prison. Male prisoners have generally had a wife or other family who can continue to maintain their home and support their children. Husbands or partners of women prisoners fulfil these obligations far less often, so imprisoned women are at a high risk of losing accommodation and of having their children taken into care. In 1982 women prisoners were the mothers of some 1600 children under 16. Women in prison are reported in numerous modern studies to retain anxieties about home, children and family. As one prisoner said; 'If women have kids outside they'll take any amount of stick off anybody.' Surviving nineteenth-century correspondence from prisoners also demonstrates concerns for children and family and shows that Victorian women prisoners had often, like their modern counterparts, been subject to domestic violence and abuse.[94] A compounding problem for the later twentieth century was the high proportion of drug and substance abuse amongst women prisoners compared to the general population. A 1967 study found that some 15 per cent of women prisoners had a major physical ailment and 20 per cent a major mental health problem.[95] In fact, modern prison populations of women demonstrate a range of the traits that at the beginning of the century were diagnosed as 'feeble-mindedness'; illegitimate children, abusive treatment by male partners and family or poverty.

Conclusion

Feminist scholars have debated the gendered implications of the punishment of women, challenging criminological and historical perspectives that emphasise 'leniency'. Historically, the experience of punishment has exceeded penal policy intentions, or even formal penologies. The far less visible micro-technologies of punishment and the punitive aspects of prison subcultures need also to be taken into account.

Gender power relations surrounding the punishment of women have been both historically persistent and highly complex. It is not possible to claim simply that women have been punished either more harshly or more leniently than men. It is also not possible to resolve the issues by looking at the penal system in isolation. Since the eighteenth century, the social forces that have resulted in (some) women becoming subject to punishment as criminal offenders have routed others into semi-penal institutions. Whether these have been philanthropic, medicalised or educational, their reformative or curative agendas have nevertheless been realised in regimes which, like institutions for female criminal offenders, have sought to discipline women into compliant femininity. This continuity in disciplinary technologies across an 'archipelago' of penal and semi-penal institutions marks out the history of women's punishment from accepted chronologies.

Both penal and semi-penal institutions have been subject to resource constraints. Even at the period when 'penal-welfarism' was most dominant and women's criminality or deviance were mostly framed through psychiatric or psychological discourses which emphasised debility, the institutional impulse to control and incarceration was limited by availability of places and the active selection of the most 'hopeful' cases. A wider view of penality takes in the social marginalisation and poor prospects of those who were ignored. To the extent that women have been thought to be incipiently weak and disorderly, their minor offending has often not been subject to heavy direct punishment. Ignoring, belittling and marginalising such women (for example, those in magistrates courts for minor charges of damage or common assault) produced a statistical finding of leniency, but abandoned them to the social suffering of materially impoverished lives. Punishment has historically been inflicted on those whose transgressions seemed most socially threatening. Consequently, this has had the effect of enabling apparent leniency to women offenders who for the most part could be understood as weaker and merely 'troublesome'. Nevertheless, on occasions where women's offending seemed to threaten the gender order, punishment could be irrationally severe.[96] Constructions of women as weaker have in the modern era often meant criminal behaviour has been explained through deficiencies in psychology, character or moral status, and led to the use of infantilising regimes which attempted to school them into dominant norms of femininity. Within penal and semi-penal institutions, those who comply with dominant gender constructions, both women and men, have tended to be more lightly punished. The penal system, like the law, works with often reductionist and outdated gender norms. Sanctioned femininity requires docility and deference, which then calls for particularly close surveillance and discipline. Women who are routed by the criminal justice system into punishable positions are those who seem most transgressive in their lives. Sexuality indicates or explains deviance. Additionally, women are normatively given responsibilities for homes and families. For women whose domestic lives are less respectable, often because of social disadvantage, their social disadvantage readily translates into a gender transgression.

8

Girls and Delinquency

In 1732 the artist William Hogarth produced a series of six engravings – entitled *A Harlot's Progress* – telling the story of the moral and physical decline of Moll Hackabout, who is first shown arriving in London as a fresh-faced country girl in her late teens (Figure 8.1). She is rapidly 'seduced' by an elderly procuress and a nobleman, descends from finery into prostitution, is imprisoned in Bridewell House of Correction for an unspecified offence, and finally dies of syphilis at the youthful age of 23. Moll Hackabout is portrayed as a victim of external circumstances and her fall depicted in sexual terms as she becomes a contagion to others. Hogarth's engravings also demonstrated parallel concerns about the disorderly behaviour of male youth, particularly apprentices, whose habits of gambling and drinking might lead to criminal offences of theft and violence (depicted in his series of engravings *Industry and Idleness*).[1] Such a gendered narrative, which drew on pre-existing concerns about the corruption of innocent youth within a decadent urban environment, was repackaged and reconfigured across the nineteenth and twentieth centuries.

This chapter is concerned with the range of criminal offences committed by young females as well as with wider notions of anti-social behaviours (not necessarily illegal in themselves) which the term 'delinquency' has come to imply. The two were implicitly connected, in that forms of deviancy were assumed to lead to experiences of criminality, either as perpetrator or (in the case of girls) as victim. Nineteenth-century debates tended to focus on male 'delinquents' and, as in the case of adult offending, it was overwhelmingly male juveniles who were accused of criminal offences. By the first half of the twentieth century, however, the figure of the deviant 'good time girl', the precocious and predatory adolescent female, had become a central figure of moral panic, seen to constitute a threat to national strength because of worries about venereal disease, illegitimate pregnancy and irresponsible parenthood. This chapter will begin by offering an overview of the ways in which the category of age combined with ideas about gender to shape attitudes towards the girl 'delinquent', considering how this in turn affected girls' experiences of state welfare and criminal justice systems in the modern period. The chapter will then focus on a specific case study, set against the backdrop of the Second World War, to explore the relationship between the portrayal of one fictional girl 'delinquent' and the actual subject upon whom she was allegedly based.

Figure 8.1   William Hogarth, A *Harlot's Progress* (1732), plate 1. © Mary Evans Picture Library

A 'modern' problem?

Whilst the concept of juvenile delinquency it often assumed to be a very modern invention, it had earlier precedents, as the work of Paul Griffiths has demonstrated. The problem of errant youth – including child vagrants or beggars, high-spirited apprentices and independent young single women migrating to towns in search of work – had been discussed as a threat to the social order since at least the sixteenth century. Seventeenth-century strategies to 'reform' anti-social behaviour included training in charity schools, workhouses or bridewells as well as transportation to the colonies. Yet any argument about continuity needs to be offset against changes in 'legal, legislative and linguistic responses', as well as changing economic, social and institutional structures.[2] The precise term 'juvenile delinquency' was a nineteenth-century coinage, first used in 1815 to describe a perceived increase in criminal offending by young urbanites.[3] From this decade onward government officials, social reformers and campaigners highlighted the presence of criminal youth as a distinct group and debated appropriate forms of prevention, punishment and rehabilitation. At the same time, too, increased collation of statistical data ensured that concerns about criminality received quantitative expression. Offenders and prisoners were not only counted but categorised into ages from the 1830s onwards. It is clear that young people were increasingly visible in the courtroom. For example, those under the age of 16 constituted 15 per cent of all those indicted at the Middlesex Quarter Sessions in 1847, compared to a mere 3 per cent in 1797. The 16–25 age group was even more prominent: they formed 46 per cent of Middlesex defendants in 1847, compared to 34 per cent in 1797.[4] At the Old Bailey, the percentage of defendants under the age of 20 had similarly risen from 21 per cent to 37 per cent between 1791 and 1822.[5] As Peter King has shown, this increase may reflect a growing willingness to prosecute juveniles (with the gradual lifting of capital sentences for thieving) as much as an actual increase in offending behaviour by young people.

Historians have also suggested that the 'discovery' of the juvenile delinquent can be linked to the economic and social transformations that accompanied industrialisation and to concerns about the decline in 'service'. The gradual breakdown in traditional patriarchal ties of authority and deference – which had shaped the system of apprenticeship within households – meant that young men in particular were no longer entrusted to the care and discipline of a 'master'. These concerns certainly shaped adult perceptions of the problem of youth, although an exact correlation between the breakdown of 'traditional' ties and changes in young people's behaviour is difficult to evidence.[6]

Whilst policies to reform deviant youth had been developed at a local level in the Early Modern period, the nineteenth century saw an intensive discussion of a national legislative response, albeit one that was ultimately delivered at the local level. The provision of separate penal institutions for juveniles (including prisons and reformatories) from the mid-nineteenth century onwards was followed by the creation of the juvenile court in 1908, which provided a distinctive legal system and status for young people. Young people were constituted simultaneously as social victims and social threats through the complex of legislation and policy initiatives that sought to protect and rehabilitate dangerous and endangered children.[7] Criminal justice was simply one strand in the wider net or 'penal-welfare' complex which sought, by the end of the nineteenth century to regulate the behaviour of children and their parents.[8] In this sense, then, the 'juvenile delinquent' was created as a separate legal entity through the bureaucratic and regulatory mechanisms of the modern state.

The construction of juvenile delinquency as a social problem must be set alongside the Victorian idealisation of childhood as a protected period of innocence that was also legally constituted. During the course of the nineteenth century those under the age of 12 were transformed from workers into scholars and separated institutionally and spatially from adults as a result of the factory legislation of the 1840s and the introduction of compulsory schooling after 1870. The 'romantic' view of childhood, associated with the poet William Wordsworth, suggested that humans were innately good; corruption was a result of environment, bad parenting or poor education. This optimistic account of human nature was reflected in initiatives to 'save' and rehabilitate street children before they were too far 'fallen' or 'corrupted' into a life of immorality or criminality. The 'juvenile delinquent' was the young person who was not really a child at all; he or she was assumed to be precocious or prematurely adult, possessing inappropriate forms of knowledge or experience. The juvenile delinquent was often stereotyped as being of teenage years, on the cusp or borderline between childhood and adulthood, but with many of the cares and responsibilities associated with maturity – including economic ones given that the school leaving age, set at ten in 1880, only rose to 12 in 1899, 14 in 1921, and 15 in 1947. Paid work was not in itself seen as problematic for young people in the nineteenth century; rather certain kinds of work – such as street selling or work in the entertainments industry – were viewed as potentially corrupting.[9] 'Industry' was to be cultivated as a key character trait and as an antidote to idleness. The exact age of the 'juvenile', 'child' or 'young person' has shifted across time as a result of legislative changes.[10] Significantly, however, the young delinquent was assumed to be a member of the urban working class. Middle-class or wealthy children who committed acts of vandalism or theft were unlikely to be hauled before the courts – they were subjected to the disciplinary mechanisms of private schools or parents, but were not seen as appropriate subjects for public scrutiny and intervention.

   The twentieth century saw a steep escalation in reported and indicted crime involving young people, particularly in the wake of the Second World War, which, it was argued had resulted in an erosion of family ties (involving both love and discipline) as a consequence of evacuation, absent fathers and working mothers (see Table 8.1). Howard Taylor has suggested that the rising statistics relating to youth offending were in part a product of policing strategies; crimes involving young people were often easier to detect and helped bolster

Table 8.1   Convictions of those under 17 for indictable offences, England and Wales

	Male/Female	1938	1947	1956	1965
Violence against the person	M	110	167	596	1888
	F	6	4	12	116
Sexual offences*	M	472	575	1,069	900
	F	3	4	4	1
Receiving, fraud and	M	553	747	1,331	3,019
false pretences	F	49	88	128	430
Breaking and Entering	M	6,683	10,323	9,210	18,178
	F	110	343	322	547
Larceny	M	18,191	19,557	22,432	30,067
	F	1,559	2,595	2,447	6,488
All	M	26,369	32,594	35,842	55,194
	F	1,747	3,100	2,973	7,676
Female convictions as % of juvenile convictions		6.2	8.7	7.7	12.2

Source: BPP, Criminal Statistics.
* Indictable sexual offences included rape, indecent assault, unlawful carnal knowledge and sodomy. The infrequency with which girls were convicted for these types of indictable offences was counterbalanced by their appearance in the juvenile courts for 'status offences' in which they were deemed to require 'care or protection'.

data relating to police efficiency, which was used by forces to argue for increased funding.[11] Male youths – whether stereotyped as 'teddy boys', 'mods' or 'rockers' – were presented in the press as violent threats to 'adult' society. The 'juvenile delinquent' moved centre stage as a target of social concern, epitomising all that was perceived to be 'wrong' with an increasingly affluent, consumerist and Americanised postwar society.

A 'girl' problem?

Females under 16 formed 17 per cent of all juveniles indicted at the Middlesex Sessions in 1791, rising to a high of 47 per cent in 1805 and then falling to 12 per cent in 1821 and to 15 per cent in 1841.[12] Like adult women, they disappeared from view by the twentieth century, girls under 17 constituting only 6.2 per cent of those convicted of indictable offences in 1938, although this figure rose again in the aftermath of the Second World War to 12.2 per cent by 1965 (see Table 8.1) and to 14 per cent by 2001. Girls, like adult women, have been subjected to disciplinary mechanisms that have both circumscribed their movements within public space and stressed the significance for personal reputations of 'good' behaviour. The continued employment of young women as domestic servants meant that household hierarchies continued to structure and discipline their lives even when apprenticeship was in decline for young men.

Case evidence for the eighteenth century suggests that young female servants were only prosecuted for theft by employers when previous attempts to resolve the matter informally had failed. William Fricker prosecuted his 17-year-old servant in 1766, declaring that 'she would not own any thing [confess] to it at first [...] I said, if she would, I would be kind to her'.[13] Cases tended to come to court, therefore, when servants refused to accept the kadi-justice of their masters. Employers often indicated awareness of a duty of care towards young female servants. In 1765 Henry Stroud told the Old Bailey that he had not intended to prosecute 16-year-old Elizabeth Gould whom he had known 'from a baby', requesting she should be treated mercifully because 'she is very young'; he stated that he had been coerced into the prosecution by 'thief-takers'.[14] Perceptions of female vulnerability may have meant that girls were less likely to be prosecuted than juvenile males or adult women.

Local reputations, evaluated in terms of gender, class and age, affected decisions to prosecute. In September 1690 Margaret Beard, described as 'a little Girl, aged 11 Years' was tried at the Old Bailey for stealing cloth from a shop. It was alleged in court that 'she was known to be a pilfering idle Wench'; in the context of the seventeenth century, an 11-year-old was expected to be in proper employment. Sentenced to a whipping on this occasion, she was prosecuted by another draper nine months later for lifting silk from his shop. She was described as 'very impudent in her Behaviour when taken, and had been an Old Offender, though Young'. It was claimed she might be 'quick with child' and the death sentence was commuted to transportation in January 1692. The details of Beard's case suggest that informal mechanisms had been used on repeated occasions; as her offending continued, shopkeepers opted for prosecution since her 'impudence', 'idleness' and adult lifestyle outweighed the sympathy they extended to those young in years.[15]

As prosecutions rose in the nineteenth century, the offences with which girls were charged, like boys, overwhelmingly involved theft, particularly from domestic premises (in the case of domestic servants) or shops (see also Chapter 2 on property offences). Servants in their early teens sometimes alleged poor treatment by their employers as a defence. In 1845 13-year-old Louisa Baker told the Old Bailey that her employers had 'half starved me, and gave me no clothes' (sovereign coins belonging to her master were found in her box).[16] In other cases, masters claimed they had taken young women on as servants to relieve them from existing poverty: 'we took the prisoner in because her father and mother were very poor – they had no bed to lie on – we allowed her wages every week'.[17] Whilst financial need may well have acted as an incentive, shoplifting, particularly in pairs or groups, might result from girls' interest in fashionable items, desire for excitement or from simply 'larking about'. In April 1834, 14-year-old Caroline Beaton and her friend 16-year-old Mary Ann Cain made away with lengths of green, pink and black satin ribbon after teasing a shop-owner's daughter, pretending they were intending to buy goods.[18]

The records of the twentieth-century juvenile courts show that boys were more likely to be accused of stealing sweets, cigarettes or tools after breaking and entering establishments, whilst girls tended to be prosecuted for taking clothing, accessories or cosmetics from self-service stores. A case heard before the Manchester juvenile court in December 1960 was not untypical. A girl of 15, her 11-year-old sister and another 11-year-old female friend went on a shoplifting spree in Piccadilly, visiting first Woolworths and then Little-woods stores. They were arrested in possession of a range of items including lipsticks, perfumes, shampoos, hair laqueur, deodorant, talcum powder, bath cubes, mascara, nail varnish, a beauty pack and powder puffs.[19] If the wearing of cosmetics acted as a marker of adult female identity, glamour and desirability, juveniles were attracted to these fetishised objects through aspiration, fantasy and romance.[20]

Girls were much less likely than boys to be prosecuted for offences involving violence (Table 8.1). As Andrew Davies has argued, this was in part a result of gendered assumptions that aggression was a masculine attribute and that women and girls were unlikely instigators of brawls, assaults or fights. Late nineteenth-century concerns about 'scuttling gangs' tended to focus on violent male youth. Yet reports of court hearings show that young women in their late teens were involved in disputes and had a highly visible presence in street life, an important arena for sociability and courtship within working-class culture. Davies suggests that female 'scuttlers' tended to fight with clogs and boots rather than the knives and belts favoured by male gang members. Girls constituted 6.3 per cent of those charged with gang-related crime in Davies's sample of Manchester cases for the years 1870–1900. When they did appear in the courts they were described in the local press as 'viragos' and 'amazons', terms that drew attention to their contravention of conventional gender norms.[21]

The extremely rare cases in which young women have been accused of homicide have led to a quest for motive and explanation within the modern news media. The exceptional case of Constance Kent – who admitted in 1865 that she had murdered her four-year-old step-brother five years previously, when she herself was only 15 – was a landmark for the development of both sensationalist crime reporting and also crime fiction. Kent, unlike the majority of the young women discussed in this chapter, was associated with the genteel middle classes. The boy's body was discovered strangled, mutilated and forced down an outside privy. Both the original murder of 1860 and Kent's trial in 1865 were covered in the national and local press; a flurry of pamphlet literature and popular ballads were illustrative of popular fascination with the case, elements of which were adapted by Wilkie Collins for his novel *The Moonstone* (1868). The sympathy that was evinced towards Kent (she was reprieved from execution and left England for Australia in 1885 after serving a 20-year prison sentence) is understandable in terms of the Victorian normalisation of genteel female passivity which, as in the case of the kleptomania diagnosis (see Chapter 2), meant that the criminality of otherwise 'innocent' middle-class women could only be explained through the language of 'madness'. Some newspapers were quick to condemn Kent; but there was also considerable speculation that the act was one of insanity, arising from a hereditary disposition that had been compounded by the tribulations of puberty, which was more likely in girls than in boys to lead to 'homicidal mania'.[22]

Despite the empirical fact that the majority of prosecutions involving female juveniles have been for theft, the working-class 'girl delinquent' has been consistently stereotyped across the modern period as sexually predatory or dangerous: as a 'flash-girl' (1830s), 'vicious girl' and 'minx' (1880s) or 'good time girl' (1940s) who seduces and corrupts both younger boys and older men to extract gifts and financial reward.[23] Commenting on the Teddy-boy gangs of the 1950s, the journalist T. R. Fyvel wrote that 'the equivalent to the boy [thief...] is the girl who slides into prostitution [...who] may end up on the streets, or else she may become a slut and an inadequate wife and mother, so perpetuating the evil'.[24] Girls, it was argued, did not appear in the criminal justice statistics for the reason that their transgressions were of a sexual rather than criminal nature. This did not mean that they were ignored by the state. Rather, the association of girls with transgressive sexuality has meant there has been a tendency to police girls 'through welfare mechanisms rather than criminal justice mechanisms'.[25] Girls judged sexually delinquent have, however, been increasingly subjected to similar levels of institutionalisation as boys convicted of criminal offences.

Whilst the early nineteenth century had seen a focus on the social problem of male delinquency, the late nineteenth and early twentieth century produced a set of moral panics centring on the sexualised figure of the adolescent girl. The sociologist Stanley Cohen has defined the concept of a 'moral panic' as a phenomenon in which:

> a condition, episode, person or group of persons emerge to become defined as a threat to societal values and interests; its nature is presented in a stylised and stereotypical fashion by the mass media; the moral barricades are manned by

editors, bishops, politicians and other right-thinking people; socially accredited experts pronounce their diagnoses and solutions [and] ways of coping are evolved or (more often) resorted to.[26]

Cohen used the concept of 'moral panic' to analyse the media hysteria surrounding a series of violent clashes between young male mods and rockers in Brighton in May 1964. Over-zealous use of the concept has been criticised, since there has been a tendency to label any media frenzy as 'moral panic'. However, Cohen's original definition is helpful in understanding particular instances in which 'the moral barricades' were 'manned' to prevent the corruption of female youth as well as their male counterparts, whose activities have tended, until comparatively recently to dominate historical and sociological work.

In 1885 the attentions of newspapers, lobby groups, and the institutions of church and state centred on the problem of what was euphemistically termed 'juvenile prostitution' as a result of the sensationally entitled series of articles 'The Maiden Tribute of Modern Babylon', published in the *Pall Mall Gazette* by campaigning editor W. T. Stead. The reports coincided with the passage through parliament of the Criminal Law Amendment Bill, which sought to raise the age of consent for females from 13 to 16. Stead depicted the daughters of the labouring poor as melodramatic victims of a predatory aristocratic masculinity. Yet he contrasted a stereotype of corrupted femininity – the 'brazen faced harlot' – with the girl who had not yet lost her 'maiden bloom' or 'pathetic eyes, where still lingered the timid glance of a frightened fawn'.[27] Concerns about girls as victims of what we now term sexual abuse merged with fears of precocious female sexuality, viewed as dangerous or corrupting of others.

The 'moral panic' of the 1880s was in part resolved by the raising of the age of consent to 16, leading to concerns in some quarters that 'precocious' girls would use the Criminal Law Amendment Act of 1885 for the purposes of blackmail.[28] It also saw the development of institutional remedies, designed to prevent contamination of girls and young women through the evil effects of street life. Whilst reformatories had been set up to rehabilitate 'dangerous' children who had criminal convictions, the industrial school system was developed to deal with endangered children who might become 'criminal'. From the 1880s onwards, legal and institutional mechanisms were introduced to 'save' girls deemed to be sexually delinquent or in danger of moral corruption. The 1880 Industrial Schools Amendment Act legislated for magistrates to commit children to a certified industrial school if they were found living 'in immoral surroundings' with prostitutes or frequenting their company. Anxieties relating to the fear of a 'white slave trade' continued into the twentieth century as young women were constructed interchangeably as victims and threats. Particular leisure venues, such as cafes, nightclubs and ice-cream parlours were to be earmarked as sites of sexual danger, from which young girls required rescue and careful supervision to prevent any future 'fall'.

Whilst the chivalric discourse of the late-Victorian period had emphasised the vulnerability of the melodramatic female victim, the First World War saw a recasting of youthful femininity in terms of sexual agency. Anxiety related to the 'amateur prostitute' – the young woman in her late teens who, excited by 'khaki fever', hung around military bases with the intent of seducing soldiers in exchange for drinks and entertainment. As an 'amateur prostitute' she was seen as a contagion, transmitting venereal disease to the country's finest fighting men. The resolution that was proposed to this 'sanitary' and 'moral panic' involved the introduction of medical inspections and forced detention for young women who were infected (under the Defence of the Realm Acts). It also involved the introduction of curfews, policed by 'respectable' women undertaking regular foot patrol (these women creating a precedent for women's involvement in the police service).[29]

During the Second World War concerns were raised yet again about 'good time girls', some as young as 13, who were once again drawn to military encampments, railway stations and the main sites of urban entertainment, spreading venereal disease to American GIs. In 1943 East London juvenile court magistrate Basil Henriques argued that 'War fever has affected girls far more than boys [...] They are attracted by anybody in uniform, and particularly a soldier who can give them a good time'. He blamed poor parenting and the American film industry for 'the promiscuous intercourse and even prostitution of girls from 14 to 17'.[30] Head of the Metropolitan Women Police, Dorothy Peto, wrote that 'the semi-delinquent type of girl and young woman [...] is a greater danger than the prostitute in spreading venereal disease'.[31] The concern was both medical and moral. Exercise of sexual restraint and continence by all women, including the young, was equated with virtuous citizenship and national strength.[32] This representation of young women as sexually predatory might also be linked to concerns about the preservation of gender norms as young working-women's earning and purchasing powers appeared to increase and as their opportunities for pleasure and leisure expanded, partly as a consequence of war. Concerns about miscegenation – sexual relationships between young white women and other racial groups – were regularly voiced as part of the popular anxiety about the 'good time girl' and her alleged attraction to black American GIs. The *Liverpool Post* quoted from a report that 'large numbers of very young girls flock into the city night after night, in search of excitement and the company of servicemen and seamen of all nationalities', whilst the *South Wales Argus* recorded claims that 'there are many girls, painted up to the eyes, walking out arm-in-arm with coloured men. It ought to be stopped.'[33] 'Moral panics' are phenomena through which ideas about social identities, involving distinctions such as gender, class and 'race' are negotiated and repositioned. They have served, historically, to focus attention on a specific target – femininity as victim or threat – whilst diverting attention away from the inequalities or forms of exploitation (such as sexual abuse) that in part have structured young women's lives.

Danger and reform

Continued concerns about young women's sexuality led to the intensification of welfare responses that sought to prevent their moral 'fall'. From 1889 until 1963, child protection legislation permitted parents to bring their own children before the courts if they felt they were 'beyond control' and in need of specialist discipline. In the case of girls, this invariably meant staying out late at night. The 1933 Children and Young Persons Act broadened the categories of those who could be defined as 'in need of care or protection' to include those under 17 with an 'unfit' parent or guardian and who were in 'moral danger'. The term 'moral danger' was assumed to mean underage sex and girls who were proved to need the protection of this clause could be sent to an approved school (the name given to institutions which had formerly operated as either industrial schools or reformatories). Whilst this clause was not in itself gendered, it was rarely used in relation to male youth. Thus regulatory strategies targeted at adolescent girls 'aimed to moralise rather than criminalise'.[34] As Cox has shown, a far greater proportion of girls than boys were brought before the courts or were referred to institutions in relation to what can be characterised as 'status offences' involving those 'in need of care or protection' or 'beyond' parental control. In 1936 just over 50 per cent of girls were sent to approved schools for these reasons compared to 10 per cent of boys; in 1964 only 5 per cent of boys were 'non-offenders' compared to 62 per cent of girls.[35] In 1955 the British Social Biology Council suggested the juvenile courts were still 'being used with an excess zeal to deal with mature, well-developed girls of 16 who stayed out all night with their boyfriends'.[36] The clause concerning those 'in moral danger' stayed on the statute book in child protection legislation until 1989, when it was replaced with rhetoric relating to harm and abuse. Its ultimate demise was a result of slowly changing attitudes towards the sexual agency of young people.

The institutional regime of the certified institutions set up for girls (reformatories or industrial schools and, after 1933, borstals and approved schools) similarly demonstrated a gendered approach to delinquency and its reform. Working-class girls were trained in domestic skills including laundry, needlework and household duties as a preparation, firstly, for employment in domestic service (in the period before the Second World War) and, subsequently, marriage and motherhood. Boys were trained to move into trades such as carpentry and metalwork.[37] Whilst austere uniforms were phased out in the twentieth century, hair was still kept short to avoid lice and there was considerable continuity in girls' experiences of institutionalisation. As Cox has commented 'through a regular diet of domestic labour, religious teaching, fair punishment and deserved rewards, they were gradually to learn the value of hard work, self-restraint and familiar routine'.[38] The motives of those who set up, ran or worked in girls' certified institutions has been subject to much debate. Whilst their function was clearly regulatory, it is also likely, as Michelle Cale has argued, that many staff hoped to improve the lives of those whom they viewed as less fortunate. In the Victorian period such work was equated with missionary work and 'well-meaning amateurs' worked with delinquents to 'wipe away their sins and make them love Jesus Christ'.[39] Religious motivation probably diminished as paid workers of lower social status took up posts in the Edwardian period, viewing their work in terms of a vocational career. By the mid-twentieth century residential social work was being recast as a profession, requiring specialist training. Whatever their aims, it is clear that institutional provision was shaped by class and gender norms, including fears of sexuality. Those girls who had 'fallen' (in Victorian terms) or had direct sexual experiences were sent to specialist institutions and were forbidden to talk of past lives. All residential institutions developed mechanisms to manage or police the 'problem' of sexuality: age groups were carefully segregated, hygiene and cleanliness were stressed, dormitories were partitioned and closely supervised at night, and diet was manipulated to encourage restraint (for example, red meat was avoided).

A number of scholars have emphasised the agency, initiative and forms of resistance of those who came within the remit of certified institutions.[40] If matrons were shocked by the 'bad language', absconding and petty thieving of some of their charges, these can be interpreted as tactics that subverted reforming intentions. Yet for some girls, particularly those removed from brutality or destitution in the late nineteenth century, the industrial and reformatory school system may have provided a more stable environment and some element of social mobility as a route into future employment. Correspondence located in case files suggests that some girls built affective bonds with staff in the home.[41] If reformers and, later, social workers aimed to prevent sexual experimentation this was, in part, because they recognised the social stigma and economic difficulties associated with single motherhood. Clearly, any notion of agency must be qualified in relation to the marginal position and limited choices of the young women sent to certified institutions. Nevertheless, the relationship between young women, their female charges and the institutional regime was a complex one that cannot be reduced to a simple model of 'social control'. As the final section of this chapter will demonstrate, however, one of the most significant effects of referral to an industrial or approved school was a change in legal status: bound by a committal order, girls were brought within the penal system even when they had not in fact committed a criminal offence. Labelling as 'delinquent' might act as a self-fulfilling prophecy, affecting girls' own sense of themselves and hence their life-chances.

Ideas about the causes of delinquency were subject to shifts across time. The explanatory power of 'nature' versus 'nurture' was constantly under debate and the ways in which these debates played out in relation to gender, class and sexuality clearly impacted on the experience of juveniles. Late-Victorians and Edwardians tended to argue that 'if a child is rescued whilst it is young, environment will overcome heredity'.[42] Where rehabilitation failed, however, juveniles were likely to be labelled as 'hardened' or of 'bad stock'. The influential text *The Young Offender*, written by London County Council Psychologist Cyril Burt and first published in 1925, viewed delinquency as caused by a multiplicity of factors – inherited, environmental, physical, intellectual and temperamental. Nevertheless, as concerns about eugenics gained currency in the interwar period and as medical explanations of delinquency gained some ground, young women whose precocity was interpreted in terms of 'mental deficiency' were in some instances institutionalised within psychiatric hospitals.[43] In the 1940s and 1950s delinquent girls were often stereotyped as 'feeble-minded' or 'unstable'. The influence of John Bowlby's work, which stressed the importance of motherly love on the social and psychological development of the child, led to attempts to supervise 'delinquents' within families through the increased use of supervision or probation orders instead of institutionalisation. For girls and young women, however, it resulted in a continued emphasis on the undesirability of single motherhood, on the need for appropriate training in maternal skills and on girls' sexual and reproductive function. Juvenile Liaison Schemes, involving cautions and at-home visits, were set up by some police forces in the post-war period as a multi-agency measure to prevent further offending. In Liverpool, where the first scheme had started in 1949, a Moral Welfare Section was added in 1957, making use of women police officers. Of the 461 female juveniles who were supervised between November 1957 and December 1958, only a third had been linked to criminal activity; the majority were supervised within the scheme for running away from home, being victims of indecent assault, being 'in moral danger' or 'beyond control' of their parents, or for other 'behavioural difficulties'.[44] Thus the sexualisation of the 'girl delinquent' has remained a common thread across the nineteenth and twentieth centuries.

Good Time Girl: a movie, a murder and a moral panic

In May 1947 the illustrated magazine *Picture Post* published a series of photographs, taken on the set of a new film, which depicted a fight in a girls' approved school.[45] *Good Time Girl*, produced for Gainsborough Pictures by Sydney Box, presented the ill-luck story of 16-year-old Gwen Rawlings (played by Jean Kent), who runs away from home after a beating from her father, falls in with a series of criminal lovers, and is implicated in a theft when she agrees to pawn jewellery that she does not realise is stolen. Gwen is tried at the juvenile court and sentenced to three years' detention at an approved school, where she is hardened by her encounters with an older girl. After absconding, she is drawn further into a cycle of robbery and violence by two American army deserters, until she is finally convicted of a murder that she did not do. Gwen's story is narrated by juvenile court magistrate, Miss Thorpe (played by Flora Robson), as a warning to other young women of the dangers that may befall them away from the protection of friends and family.

The film *Good Time Girl* was loosely based on the heavily sensationalised 'Cleft Chin Murder', which had led to the conviction at the Old Bailey in January 1945 of a London-based 'Bonnie and Clyde' – American GI Karl Hulten and 18-year-old Elizabeth Maud ('Marina') Jones – for the murder of taxi driver George Heath. Hulten was found to have fired the shot, but Jones was also viewed as culpable since she had dragged the body into a ditch and robbed it. After the trial verdict it emerged that they had been involved in other violent attacks during the course of the week that they had been together. The court had been packed throughout the trial, and the tabloid press had avidly followed proceedings. The case was partly of note because the American authorities had waived their right to deal with Hulten in a court martial – he had been handed over to the British police on the grounds that both defendants should be tried together in a criminal court. Hulten's appeal was turned down and he was executed at Pentonville Prison in March 1945. Jones was reprieved two days before she was due to hang and the death sentence was commuted to life imprisonment. Jones had spent a period of time in a girls' approved school in Sale, Cheshire, before moving to London where she had met Hulten, who alleged she had said 'she would like to do something exciting like becoming a "Gun Moll"' (a claim that reinforced perceptions of the damaging effects of

American gangster films).[46] While the case has some similarity with that of Constance Kent in terms of age (late teens) and the public interest in culpability and hence agency, the social, cultural, political and geographical landscapes were markedly different. For the writer George Orwell, the 'Cleft Chin Murder' was 'pitiful', 'sordid' and meaningless' rather than tragic and emotional, signifying the 'decline of the English murder'.[47] It was the apparently ordinary and almost accidental nature of the case that guaranteed its appeal. Attention focused on Elizabeth Jones. When war broke out she had been a 12-year-old schoolgirl; when it ended she was serving a life sentence for murder in Holloway prison. For Minister of Labour Ernest Bevin, Elizabeth Jones was the girl victim of a failed social system. For those who chalked 'she should hang' on the walls of her hometown, she was a manipulative, deceitful, callous and immoral woman, experienced beyond her 18 years.[48]

The controversy continued as Jones's life was fictionalised, first through a novel and then through film.[49] *Good Time Girl* attracted debate even before its release as a result of the advanced *Picture Post* publicity. In Newcastle, a local branch of the National Council of Women called for the film to be banned, arguing that the fight scene portrayed the work of approved schools in a wholly negative light. Supporters of Elizabeth Jones's family also suggested it was libellous in its claim, printed in *Picture Post*, that it was 'based on the recent Cleft-chin Murder'.[50] As a result of letters to the Home Secretary, four civil servants viewed an early version of the film in July 1947, which they described as a 'travesty'. Not only did it depict approved schoolgirls as violent and out of control, smoking and drinking alcohol in the dormitories; it also showed the juvenile court committing a miscarriage of justice in its wrongful conviction of Gwen Rawlings. Whilst it was seen as inappropriate for the film to be censored for simple 'misrepresentation', suggestions were made that the 20-minute approved school scene could be cut. Whilst keen to respond to criticism, the producers simply made the matter worse in the Home Office's opinion: by introducing a further scene in which the school's headmistress addressed a conference on the difficulties of recruiting adequate staff.[51]

Good Time Girl was finally released in April 1948 to mixed responses. Reviewers from the quality papers tended to agree it was extremely well performed. The issue for debate, however, was whether it was a 'moral' story and, indeed, a socially responsible one. Sydney Box and his crew had visited both an approved school and the girls' borstal (at Aylesbury) as part of their research, and they defended the film as representing 'fairly and honestly the truth about one of the greatest social problems of our time'.[52] A number of reviewers suggested the film offered a necessary realism as 'an argument against depriving exuberant young people of their liberty'.[53] In this it was seen as an important comparison to the earlier documentary *Children on Trial*, which had presented an extremely optimistic vision of the approved school system. It was difficult not to read the film as critique: 'Is this an indictment against Juvenile Courts and the way in which approved schools are run?'[54] Any complexity was lost on the tabloid press, which tended to view *Good Time Girl* as 'an unpleasant picture of the seamy side of life' and 'the latest British film course in advance thuggery'. Along with *Brighton Rock* (1947) and *No Orchids for Miss Blandish* (1948) it was identified as offering an Americanised diet of 'gangsters, razor-slashings

Figure 8.2   *Good Time Girl* (1947), production still. © ITV Global Entertainment

[and] beatings-up' to British audiences.[55] Some social workers warned that it would act as a malign influence rather than a cautionary tale. It was alleged that two remand home girls in Bristol had decided 'they would abscond [...] to London [...], pick up a spiv and enjoy life as seen in *Good Time Girl*'.[56] Here-fordshire Council refused to license the film; similar attempts in Newcastle were unsuccessful.[57] Tellingly, one married woman wrote to the *Newcastle Journal* in support of the film, which she had seen in London: 'I am only sorry I didn't have the chance of seeing it when I was 14 or 15. It would have made a lot of things clear to me that I learned only later on the hard way [...] No girl after seeing it would believe men's stories about having a good time [...].'[58]

Good Time Girl evinced a range of strong reactions in audiences; its meanings were contingent and shaped by personal experiences. Yet the interest surround-ing both the film and the original murder case was illustrative of the way in which the 'girl delinquent' had become a central figure of moral panic against the backdrop of the Second World War. The 'good time girl' was a stereotype or cultural representation that was specific to a particular historical moment. However, there were deep resonances with an earlier epoch, which gave it wider cultural significance. The narrative of decline and fall that was mapped onto the life of the fictional Gwen Rawlings presented her as an increasingly hardened vic-tim of male violence, seduction and trickery against the backdrop of a dystopian urban landscape (see Figure 8.2). Hogarth's Moll Hackabout had been repack-aged for mid-twentieth-century viewers. The result was unsettling. Despite the creation of the welfare state, neither official social/penal interventions nor the private realm of the family were seen to provide a realm of safety. Like *The Harlot's Progress, Good Time Girl* placed responsibility directly on the individual to exercise moral restraint within a malign society. The Cleft Chin Case – and the film that followed – were symptomatic of the collapse of certainties that was to mark the post-war period.

Whilst responses to the figure of the 'good time' girl are indicative of her wider cultural 'meaning', the life story of the 'real' Elizabeth Jones is also worthy of study since it reveals one young woman's experiences within the penal-welfare system. Jones was born in Canada in 1926, but had returned to Britain with her family when she was six to live in Neath, South Wales. She first came to police attention in February 1940, aged 13, when she was found by police in the nearby city of Swansea after running away from home following an allegation of sexual abuse that she had made against an older man. She was returned home and the man was subsequently charged with sexual assault (a medical examination confirmed she was not *virgo intacta*) but the case was dismissed by magistrates. Three weeks after the court case she 'was found lying unconscious in the gutter at a late hour of the night in the town centre'.[59] When her absconding continued, her mother complained to police that she had no control over her. On 30 May 1940 the juvenile court decided she was 'in need of care or protection' and sent her to an approved school for two years, where her absconding continued. On one occasion she 'said she had spent the night in a field with a soldier' and on another she was 'found by police travelling on the railways without paying fares'. She married a friend of her family within three months of leaving the approved school, taking her, as a 16-year-old bride, outside the scope of the Children and Young Persons Acts (which would otherwise have offered 'moral' protection until she reached 17). She abandoned her husband on her wedding day, moving to London in 1943 to take up various forms of casual labour, including unsuccessful work as a cabaret or 'striptease' dancer under the assumed name of 'Georgina Grayson', which was the name she also used when she met Hulten. The approved school authorities continued to exercise their duty of care, the headmistress visiting her in London and attempting to effect a reconciliation with her husband. By the time she met Hulten she had contracted venereal disease, visible as a rash on her body. Jones had not been convicted as a juvenile of any criminal offence; rather she had been brought before juvenile court magistrates because she was deemed to be a 'wayward girl' in need of protection. Her rebellion against the processes of 'institutionalisation', however, had led her into further trouble as she was charged with absconding from an approved school. Indeed, the themes of escaping and running away recurred during her teenage years.

The story of Elizabeth Jones chimes with the narratives told by female offenders who were interviewed by the criminologist Pat Carlen in the 1980s, many of whom had experienced forms of institutional care as adolescents in the 1950s and 1960s.[60] As Carlen argues, institutionalisation led to 'stigmatisation as a delinquent' as well as 'social isolation' (away from family and friends). Whilst committal to an approved school for a 'status offence' such as being 'in moral danger' was technically a protective initiative, the line between penality and welfare (in terms of policy, institutional regimes and individual experience) was often an extremely fine one. Absconding might be a way of trying to reassert control: 'determined to be neither "put away" nor "filed away", spirited young women in Care repeatedly abscond, "cause trouble" and come to the attention of the police'.[61] Its frequency is illustrated by figures for the year 1942, during which girls absconded from approved schools on 528 occasions. Such a figure was deemed particularly high, given that the female population in approved schools was just 800 in that year, and it was blamed on the dislocations and excitement of war; girls who were returned to schools were systematically examined for venereal disease.[62] Other forms of resistance included the use of violence or destructive behaviour, experienced by residential social worker 'Jane Sparrow' who worked in a girls' approved school in the mid-twentieth century.[63] Within the approved school environment girls acquired knowledge of how to run away, where to abscond to, as well as possible survival strategies from 'recalls' who had been caught and sent back. For young women with little or no money, sexuality became a resource or form of 'capital' for getting by as well as a possible source of vulnerability when they absconded, as Elizabeth Jones found out. Clearly, not all girls committed to approved schools or other forms of institutional care ended up in further 'trouble'. The account of 'Jane Sparrow' also refers to girls who sought recognition and approval from staff or for whom the regime provided a form of structure and organisation that had been missing from previous lives. It is likely that committal to an approved school was as much symptomatic as causal of later offending behaviour. Carlen argues that four major factors have tended to contribute to women's criminality in the second half of the twentieth century. They are (in order): poverty; addiction (to alcohol or drugs); being 'in care' as a child or adolescent; and desire for excitement (perhaps rejecting conventional gender norms).[64] Clearly, the latter two were contributory factors in the case of Elizabeth Jones.

For the popular press, the case triggered debate and investigation into the personal circumstances of Jones's life – personal diaries were leaked to the press, which it was claimed included lists of all the American servicemen with whom Jones had become acquainted. It also led to discussion of the approved school system and, further, careful coverage of cases involving girl delinquents that were coming before London's juvenile courts. As the *News of the World* campaigned to raise money for the widow and sons of George Heath in March 1945, it also reported similar cases involving runaway schoolgirls who looked older than their years who were 'out for adventure' seeking sexual relationships with older men.

It is not possible to piece together why, exactly, Elizabeth 'Marina' Jones behaved as she did. The competing narratives surrounding her life – that packaged her in turn as innocent victim, delusional and 'wayward' girl, or scheming and precocious adult – were well-worn stereotypes that offered alternative trajectories of causation. She told the Old Bailey in a barely audible voice that Hulten, who she had known as 'Ricky' and of whom she was frightened, was responsible for what had happened. The letter that she had written to him in prison, begging him to accept culpability, and which was used against her at her trial as evidence of her duplicity, can also be interpreted as a young woman's desperate plea to return to her mother and family.[65]

Debates surrounding the film resulted from a convergence of moral panics – about the 'folk devil' of the 'good time' girl, the demoralising effects of cinema and the impact of Americanisation on young people's behaviour. These met the Home Secretary's specific concerns about the misrepresentation of Home Office approved schools and the protests of social workers that their professionalism and authority were being undermined. The press unwittingly launched the furore, as pre-publicity led to complaints from interest groups. The film itself offered a stereotyping of the 'good-time' girl, as its content led to further media debate upon release. Whilst Orwell was quick to suggest that the Cleft Chin murder case was limited in appeal, its resonance has been enduring. The 1990 movie *Chicago Joe and the Showgirl* (starring Emily Lloyd, Patsy Kensit and Kiefer Sutherland) was yet a further retelling of the Jones/Hulten case. One is struck by the apparently postmodern narrative that the case offered – competing accounts of events in which 'the truth' was never paramount, a series of assumed identities and staged performances that were inspired by Hollywood fantasies, and which were subsequently further fictionalised on screen.

Conclusion

The need to protect girls and young women from sexual danger became a focal point of regulatory frameworks, promoted, firstly, by voluntary agencies (in the nineteenth century) and subsequently by the state through the 'moral danger' clauses of the Children and Young Persons Acts (in the first half of the twentieth century). This work was packaged as preventative in function: to stop the 'endangered' or 'wayward' girl from completing her descent into prostitution and criminality. When she did cross the line into offending behaviour, the 'girl delinquent' was associated with shoplifting rather than violence. Indeed, girls' participation in violence was sidelined or, in exceptional cases, presented as extreme aberration. This was apparent in the cases of Constance Kent, Elizabeth Jones and, in 1968, that of 11-year-old Mary Bell, who was sentenced to life detention for the manslaughter of two infant boys in Newcastle. Tried in an adult court despite her age, Bell was acquitted of murder: on the grounds of diminished responsibility linked to a psychopathic disorder. She was depicted in the press as an 'unnatural monstrosity' and 'freak of nature', contravening assumptions about children as innocent as much as those about femininity.[66] Generally, however, the 'girl delinquent' was depicted as being on the edges of criminality.

Yet the late twentieth and early twenty-first centuries have seen a noticeable shift in paradigm, as the criminologist Anne Worrall has argued. Firstly, girls' behaviour is now being interpreted differently. As Worrall puts it 'no longer "at risk" and "in moral danger" from the damaging behaviour of men, increasing numbers of young women are being assigned to the same categories as young men ("violent girls", "drug-abusing girls", "girl robbers", "girl murderers" – "girl rapists" even').[67] Secondly, the same measures are being invoked as for boys: 'we are seeing increasing numbers of young women being incarcerated, not on spuriously benevolent welfare grounds, but on spuriously equitable "justice" grounds'.[68] Nevertheless, as this chapter has sought to demonstrate, an apparently 'softer' welfarist approach meant that girls' lives were regulated through institutional and preventative mechanisms despite their invisibility within criminal justice statistics.

The case of Elizabeth 'Marina' Jones is emblematic of many of the themes than have shaped this book. The stereotypes of the hypersexual 'good time' girl and the duplicitous *'femme fatale'* were indicative of the continued significance of sexuality in the construction of female reputations. The prurient interest in her private life that shaped public debates as to whether she should escape the death sentence involved an evaluation of her culpability as 'mad', 'bad' or duped victim. Ultimately, the reprieve appears to have been a function of leniency on the grounds of age not gender – had she been six months younger she could not have been sentenced to death at all.

Afterword

We began this book by pointing to three modern areas of concern that linked women and crime. These were, firstly, the growing numbers of women in prison; secondly, the very low percentage of rape and sexual assault cases that currently produce a guilty verdict; and thirdly, the recent press attention to the (unfeminine) violence of 'girl gangs'. These are all issues that, we argued, are hard to understand without an appreciation of the history of gender. Sexual violence against women, violence as a component of female juvenile deviance and the penal incarceration of women are separate and distinct subjects. However, viewed historically it becomes clear that each of them have depended on the dispositions of power by gender which have constituted (some) women and girls as deviant and punishable; these include the field of criminal justice but also exceed it.

In our first chapter we looked at the uneven and uncertain hearing that women complaining of sexual assault have received over centuries. The scant attention paid by the criminal justice process to sexual violence (and indeed to domestic violence) in the twenty-first century, despite recent comprehensive legislation that was at least in part informed by the research of feminist criminologists over several decades, indicates the disjunction between the generation of new knowledge and the actual effects for women subjected to sexual violence. It also indicates how knowledge produced with the intention of empowering women can become incorporated into dominant systems which marginalise them.

In Chapters 3 and 8 we commented on how girls were involved in late nineteenth-century youth 'gangs'. There is a documented history to these kinds of violence by young women, despite the tendencies of modern media to present the phenomenon as new and therefore symptomatic of worrying modern fractures in social order – 'Broken Britain' to quote the tabloid *Sun* newspaper.[1] In the last half century, for example, the late 1960s and early 1970s and the mid-1980s were also moments when the media discovered 'new' levels of violence amongst girls and young women and repeatedly the phenomenon has been loosely, and for the most part inaccurately, associated with 'women's liberation' or 'girl power'.[2] The 'girl gang' story has been a feature of press coverage of violent youth culture in the first decade of the 2000s; for example, the 'about 25' teenage girls reported to have been fighting with weapons fashioned from snooker balls in socks in the railway station in the small, fairly affluent and peaceable town of Shoreham.[3] Young women have certainly been involved in violent disputes between groups of teenagers and adolescents and there have been fatalities.[4] However, despite legitimate concerns about the use of knives and guns and the ready resort to violence in youth culture, the scare stories of predatory, criminal gangs of female teens armed to the teeth are hyperbolic. Because 'girl gangs' are always 'new' and sensational, they provide another means of marking anxieties about the gender order and indicating the destabilising consequences of feminist arguments. In the current coverage, anxieties about gender disorder amplify and sensationalise concerns about youth violence, which for the most part involves young men. To quote a recent commentator: 'It is a sad indictment of our society that girls who are meant to be nurturing, caring and supportive are becoming involved in very aggressive activity.'[5]

Our review of the history of women in prison in Chapter 7 has shown continuities in the ways that women have been anomalies in the penal system and have been subjected to infantilising regimes in both penal and semi-penal institutions that aimed to produce docile and subordinated femininities as evidence of rehabilitation. The major change over the twentieth century has been the rise in the women's (and of course men's) prison population over the last 30 years as the surrounding 'archipelago' of semi-penal and welfare institutions have been progressively dismantled and as penal regimes in general have become more punitive. In ways corresponding to the question of sexual violence, the very issues that feminist criminologists were raising 30 years ago about the particularly deleterious consequences of carceral sentences for most imprisoned women can be seen to figure in the professional knowledges of the prison service, boards of visitors and prison inspectorate, but make virtually no impact on the rapidly worsening conditions for women prisoners.

Mirroring worldwide trends, the numbers and the proportion of women in the prison population have increased rapidly over recent decades. Daily averages in 1980 were 42,180 males and 1580 females. In 1997, excluding remand prisoners, there were over 46,400 men serving prison sentences compared to 2100 women, including young offenders.[6] More striking are the gender differentials in the rates of increase of prison populations – 45 per cent for men compared to 100 per cent for women between 1993 and 1998. The female prison population was at 4045 in 2001 and prisons that formerly accommodated men were converted to hold women.[7] In 2008, over 4300 women were held in English and Welsh prisons, around a fifth of these on remand. The rapid increase in the women's prison population has significantly outstripped the much slower rate of increase in women's offending. A growing proportion of women in prisons were foreign nationals or from ethnic minorities and/or were sentenced for drug trafficking offences. The greater majority of women in prison have mental health problems – 78 per cent of a recent study of 500 women compared to around 15 per cent of the female population in general. This study also found that women coming into prison were generally in very poor physical health; 58 per cent were regular users of illegal drugs and 42 per cent had alcohol problems.[8] Rhetorics of 'equal treatment' with which policy makers have met feminist calls for social equality by gender have resulted in the erosion of measures which appeared to be lenient to women rather than any rethinking of the full effects for both female and male offenders of punitive penal regimes.[9] Recent findings underline how far women in prison are already heavily socially disadvantaged. In 2007–08 the high levels of self-harm (incidents increased by 48 per cent in the previous five years) and suicides by women prisoners drew press attention.[10] Current public discourse does now recognise that social marginality rather than any intrinsic gendered disorder routes women into prison. Nevertheless, the female prison population that policy makers and professionals address is still multiply debilitated and penal regimes remain particularly punitive for women for a range of reasons from the loss of their children to the inadequacy of facilities for personal hygiene in prison. The government-commissioned report by Baroness Corston, published in 2007, recommended the closure of all existing women's prisons over a ten-year period, replacing them with smaller custodial units. However, these recommendations clashed with the prevailing government policy centred on the development of three huge 'titan' prisons.[11]

Female sexuality has been a recurrent theme throughout this book. It arises no less as an issue in our discussion of property crime (by far the most frequent criminal offence committed by women over three centuries) as in other areas. Ideologically constituted as deviant, sexuality has explained both dangerous criminal activity by women and behaviours that have seemed to arise out of feminine weakness and debility. The instabilities of female sexuality have provided a sufficiently powerful and flexible explanatory framework to have effects as diverse as silencing or deflecting complaints of sexual violence, shaping dominant and professional understandings of what constituted deviance in teenage girls, and rendering women an especially problematic and poorly managed category of prisoners in the penal system. We have often returned to and re-examined the concept of 'double deviance'. As we have traced the gendering of deviance over the preceding eight chapters we have found that double deviance is a relevant, but also a far more nuanced framework for understating women and crime than has sometimes been assumed. Our historical survey concurs with some of the more thoughtful uses of the concept being devised by feminist criminologists, who have argued that social transgressions (crime and deviance) and gender transgressions have overlapped and in many cases been mutually constituted. This doubled transgression has been argued to subject women to double punishment, either in the sense of especially stringent sentences or in that of the reinforcement of formal punishments, which might on the face of it seem lenient, with informal or more diffuse punitive consequences such as marginalisation, material hardship, and social suffering either inside or outside the criminal justice process.

Such perspectives rethink the model of women as merely victims of a monolithic and patriarchal criminal justice system. They move away from the (in the end) sterile debate about whether women criminals have been leniently punished. They also underline how the topic of 'women and crime' cannot be separated from a consideration of how gender works in shaping cultures of penality.[12] It becomes possible to situate the workings of gender against other processes of marginalisation and the production of deviance in a world increasingly shaped by the movements, inclusions and exclusions labelled as 'globalisation'. We have not had space in this comparatively short volume to consider trafficking and the global dimensions of the twenty-first-century sex trade. The balance between exploitation and agency is complex, and the construction of women and children involved in sex work as perennial victims hampers understanding of the trade.[13] However, it seems clear that the social marginality we have observed historically in women turning to prostitution is amplified in the ways that women and young people who are already socially disadvantaged in their home societies are becoming particularly vulnerable to violence, coercion, exploitation and criminalisation in Britain and other Western societies through trafficking in people, sex and drugs. Indeed, the perspective from the early twenty-first century is a pessimistic one, even aside from the very poor situation in women's prisons which remains in the public eye through a series of inquests on women committing suicide in prison, most of them heavily critical of the penal system. The Rape Crisis Network of England and Wales had 38 centres in 2007, compared to 60 in 1996. Recent findings suggest that 85 per cent of women in British brothels are foreign born, yet the biggest charity providing refuge accommodation for trafficked women trying to leave prostitution had only 35 beds in the whole country in 2008.[14]

The long chronology we have discussed saw major historical transitions associated with modernisation and the shaping of late (or post-) modernity in England, not least industrialisation and more recently areas of de-industrialisation, population growth and changes in demographic structure, the growth of the state (including the elaboration and professionalisation of the criminal justice system), and shifting and increasingly complex interactions between the media, culture and the criminal justice process. All these historical developments contributed to changes in the ways that women's criminality has been defined, positioned and managed by criminal justice and penal systems. No twenty-first-century British courts contemplate the kind of supernatural forces that seventeenth-century witches were held to manipulate, neither do they pass capital sentences that result in the spectacle of women executed on a public gallows. However, placing the historical experience of women and its signification at the centre of analysis also disturbs some of the better established historical narratives of modernisation and criminal justice. The history of women and violence (either as perpetrators or as victims) does not fit well with the idea of a 'civilising process'. The history of penal institutions and regimes as applied to women qualifies not only more progressive historical paradigms but also those more pessimistic models which owe an intellectual debt to Foucault's ideas. Overall, the rates and incidence of women's crime have not necessarily mirrored general trends. Women seeking a professional role in the modern criminal justice process have not participated on the same terms, or even in the same ways as have men.

What, then, do we conclude from this historical survey of women and crime? In many ways we are reluctant to construct any overarching metanarrative from the discrete yet interlinked thematic chapters. So much research in gender history points to the unevenness and even reversibility of historical change as regards the social position of women. We have discovered complex relationships between continuity and change, and between criminal justice and other disciplinary institutions directed towards women. Social change and institutional change within the criminal justice process have by no means always kept pace. The letter of the law has by no means always accorded with the practice of criminal justice. Gender subordination has been a feature of society throughout the long period we are discussing, though it has varied by class and race and been tempered by prevailing social and economic conditions. The women that have come to the attention of the criminal justice system for criminal(ised) behaviour have very often already been especially marginalised or disadvantaged. The exceptions have for the most part been women who have used law-breaking as a means of protest or those who (maybe despite a comparatively privileged social position) have been in socially or emotionally painful situations because of the gendered workings of power in their intimate relationships. Contradictory and not infrequently muddled constructions of the social and psychological outcomes of female sexuality have recurrently intervened in both the institutional treatment and the professional and public knowledges of women accused of crime. Though the outcomes for individual women have been variable, more often than not the social and penal effects of such constructions have been to women's disadvantage.

Notes

Introduction: 'Vice' and 'Virtue'?

1. Home Office (2003), 'Statistics on Women and the Criminal Justice System': http://www.homeoffice.gov.uk/rds/pdfs2/s95women03.pdf.
2. L. Kelly, J. Lovett and L. Regan (2005) 'A gap or chasm? Attrition in reported rape cases': http://www.homeoffice.gov.uk/rds/pdfs05/hors293.pdf.
3. For an overview, see C. Alder and A. Worrall, *Girls' Violence* (New York: SUNY, 2004).
4. We use the term 'the past' to refer to events and occurrences that are previous; we use the term 'history' specifically to mean the academic study of the past.
5. T. B. Macaulay, *The History of England from the Accession of James II* (London, 1849), vol. 1, pp. 420–3.
6. L. O. Pike, *A History of Crime in England, illustrating the Changes of the Laws in the Progress of Civilization*, 2 vols (London, 1873-66); L. Radzinowicz, *A History of English Criminal Law and its Administration from 1750*, 5 volumes (London: Stevens & Sons, 1948).
7. D. Hay, 'Property, Authority and the Criminal Law', in D. Hay, P. Linebaugh and E. P. Thompson (eds), *Albion's Fatal Tree: Crime and Society in Eighteenth-Century England* (London: Allen Lane, 1975), pp. 13–63.
8. P. King, 'Decision-Makers and Decision-Making in the English Criminal Law, 1750–1800', *The Historical Journal*, 27 (1993), 25–58. Important work on the Early Modern courts was undertaken by J. Sharpe, *Crime in Seventeenth-Century England* (Cambridge: Cambridge University Press, 1983).
9. M. Vicinus (ed.), *Suffer and Be Still: Women in the Victorian Age* (London and Bloomington: Indiana University Press, 1972).
10. C. Cockburn, *Brothers: Male Dominance and Technological Change* (London: Pluto, 1983).
11. J. Kelly-Gadol, 'Did Women Have a Renaissance?', in R. Bridenthal, C. Koonz and S. Stuard (eds), *Becoming Visible: Women in European History* (Boston, MA: Houghton Mifflin, 1977).
12. S. Brownmiller, *Against Our Will* (Harmondsworth: Penguin, 1976); M. Daly, *Gyn/Ecology* (London: Women's Press, 1978).
13. A. Clark, *Women's Silence, Men's Violence: Sexual Assault in England 1770–1845* (London: Pandora, 1987); S. Jeffreys, *The Spinster and Her Enemies: Feminism and Sexuality 1880–1930* (London: Pandora, 1985). Both Clark and Jeffreys were involved in the London Feminist History Group.

14. K. Thomas, *Religion and the Decline of Magic* (Harmondsworth: Penguin, 1971); A. Macfarlane, *Witchcraft in Tudor and Stuart England* (London: Routledge, 1970).

15. M. Gaskill, 'Witchcraft and Evidence in Early Modern England', *Past and Present*, 198:1 (2008), 33–77.

16. J. Sharpe, *Instruments of Darkness: Witchcraft in England 1550–1750* (London: Hamish Hamilton, 1996).

17. Recent overviews include D. Oldridge (ed.), *The Witchcraft Reader* (London: Routledge, 2002); and J. Barry and O. Davies (eds), *Witchcraft Historiography* (Basingstoke: Palgrave Macmillan, 2007).

18. Clark, *Women's Silence*. For important statements that discuss the theorisation of gender see J. W. Scott, 'Gender: A Useful Category of Historical Analysis', *American Historical Review* 5 (1986), pp. 1053–75 and C. Hall, 'Feminism and Feminist History', in her *White, Male and Middle Class: Explorations in Feminism and History* (Cambridge: Polity, 1992).

19. Scott, 'Gender', p. 1067.

20. C. Smart, *Women, Crime and Criminology: A Feminist Critique* (London: Routledge, 1976); F. Heidensohn, *Women and Crime* (Basingtoke: Macmillan, 1986).

21. M. Arnot and C. Usborne (eds), *Gender and Crime in Modern Europe* (London: UCL Press, 1999); S. D'Cruze (ed.), *Everyday Violence in Britain, 1850–1950: Gender and Class* (Harlow: Longman, 2000); M. Wiener, *Men of Blood: Violence, Manliness and Criminal Justice in Victorian England* (Cambridge: Cambridge University Press, 2004); C. Emsley, *Hard Men: Violence in England since 1750* (London and New York: Hambledon, 2005).

22. M. Foucault, *Discipline and Punish: The Birth of the Prison*, trans. Alan Sheridan (Harmondsworth: Penguin, 1977). See also M. Foucault, 'The Eye of Power', in C. Gordon (ed.), *Power/Knowledge: Selected Interviews and Other Writings* (New York: Pantehon, 1980).

23. The work was published in three volumes as *The History of Sexuality* between 1976 and 1984.

24. By 'hermeneutic' we mean analysis that focuses on the interpretation of texts and the decoding of their meanings.

25. J. Walkowitz, *Prostitution and Victorian Society* (Cambridge: Cambridge University Press, 1980), p. 5.

26. Ibid., pp. 55–7.

27. J. Walkowitz, *City of Dreadful Delight: Narratives of Sexual Danger in Late-Victorian London* (London: Virago, 1992), p. 5. For the 'cultural turn', see L. Hunt (ed.), *The New Cultural History* (Berkeley: University of California Press, 1989).

28. Walkowitz, *City of Dreadful Delight*, p. 13.

29. Ibid., p. 220.

30. The murders occurred in the urban areas of Leeds and Bradford in West Yorkshire; the term 'the Yorkshire Ripper' was used by the press as the investigation continued because of the mutilation of victims' bodies which was deemed comparable to the murders of 1888.

31. Ibid., p. 245.

32. J. W. Scott, 'The Evidence of Experience', *Critical Enquiry*, 17 (1991), 773–97.

33. T. R. Gurr, 'Historical Trends in Violent Crime: A Critical Review of the Evidence', *Crime and Justice: An Annual Review of Research*, 3 (1981), 295–353; M. Eisner, 'Long-Term Trends in Violent Crime', *Crime and Justice: A Review of Research*, 30 (2003), 83–142; G. Schwerhoff, 'Criminalised Violence and the Process of Civilisation: A Reappraisal', *Crime, Histoire et Societés*, 6 (2002), 103–26.

34. N. Elias, *The Civilizing Process: The History of Manners and State Formation and Civilization*, trans. E. Jephcott, 2 vols (Oxford: Blackwell, 1978, 1982).

35. J. Carter Wood, *Violence and Crime in Nineteenth Century England: The Shadow of Our Refinement* (London and New York: Routledge, 2004); J. Adler, 'Foreword', in E. Avdela et al. (eds), *Crime, Violence and the Modern State, 1780–2000* (Lampeter: Mellen, 2009).

36. Discussions of the Elias thesis include P. Spierenburg, 'Violence and the Civilising Process: Does it Work?', *Crime, Histoire et Societés*, 5 (2001), 87–105; J. Carter Wood, 'Its a Small World After All? Reflections on Violence in Comparative Perspectives', in B. Godfrey, C. Emsley and G. Dunstall (eds), *Comparative Histories of Crime* (Cullompton: Willan, 2003), pp. 36–52; S. Carroll, 'Introduction', in S. Carroll (ed.), *Cultures of Violence: Interpersonal Violence in Historical Perspective* (Basingstoke: Palgrave Macmillan, 2007), pp. 1–46; E. Avdela et al., 'Introduction: De-Centring Violence History', in Avdela et al. (eds), *Crime, Violence and the Modern State*.

37. D. Wahrman, *The Making of the Modern Self: Identity and Culture in Eighteenth-Century England* (New Haven, CT, and London: Yale University Press, 2004); R. Shoemaker, 'Male Honour and the Decline of Public Violence in 18th-Century London', *Social History*, 26 (2001), 190–208.

38. Carter Wood, *Violence and Crime in Nineteenth Century England*; J. Rowbotham, 'Criminal Savages? Or "Civilising" the Legal Process', in J. Rowbotham and K. Stevenson (eds), *Criminal Conversations: Victorian Crimes, Social Panic, and Moral Outrage* (Columbus, OH: Ohio State University Press, 2005), pp. 91–105.

39. J. Rowbotham, 'Only When Drunk': The Stereotyping of Violence in England, c.1850–1900', in D'Cruze (ed.), *Everyday Violence*, pp. 155–69, here p. 159.

40. S. D'Cruze, *Crimes of Outrage: Sex, Violence and Victorian Working Women* (London: UCL Press, 1998), pp. 52–3.

41. Wiener, *Men of Blood*.

42. Walkowitz, *Prostitution*, p. 8.

43. P. Carlen (ed.), *Criminal Women: Autobiographical Accounts* (Cambridge: Polity, 1985).

44. P. Priestley (ed.), *Victorian Prison Lives: English Prison Biography, 1830–1914* (London: Methuen, 1985).

45. J. Henry, *Who Lie in Gaol* (London: Victor Gollancz, 1952); the book was published in the United States as *Women in Prison* (New York: Doubleday, 1952).

46. Those adopting communist or Irish nationalist political perspectives did not campaign for women police, judges and magistrates; their opposition was concerned with the political legitimacy of the state itself, not of the gender order.

1 Women and Criminality: Counting and Explaining

1. Quoted in L. Zedner, *Women, Crime and Custody in Victorian England* (Oxford: Clarendon Press, 1991), p. 2. Ellis was influenced by the Italian criminologist Cesare Lombroso, who viewed criminality in terms of a hereditary biological disposition and for whom 'criminal' women were more degenerate (primitive) than men. *The Female Offender* by Lombroso and William Ferrero was translated into English in 1895; its emphasis on degeneration theory was accepted by few in England other than Ellis.

2. F. P. Wensley, *Detective Days: The Record of Forty-Two Years' Service in the Criminal Investigation Department* (London: Cassell, 1931), p. 143.

3. Zedner, *Women, Crime and Custody*, p. 1.

4. N. Davie, *Tracing the Criminal. The Rise of Scientific Criminology in Britain, 1860–1918* (Oxford: Bardwell Press, 2005). Lombroso and Ferrero's *Female Offender* was a rare exception in discussing women.

5. In May 1966 Myra Hindley was sentenced to life imprisonment at the Chester Assizes for the murder of two young people (aged 17 and 10) and for acting as an accessory to the murder of another (aged 12); Ian Brady was convicted of all three murders, which had taken place between November 1963 and October 1965. In November 1995 Rosemary West was sentenced to life imprisonment for murdering ten young women in Gloucester over a 20-year period; her husband Frederick escaped trial by committing suicide.

6. J. M. Beattie, 'The Criminality of Women in Eighteenth-Century England', *Journal of Social History*, 8 (1974–5), 80–116.

7. G. Walker, *Crime, Gender and Social Order in Early Modern England* (Cambridge: Cambridge University Press, 2003); G. Morgan and P. Rushton, *Rogues, Thieves and the Rule of Law: The Problem of Law Enforcement in the North-East of England 1718–1800* (London: UCL Press, 1998); P. King, *Crime, Justice and Discretion in England 1740–1820* (Oxford: Oxford University Press, 2000).

8. R. B. Shoemaker, *Prosecution and Punishment: Petty Crime and the Law in London and Rural Middlesex, c. 1660–1725* (Cambridge: Cambridge University Press, 1991).

9. *Old Bailey Proceedings Online* (www.oldbaileyonline.org), hence *OBP*.

10. A. Kilday, *Women and Crime in Enlightenment Scotland* (London: Boydell & Brewer, 2007).

11. M. Feeley and D. Little, 'The Vanishing Female: The Decline of Women in the Criminal Process, 1687–1912', *Law and Society Review*, 25 (1991), 719–57.

12. King, *Crime, Justice and Discretion*, pp. 192–9.

13. Beattie. 'Criminality of Women'.

14. King, *Crime, Justice and Discretion*.

15. B. Godfrey, S. Farrall and S. Karstedt, 'Explaining Gendered Sentencing Patterns for Violent Men and Women in the Late Victorian and Edwardian Period', *British Journal of Criminology*, 45 (2005), 696–720.

16. S. Grace, 'Female Criminality in York and Hull 1830–70' (University of York, unpublished DPhil thesis, 1998), p. 120.

17. M. J. Wiener, 'The Victorian Criminalisation of Men', in P. Spierenburg (ed.), *Men of Violence: Gender, Honour and Rituals in Modern Europe and America* (Columbus: Ohio State University Press, 1998).

18. London Metropolitan Archives, Thames Police Court Registers, PS/TH/A/01/11 and PS/TH/A/01/12.

19. Some criminologists choose to exclude statistics for motoring offences from the data for summary offences since they see it as skewing comparisons over time. To do so, however, is to imply that motoring offences uniquely are not really 'criminal' activities. We argue, however, that judicial statistics are always social constructs or mediations reflecting the historical contexts in which they were produced (including the changing technologies associated with public order and systems of regulation).

20. *Statistics on Women and the Criminal Justice System 2003* (London: Home Office, 2004): www.homeoffice.gov.uk/rds/pdfs2/s95women03.pdf (accessed 10 Oct. 2008).

21. R. Thornhill, *A Natural History of Rape: Biological Bases of Sexual Coercion* (Cambridge MA: MIT Press, 2000).

22. R. Scot, *The Discoverie of Witchcraft*, republished with an introduction by Montague Summers (New York: Dover Publications, 1972; first pub. 1584).

23. P. Bartley, *Prostitution: Prevention and Reform in England 1869–1914* (London: Routledge, 2000). It remains unlikely, however, that a sizeable proportion of women were diverted in this way; the populations of institutions for the feeble-minded remained comparatively small.

24. J. Carter Wood, 'The Limits of Culture? Society, Evolutionary Psychology and the History of Violence', *Cultural and Social History*, 4 (2007), 104.

25. Quoted in E. P. Thompson, *Customs in Common: Studies in Traditional Popular Culture* (New York: New Press, 1993), p. 479.

26. A. J. Hammerton, 'The Targets of Rough Music', *Gender and History*, 3 (1991), 23–44.

27. *East London Observer*, 15 May 1880.

28. O. Davies, *Witchcraft, Magic and Culture 1736–1951* (Manchester: Manchester University Press, 1999).

29. P. King, 'Gender, Crime and Justice in Late-Eighteenth and Early-Nineteenth-Century England', in M. Arnot and C. Usborne (eds), *Gender and Crime in Modern Europe* (London: UCL Press, 1999), pp. 44–74.

30. Zedner, *Women, Crime and Custody*, p. 308.
31. J. Sharpe, *Crime in Seventeenth-Century England* (Cambridge: Cambridge University Press, 1983).
32. Godfrey et al., 'Explaining Gendered Sentencing Patterns', p. 718.
33. C. Hall, 'Feminism and Feminist History', in her *White, Male and Middle Class: Explorations in Feminism and History* (Cambridge: Polity, 1992), p. 33.
34. This can now be tested and evidenced quickly using *OBP*. For example, between 1850 and 1860 a 71 per cent conviction rate was secured in cases tried at the Old Bailey involving girls under 12, compared to a 40 per cent conviction rate in cases known to involve women over the age of consent.
35. L. A. Jackson, *Child Sexual Abuse in Victorian England* (London: Routledge, 2000), pp. 22–3.
36. C. A. Conley, 'Rape and Justice in Victorian England', *Victorian Studies*, 29 (1986), 519–37; see also S. D'Cruze, *Crimes of Outrage: Sex, Violence and Victorian Women* (London: UCL Press, 1998).
37. Zedner, *Women, Crime and Custody*, p. 297.
38. A. Ballinger, *Dead Woman Walking: Executed Women in England and Wales, 1900–1955* (Aldershot: Ashgate, 2000), p. 239.
39. A. Ballinger, 'Masculinity in the Dock: Legal Responses to Male Violence and Female Retaliation in England and Wales, 1900 to 1965', *Social Legal Studies*, 16 (2007), 475.
40. L. Gowing, *Domestic Dangers: Women, Words and Sex in Early Modern London* (Oxford: Clarendon Press, 1996), p. 265.
41. S. M. Waddams, *Sexual Slander in Nineteenth-Century England: Defamation in the Ecclesiastical Courts 1815–55* (Toronto: University of Toronto Press, 2000).
42. J. Davis, 'A Poor Man's System of Justice: The London Police Courts in the Second Half of the Nineteenth Century', *Historical Journal*, 27 (1984), 309–35; D'Cruze, *Crimes of Outrage*.
43. *East London Observer*, 21 July 1888.
44. The increased number of complainants in the first half of the nineteenth century (Table 1.2) can be linked to the gradual removal of the capital sentence for property offences (which had made individuals reluctant to prosecute and juries reluctant to convict). The decrease in the number of complainants coming before the Old Bailey in the second half of the nineteenth century is a likely reflection of the rise of summary justice.
45. *OBP* (accessed 10 Oct. 2008), October 1699, trial of Mary Pemberton and Jane Chatterton (t16991011-34).
46. Peter King, 'Decisions and Decision-Making in the English Criminal Justice system', *Historical Journal*, 27 (1984), 25–58; J. Brewer and J. Styles (eds), *An Ungovernable People: The English Law in the Seventeenth and Eighteenth Centuries* (London: Hutchinson, 1980).
47. Jackson, *Child Sexual Abuse*.
48. British Parliamentary Papers (BPP), Criminal Statistics, England and Wales.

49. Cited in L. A. Jackson, *Women Police: Gender, Welfare and Surveillance in the Twentieth Century* (Manchester: Manchester University Press, 2006), p. 189.
50. Cited in V. A. C. Gatrell, *The Hanging Tree: Execution and the English People 1770–1868* (Oxford: Oxford University Press, 1994), p. 471.
51. L. Kelly, J. Lovett and L. Regan (2005) 'A Gap or Chasm? Attrition in Reported Rape Cases', www.homeoffice.gov.uk/rds/pdfs05/hors293.pdf (accessed 10 Oct: 2008).
52. Kilday, *Women and Crime*, p. 24.

2   Women and Property Offences

1. D. Defoe, *Moll Flanders* (Harmondsworth: Penguin, 1989), p. 268.
2. G. Howson, *Thief-Taker General: Jonathan Wild and the Emergence of Crime and Corruption as a Way of Life in Eighteenth-Century England* (London: Hutchinson, 1970).
3. Defoe, *Moll Flanders*, p. 229.
4. N. McKendrick, J. Brewer and J. H. Plumb, *The Birth of a Consumer Society: The Commercialization of Eighteenth-Century England* (Bloomington: Indiana University Press, 1982); L. Weatherill, *Consumer Behaviour and Material Culture in Britain, 1660–1760* (London: Routledge, 1988).
5. J. M. Beattie, 'The Criminality of Women in Eighteenth-Century England', *Journal of Social History*, 8 (1974–5), 80–116, here p. 89.
6. G. Walker, *Crime, Gender and Social Order in Early Modern England* (Cambridge: Cambridge University Press, 2003); Beattie, 'Criminality of Women'; L. Zedner, *Women, Crime and Custody in Victorian England* (Oxford: Clarendon Press, 1991).
7. By 2003, women constituted around a quarter of those arrested for theft, forgery and handling stolen goods. See *Statistics on Women and the Criminal Justice System 2003* (London: Home Office, 2004): www.homeoffice.gov.uk/rds/pdfs2/s95women03.pdf (accessed 10 Oct 2008).
8. G. Morgan and P. Rushton, *Rogues, Thieves and the Rule of Law: The Problem of Law Enforcement in the North-East of England 1718–1800* (London: UCL Press, 1998).
9. G. Walker, 'Women, Theft and the World of Stolen Goods', in J. Kermode and G. Walker (eds), *Women, Crime and the Courts in Early Modern England* (London: UCL Press, 1994), pp. 81–105; L. MacKay, 'Why They Stole: Women in the Old Bailey, 1779–89', *Journal of Social History*, 32 (1999), 623–39.
10. BPP, Judicial Statistics for England and Wales.
11. Walker, 'Women, Theft and the World of Stolen Goods'.
12. Morgan and Rushton, *Rogues, Thieves and the Rule of Law*, pp. 67 and 91.
13. BPP, Judicial Statistics.
14. *OBP* (accessed 10 Oct. 2008), 31 October 1792, trial of Martha Hall (t17921031-19).

15. P. King, 'Female Offenders, Work and Life-Cycle Change in Late-Eighteenth-Century London', *Continuity and Change*, 11 (1996), 61–90.

16. D. Philips, *Crime and Authority in Victorian England: The Black Country, 1835–60* (London: Rowman & Littlefield, 1977).

17. Manchester City Archives, Manchester Quarter Sessions, M116/2/5/22, 15 May 1911, deposition 13.

18. Walker, 'Women, Theft and the World of Stolen Goods'.

19. *OBP*, 25 April 1688, Sarah Boram (t16880425-14).

20. B. Lemire, 'The Theft of Clothes and Popular Consumerism in Early Modern England', *Journal of Social History*, 24 (1990), 255–76, here p. 257.

21. Ellen Ross, 'Survival Networks: Women's Neighbourhood Sharing in London before World War One', *History Workshop Journal*, 15 (1983), 4–27.

22. MacKay, 'Why they Stole'.

23. G. Morgan and P. Rushton (eds), *The Justicing Notebook (1750–64) of Edmund Tew, Rector of Boldon* (London: Boydell & Brewer, 2000), 31 March 1755.

24. *OBP*, 30 May 1750, Mary Williams (t7500530-39).

25. *Manchester Evening News*, 11 April 1910.

26. *OBP*, 17 October 1750, Elizabeth Smith (t17501017-4).

27. Morgan and Rushton, *Justicing Notebook*, 14 May 1763.

28. Ibid., 17 May 1762, warrant against James Henderson; and 20 June 1763, warrant against Margaret Moray.

29. B. Godfrey, 'Workplace Appropriation and the Gendering of Factory "Law": West Yorkshire, 1840–80', in M. Arnot and C. Usborne (eds), *Gender and Crime in Modern Europe* (London: UCL Press, 1999), pp. 137–50. Godfrey found that the conviction rate for women was higher than that for men, although women were charged in far fewer numbers.

30. Manchester City Archives, Manchester Quarter Sessions, M116/2/5/7, 29 January 1896, Depositions 17–18.

31. J. Gay, *The Beggar's Opera* (Harmondsworth: Penguin, 1986), first performed 1728, p. 76.

32. The National Archives (NA), London, ASSI 45/25/2, Deposition 40. Shalloon was a light-twilled woollen cloth.

33. Davie, *Tracing the Criminal*.

34. T. C. Whitlock, *Crime, Gender and Consumer Culture in Nineteenth-Century England* (Aldershot: Ashgate, 2005), pp. 149–50.

35. P. O'Brien, 'The Kleptomania Diagnosis: Bourgeois Women and Theft in Late Nineteenth-Century France', *Journal of Social History*, 17 (1983), 65–77, here p. 70.

36. Whitlock, *Crime, Gender and Consumer Culture*.

37. J. Walkowitz, *City of Dreadful Delight: Narratives of Sexual Danger in Late-Victorian London* (London: Virago, 1992).

38. Whitlock, *Crime, Gender and Consumer Culture*, pp. 74–80.

39. C. Smart, *Women, Crime and Criminology: A Feminist Critique* (London: Routledge, 1976), pp. 9–10.

40. T.C.N. Gibbens and J. Prince, *Shoplifting* (London: Institute for the Study and Treatment of Delinquency, 1962), p. 150. The study was based on records of 532 cases involving women convicted of shoplifting in three Greater London courts in the year 1959–60 (as well as a range of other samples).
41. Ibid., p. 59.
42. Ibid., p. 86.
43. Ibid., p. 15.
44. P. Carlen (ed.), *Criminal Women. Autobiographical Accounts* (Cambridge: Polity, 1985), p. 14.
45. S. Boseley, 'Why do Women Steal?', *Guardian*, 21 July 2003; T. Stuttaford, 'Theft as a Cry for Help', *The Times*, 7 February 2002, Features.
46. J. Swetnam, *The Arraignment of Lewd, Idle, Froward and Unconstant Women: or the Vanitie of them* (London: Thomas Archer, 1615), p. 28.
47. O. Pollak, *The Criminality of Women* (Philadelphia: University of Pennsylvania Press, 1950), p. 9. For a full critique of Pollak, see Smart, *Women, Crime and Criminology*, pp. 46–51.
48. H. Fielding, *An Enquiry into the Causes of the Late Increase in Robbers with some proposals for remedying this growing evil* (Dublin: J. Faulkner, 1755), p. 5.
49. F. Dabhoiwala, 'The Construction of Honour, Reputation and Status in Late Seventeenth- and Early Eighteenth-Century England', *Transactions of the Royal Historical Society*, 6 (1996), 201–13.
50. Morgan and Rushton, *Justicing Notebook*, notebook, 24 June 1754 and 8 August 1757.
51. NA, ASSI 45/25/2, deposition 100.
52. See 'The case of Mary Carleton', reproduced in J. Todd and E. Spearing (eds), *Counterfeit Ladies* (London: Pickering & Chatto, 1994), pp. 131–56.
53. Defoe, *Moll Flanders*, p. 277.
54. Captain Alexander Smith, *A Compleat History of the Lives and Robberies of the Most Notorious Highway-men, Foot-pads, Shop-lifts, and Cheats, of both Sexes*, 5th edn (London: Sam Briscoe, 1719), vol. 1, p. 146.
55. 'The Life and Death of Mary Frith, alias Mal Cutpurse', in Todd and Spearing (eds), *Counterfeit Ladies*, p. 17.
56. Anon., *An Authentic Narrative of the Most Remarkable Adventures and Curious Intrigues Exhibited in the Life of Miss Fanny Davies* (London: R. Jamieson, 1786), pp. 9 and 32.
57. W. Blackstone, *Commentaries on the Laws of England* (Oxford: Clarendon Press, 1765–69), vol. 1, p. 430.
58. King, 'Female Offenders, Work and Lifecycle Change', pp. 67–8.
59. Blackstone, *Commentaries*, vol. 1, p. 430.
60. Whitlock, *Crime, Gender and Consumer Culture*, p. 170.
61. V. A. C. Gatrell, *The Hanging Tree: Execution and the English People 1770–1868* (Oxford: Oxford University Press, 1994), p. 133.
62. W. D. Morrison, *Crime and Its Causes* (London: Sonnenschein, 1891), quoted in Philips, *Crime and Authority*, p. 150.

63. *Sunday Dispatch*, 9 December 1928; *Liverpool Weekly Post*, 13 April 1929.

64. *Pearson's Weekly*, 25 October 1919.

65. C. Bishop, *Women and Crime* (London: Chatto & Windus, 1931), pp. 24 and 13.

3 Women and Violence

1. J. M. Beattie, *Crime and the Courts in England, 1660–1800* (Oxford: Clarendon, 1986), p. 97.

2. E. Stanko, 'Introduction', in E. Stanko (ed.), *The Meanings of Violence*, (London: Routledge, 2003), p. 12; Richard Jackson (ed.), *(Re)constructing Cultures of Violence and Peace* (Amsterdam: Rodopi, 2004), p. 3.

3. See discussion in Chapter 4.

4. S. D'Cruze and A. Rao, 'Violence and the Vulnerabilities of Gender', in *Violence, Vulnerability and Embodiment, A Special Issue of Gender & History*, 16 (2004), 495–512; P. Burke, 'Performing History: The Importance of Occasions', *Rethinking History*, 9 (2005), 35–52.

5. For a useful discussion of the concepts as regards violence by men, see E. Stanko, 'Challenging the Problem of Men's Individual Violence', in E. Stanko and T. Newburn (eds), *Just Boys Doing Business: Men, Masculinities and Crime* (London: Routledge, 1994), pp. 32–46, here pp. 41–5.

6. M. Ingram, ' "Scolding Women Cucked or Washed": A Crisis in Gender Relations in Early Modern England?', in J. Kermode and G. Walker (eds), *Women, Crime and the Courts in Early Modern England* (London: UCL Press, 1994), pp. 48–80; S. Hindle, 'The Shaming of Margaret Knowsley', *Continuity and Change*, 9 (1994), 391–419; M. Tebbutt, *Women's Talk? A Social History of Gossip in Working Class Neighbourhoods, 1880–1960*, (Aldershot: Scolar Press, 1995).

7. See Chapter 5.

8. S. Carroll, 'Introduction', in S. Carroll (ed.), *Cultures of Violence: Interpersonal Violence in Historical Perspective* (Basingstoke: Palgrave Macmillan, 2007), pp. 1–46.

9. P. King, 'Punishing Assault: The Transformation of Attitudes in the English Courts', *Journal of Interdisciplinary History*, 27 (1996), 62–4, 70; S. D'Cruze, 'Introduction: Unguarded Passions: Violence, History and the Everyday', in S. D'Cruze, *Everyday Violence in Britain, 1850-1950: Gender and Class* (Harlow: Longman, 2000), pp. 1–26.

10. R. Campbell, 'Sentence of Death by Burning for Women', *Journal of Legal History*, 5 (1984), 44–59; S. A. M. Gavigan, 'Petit Treason in Eighteenth Century England: Women's Inequality Before the Law', *Canadian Journal of Women and the Law*, 3 (1989), 335–74; S. Devereaux, 'The Abolition of the Burning of Women in England Reconsidered', *Crime, History and Societies*, 9 (2005), 73–98.

11. N. Naffine, *Law and the Sexes* (London: Allen & Unwin, 1990); S. Edwards, *Sex and Gender in the Legal Process* (London: Blackstone Press, 1996).

12. J. Sharpe, *Instruments of Darkness: Witchcraft in England 1550–1750* (London: Hamish Hamilton, 1996); J. Barry and O. Davies (eds), *Witchcraft Historiography* (Basingstoke: Palgrave Macmillan, 2007), especially Introduction and P. G. Maxwell-Stewart, 'The Contemporary Debate, 1400–1800', ch. 1.

13. For a case study, see M. Gaskill, 'Witchcraft, Politics, and Memory in Seventeenth-Century England', *Historical Journal*, 50 (2007), 289–308. For attitudes during the period of declining prosecutions, O. Davies, *Witchcraft, Magic and Culture 1736–1951* (Manchester: Manchester University Press, 1999), ch. 1.

14. The gendering of witch accusations is also evident in the trials of male witches. E. J. Kent, 'Masculinity and Male Witches in Old and New England, 1593–1680', *History Workshop Journal*, 60 (2005), 69–92.

15. L. Jackson 'Witches, Wives and Mothers: Witchcraft Persecution and Women's Confessions in Seventeenth-Century England', *Women's History Review*, 4 (1995), 63–83.

16. C. Holmes, 'Women: Witnesses and Witches', *Past and Present*, 140 (1993), 45–78; J. Sharpe, 'Women, Witchcraft and the Legal Process', in Kermode and Walker (eds), *Women, Crime and the Courts*, pp. 106–24.

17. F. Timbers, 'Witches' Sect or Prayer Meeting? Matthew Hopkins Revisited', *Women's History Review*, 17 (2008), 21–37.

18. See above, Introduction, note 15; O. Davies, 'Witchcraft: The Spell That Didn't Break', *History Today*, 49.8 (1999), 7–13; Davies, *Witchcraft, Magic and Culture*, pp. 79–86.

19. http://www.oldbaileyonline.org/static/Crimes.jsp

20. *OBP*, 29 June 1692, highway robbery, Elisabeth Lee (t16920629-7).

21. L. MacKay, 'Why They Stole: Women in the Old Bailey, 1779–89', *Journal of Social History*, 32 (1999), 623–39; M. Lambert, ' "Cast Off Wearing Apparel": The Consumption and Distribution of Second-Hand Clothing in Northern England During the Long Eighteenth Century', *Textile History*, 35, (2004), 1–26; B. Lemire, 'The Theft of Clothes and Popular Consumerism in Early Modern England', *Journal of Social History*, 24 (1990), 255–76.

22. *OBP*, 31 August 1726, highway robbery, Frances alias Mary Blacket (t17260831-3).

23. T. Henderson, *Disorderly Women in Eighteenth-Century London: Prostitution and Control in the Metropolis, 1730–1830* (London and New York: Longman, 1999), pp. 27–35.

24. *OBP*, 13 January 1727, highway robbery, Mary Mukes and Jane Dennis (t17270113-32).

25. *OBP*, 20 September 1809, highway robbery, Ann Kennington and Matilda Dyer (t18090920-28).

26. *OBP*, 5 April 1780, highway robbery, Jane Morris (t17800405-38).

27. *OBP*, 15 October 1718, highway robbery, Joseph Shannon and Elizabeth George (t17181015-13).

28. H. Shore, 'Cross Coves, Buzzers and General Sorts of Prigs: Juvenile Crime and the Criminal Underworld in the Early Nineteenth Century', *British Journal of Criminology*, 39 (1999), 10–24.

29. B. White, 'Voss, Jenny (d. 1684)', *Oxford Dictionary of National Biography* (Oxford, 2004): http:www.oxford.dnb.com/view/article/73928 (accessed 22 Feb. 2008).

30. *The German Princess Revived, or, The London Jilt: Being a True Account of the Life and Death of Jenney Voss, . . . Published From Her Own Confession* (London, 1684).

31. B. White, 'Clay, Marcy (d. 1665)', *Oxford Dictionary of National Biography* (Oxford, 2004): http:www.oxford.dnb.com/view/article/73926 (accessed 22 Feb. 2008).

32. B. White, 'Ferrers, Catherine (1634–1660)', *Oxford Dictionary of National Biography* (Oxford, 2004): http:www.oxford.dnb.com/view/article/73927 (accessed 22 Feb. 2008); S. Harper, *Picturing the Past: The Rise and Fall of the British Costume Film* (London: British Film Institute, 1994).

33. P. Linebaugh and M. Rediker, *The Many-Headed Hydra: Sailors, Slaves, Commoners and the Hidden History of the Revolutionary Atlantic* (London: Verso, 2000).

34. J. Stanley (ed.), *Bold in Her Breeches: Women Pirates Across the Ages* (London: Pandora, 1995).

35. M. Rediker, *Villains of all Nations: Atlantic Pirates in the Golden Age, 1716–1726* (London: Verso, 2004), p. 112.

36. Linebaugh and Rediker, *Hydra*, p. 167.

37. Trial witness Dorothy Thomas cited by Rediker, *Villains*, pp. 108–9.

38. D. Cordingly, 'Bonny, Anne (1698–1782)', *Oxford Dictionary of National Biography* (Oxford, 2004): http:www.oxford.dnb.com/view/article/39085 (accessed 26 Feb. 2008); D. Cordingly, 'Read, Mary (c.1695–1721)', *Oxford Dictionary of National Biography* (Oxford, 2004), online edition, January 2008: http:www.oxford.dnb.com/view/article/45454 (accessed 26 Feb, 2008).

39. D. Dugaw, *Warrior Women and Popular Balladry, 1650–1850*, 2nd edn. (Chicago and London: University of Chicago Press, 1996); L. Grant De Pauw, *Battle Cries and Lullabies: Women in War from Prehistory to the Present* (Norman: University of Oklahoma Press, 1998).

40. Rediker, *Villains*, p. 110.

41. R. Trumbach, *Sex and the Gender Revolution*, Volume 1, *Heterosexuality and the Third Gender in Enlightenment London* (Chicago and London: University of Chicago Press, 1998).

42. Stanley (ed.), *Bold in Her Breeches*.

43. L. J. Rupp, *A Desired Past: A Short History of Same-Sex Love in America* (Chicago and London: University of Chicago Press, 1999).

44. G. Walker, *Crime, Gender and Social Order in Early Modern England* (Cambridge: Cambridge University Press, 2003), pp. 118, 121, 140, 145–5.

45. Ibid., pp. 135–6.

46. M. Wiener, *Men of Blood: Violence, Manliness and Criminal Justice in Victorian England* (Cambridge: Cambridge University Press, 2004).

47. G. Robb and N. Erber (eds), *Disorder in the Court: Trials and Sexual Conflict at the Turn of the Century* (Basingstoke: Macmillan, 1999); K. Watson, *Poisoned Lives: English Poisoners and their Victims* (London and New York: Hambledon, 2004).

48. G. Frost, ' "She is But a Woman": Kitty Byron and the English Edwardian Criminal Justice System', in S. D'Cruze and A. Rao (eds), *Violence, Vulnerability and Embodiment. Special Issue of Gender and History*, 16 (2004), 538–60; A. Ballinger, *Dead Woman Walking: Executed Women in England and Wales, 1900–1955* (Aldershot: Ashgate, 2000).

49. Watson, *Poisoned Lives.*

50. Both murders were detected by toxicologist William Herapath; W. A. Campbell, 'William Herapath, 1796–1868: A Pioneer of Toxicology', *Anal. Proc* (1980), 346–8; Watson, *Poisoned Lives*, p. 205, *Hereford Times*, 2 February 2004.

51. *Daily News*, 9 August 1876, p. 3.

52. Y. Bridges, *Poison and Adelaide Bartlett* (London: Hutchinson, 1962); J. Hall (ed.), *The Trial of Adelaide Bartlett*, Notable British Trials Series (Edinburgh: William Hodge, 1927).

53. H. B. Irving (ed.), *The Trial of Mrs Maybrick*, Notable British Trials Series, (Edinburgh: William Hodge, 1922); B. O'Riain, *The Poisoned Life of Mrs Maybrick* (Harmondsworth: Penguin, 1989).

54. A James Hamerton, *Cruelty and Companionship: Conflict in Nineteenth-Century Married Life* (London and New York: Routledge, 1992).

55. G. Robb, 'Circe in Crinoline: Domestic Poisonings in England', *Journal of Family History*, 22 (1997), 176–90.

56. A. Ballinger, 'Masculinity in the Dock: Legal Responses to Male Violence and Female Retaliation in England and Wales, 1900 to 1965', *Social Legal Studies*, 16 (2007).

57. L. Bland, 'The Trial of Madame Fahmy: Orientalism, Violence, Sexual Perversity and the Fear of Miscegenation', in D'Cruze (ed.), *Everyday Violence in Britain*, pp. 185–97.

58. Ballinger, *Dead Woman Walking*; J. G. Hall and G. D. Smith, *R. v. Bywaters and Thompson* (Chichester, 1997); Lucy Bland, 'The Trials and Tribulations of Edith Thompson: The Capital Crime of Sexual Incitement in 1920s England', *Journal of British Studies*, 47 (2008), 624–48.

59. A. Logan, 'Guilty or Not Guilty? The Trial of Alma Victoria Rattenbury', Feminist Crime Research Network Seminar, May 2004, University of Greenwich; F. Tennyson Jesse (ed.), *The Trial of Alma Victoria Rattenbury and George Percy Stoner*, Notable British Trials Series (Edinburgh and London: W. Hodge, 1935). For a contrary view in a popular history, see D. Napley, *Murder at the Villa Madeira* (London: Weidenfeld & Nicholson, 1988).

60. Alma was careful of her appearance and did the work of performing middle-class femininity until the day she died; we know this because the press were also keen to describe her clothes and appearance and her letters from prison to Irene Riggs and Stoner include requests for accessories and bobby pins. F. Tennyson Jesse (ed.), *The Trial of Alma Victoria Rattenbury*, press coverage in May 1935 in *The Times, The Daily Mirror* and *The Evening Standard*, also original documents held in the National Archives at references MEPO3/736; CRIM158/1511; CRIM1/778; DPP2/263; PCOM9/2028.

61. See Chapter 1, note 5. H. Birch (ed.), *Moving Targets: Women, Murder and Representation* (London: Virago, 1993); *Scottish Sunday Mail*, 17 November 2002, p. 6.

62. L. Gowing, *Domestic Dangers: Women, Words and Sex in Early Modern London* (Oxford: Clarendon Press, 1996).

63. Wahrman, *The Making of the Modern Self.*

64. S. M. Waddams, *Sexual Slander in Nineteenth-Century England: Defamation in the Ecclesiastical Courts 1815–55* (Toronto: University of Toronto Press, 2000), p. 140.

65. A. Davis, 'Youth Gangs, Gender and Violence, 1870–1900', in D'Cruze (ed.), *Everyday Violence*, pp. 70–89, here p. 72; A. Davis, ' "These Viragoes Are No Less Cruel Than the Lads": Young Women, Gangs and Violence in Late Victorian Manchester and Salford', *British Journal of Criminology*, 39 (1999), 72–89.

66. D'Cruze, *Crimes of Outrage*, p. 117.

67. *Crewe Chronicle*, 4 September 1880, 19 March 1881, 30 April 1881; S. D'Cruze, B. S. Godfrey and D. J. Cox, ' "The Most Troublesome Woman in Crewe": Investigating Gender, Sentencing and the English Lower Courts, c.1880–c.1920', in Avdela et al. (eds), *Crime, Violence and the Modern State*, in which all names of offenders and victims have been changed.

68. *Crewe Chronicle*, 18 September 1879; B. Godfrey, D. Cox and S. Farrall, *Criminal Lives: Family Life, Employment and Offending* (Oxford: Oxford University Press, 2007).

69. B. Godfrey, S. Farrall and S. Karstedt, 'Explaining Gendered Sentencing Patterns for Violent Men and Women in the Late Victorian and Edwardian Period', *British Journal of Criminology*, Autumn (2005), 696–720.

70. V. A. C. Gatrell, 'Crime, Authority and the Policeman-State', in F. M. L. Thompson (ed.), *Social Agencies and Institutions*, The Cambridge Social History of Britain, 1750–1950 (Cambridge: Cambridge University Press, 1990), vol. 3, pp. 243–310; J. Davis, 'A Poor Man's System of Justice: The London Police Courts in the Second Half of the Nineteenth Century', *Historical Journal*, 27 (1984), 309–35; J. Davis, 'Prosecutions and Their Context: The Use of the Criminal Law in Later Nineteenth-Century London', in D. Hay and F. Snyder (eds), *Policing and Prosecution in Britain, 1750–1850* (Oxford: Oxford University Press, 1989), pp. 379–426.

4 Women and Sexuality

1. T. C. N. Gibbens and J. Prince, *Shoplifting* (London: Institute for the Study and Treatment of Delinquency, 1962), pp. 69, 74.
2. J. Walkowitz, *City of Dreadful Delight: Narratives of Sexual Danger in Late-Victorian London* (London: Virago, 1992), p. 21.
3. T. J. Gilfoyle, 'Prostitutes in History: From Parables of Pornography to Metaphors of Modernity', *American Historical Review*, 104 (1999), 117–41.
4. E. P. Thompson and E. Yeo (eds), *The Unknown Mayhew: Selections from the Morning Chronicle, 1849–1850*, (London: Merlin, 1971), pp. 116–80.
5. J. Walkowitz, *Prostitution and Victorian Society* (Cambridge: Cambridge University Press, 1980), p. 203.
6. D. Jones, 'The Conquering of "China"; Crime in an Industrial Community, 1842–64', in D. Jones, *Crime, Protest, Community and Police in Nineteenth-Century Britain* (London: Routledge & Kegan Paul, 1982), pp. 85–116, here pp. 106–8.
7. *OBP*, 9 December 1685, Elizabeth Herd alias Racket, offences against the king: seditious words (t16851209-32).
8. A. E. Simpson, 'The Ordeal of St. Sepulchre's: A Campaign Against Organized Prostitution in Early 19th-Century London and the Emergence of Lower Middle-Class Consciousness', *Social and Legal Studies*, 15 (2006), 363–87.
9. T. Fisher, *Prostitution and the Victorians* (Stroud: Sutton, 1997), p. 50.
10. W. Acton, *Prostitution: Considered in its Moral, Social and Sanitary Aspects*, 1870 edn, ed. P. Fryer (New York, Fitzroy, 1968), p. 24.
11. R. Mazo Karras, *Common Women: Prostitution and Sexuality in Medieval England* (Oxford: Oxford University Press, 1996).
12. A. Corbin, *Women for Hire: Prostitution and Sexuality in France after 1850*, trans. A. Sheridan (Cambridge, MA, and London: Harvard University Press, 1990).
13. F. Finnegan, *Poverty and Prostitution: A Study of Victorian Prostitutes in York* (Cambridge: Cambridge University Press, 1979), p. 76; Walkowitz, *Prostitution and Victorian Society*, pp. 20, 196, 209; T. Henderson, *Disorderly Women in Eighteenth-Century London: Prostitution and Control in the Metropolis, 1730–1830* (London and New York: Longman, 1999), pp. 20–7; C. H. Rolph (ed.), *Women of the Streets: A Sociological Study of the Common Prostitute* (London: Secker & Warburg, 1959).
14. Finnegan, *Poverty and Prostitution*, pp. 162–3; Walkowitz, *Prostitution*, pp. 16–17; Rolph, *Women of the Streets*, pp. 107–8; Henderson, *Disorderly Women*, pp. 18–20.
15. Walkowitz, *Prostitution*, p. 22.
16. J. Hurl-Eamon, 'Policing Male Heterosexuality: The Reformation of Manners Societies' Campaign Against the Brothels in Westminster, 1690–1720, *Journal of Social History*, 37 (2004), 1017–35.
17. Henderson, *Disorderly Women*, pp. 139–40, 165–6.

18. F. Mort, 'Scandalous Events: Metropolitan Culture and Moral Change in Post-Second World War London', *Representations*, (2006), 106–37; A. Brown and D. Barrett, *Knowledge of Evil: Child Prostitution and Child Sexual Abuse in Twentieth-Century England* (Cullompton: Willan, 2002), pp. 148, 152–6, 160–1.

19. Rolph, *Women of the Streets*; Walkowitz, *Prostitution*, p. 23; Walkowitz, *City of Dreadful Delight*, 19–22.

20. Finnegan, *Poverty and Prostitution*, pp. 56–7.

21. Mazo Karras, *Common Women*.

22. J. Miller, 'A Suffering People; English Quakers and their Neighbours, c.1650–c.1700', *Past and Present*, 188, (2005), 71–103.

23. Henderson, *Disorderly Women*, ch. 6.

24. M. M. Mowry, *The Bawdy Politic in Stuart England, 1660-1714: Political Pornography and Prostitution* (Aldershot: Ashgate, 2004).

25. T. Hitchcock, *English Sexualities, 1700–1800*, (Basingstoke: Macmillan, 1997); J. Hurl-Eamon, 'Policing Male Heterosexuality'.

26. R. Trumbach, *Sex and the Gender Revolution*, vol. 1, *Heterosexuality and the Third Gender in Enlightenment London* (Chicago and London: University of Chicago Press, 1998).

27. Hitchcock, *English Sexualities*; T. Evans, ' "Unfortunate Objects": London's Unmarried Mothers in the Eighteenth Century', *Gender and History*, 17 (2005), 127–53.

28. Walkowitz, *Prostitution*, pp. 33–4.

29. Simpson, 'The Ordeal of St. Sepulchre's'.

30. Walkowitz, *City of Dreadful Delight*, p. 22.

31. Henderson, *Disorderly Women*, ch. 8; Simpson, 'The Ordeal of St Sepulchre's'.

32. Fisher, *Prostitution*, pp. 75–9

33. Portsmouth, Plymouth, Woolwich, Chatham, Sheerness, Aldershot, Colchester, Shorncliffe and The Curragh, Cork and Queenstown in Ireland.

34. L. Mahood, *The Magdalenes: Prostitution in the Nineteenth Century* (London: Routledge, 1990); P. Howell, ' "A Private Contagious Diseases Act": Prostitution and Public Space in Victorian Cambridge', *Journal of the History of Geography*, 26 (2000), 376–402.

35. P. Levine, *Prostitution, Race and Politics: Policing Venereal Disease in the British Empire* (London and New York: Routledge, 2003).

36. L. Radzinowicz, *Sexual Offences* (Cambridge: Cambridge University Press, 1959), p. 329.

37. Walkowitz, *City of Dreadful Delight*, chs 3 and 4; P. McHugh, *Prostitution and Victorian Social Reform: The Campaign Against the Contagious Diseases Acts* (London: Croom Helm, 1980).

38. L. Bland, *Banishing the Beast: English Feminism and Sexual Morality, 1885–1914* (London: Penguin, 1995); F. Mort, *Dangerous Sexualities: Medico-Moral Politics in England since 1830* (London: Routledge & Kegan Paul, 1987).

39. S. Petrow, *Policing Morals: The Metropolitan Police and the Home Office, 1870–1914* (Oxford: Oxford University Press); Fisher, *Prostitution*, pp. 146–8; *Times*, 14 October 1895.
40. B. Braber, 'The Trial of Oscar Slater (1909) and Anti-Jewish Prejudices in Edwardian Glasgow', *History*, 88 (2003), 262–79.
41. M. Kohn, *Dope Girls: The Birth of the British Drugs Underground* (London: Lawrence & Wishart, 1992).
42. P. Bartley and B. Gwinnett, 'Prostitution', in I. Zweiniger Bargielowska (ed.), *Women in Twentieth-Century Britain* (Harlow: Longman, 2001), 214–28.
43. Street Offences Act, 1959, paragraphs 5 and 6.
44. Mort, 'Scandalous events'.
45. Walkowitz, *City of Dreadful Delight*, pp. 229–45.
46. Sexual Offences Act 1985, Section 21(1); H. Self, *Prostitution, Women and Misuse of the Law: The Fallen Daughters of Eve* (London: Frank Cass, 2003).
47. P. Bartley, *Prostitution: Prevention and Reform in England 1869–1914* (London: Routledge, 2000), pp. 25–6.
48. Glasgow 1805, Newcastle 1813, Manchester 1819, Liverpool 1834, Leeds 1842, Bristol 1870, Birmingham 1881.
49. Walkowitz, *Prostitution*, p. 59.
50. Ibid., pp. 210–13; Bartley, *Prostitution*.
51. Brown and Barrett, *Knowledge of Evil*, pp. 152–5, 178–80.
52. L. A. Jackson, *Women Police: Gender, Welfare and Surveillance in the Twentieth Century* (Manchester: Manchester University Press, 2006).
53. Brown and Barrett, *Knowledge of Evil*, pp. 176, 178–9. See also L. Agustin, *Sex on the Margins: Migration, Labour Politics and the Rescue Industry* (London: Zed Books, 2007) for an analysis of the complexities of agency and exploitation in the contemporary sex trades.
54. S. Mendelson and P. Crawford, *Women in Early Modern England, 1550–1720* (Oxford: Clarendon, 1998), pp. 148–52; L. Gowing, 'Secret Births and Infanticide in Seventeenth-Century England', *Past and Present*, 156 (1997), 87–115.
55. C. M. Clive, 'The Hidden Truths of the Belly: The Uncertainties of Pregnancy in Early Modern Europe', *Social History of Medicine*, 15 (2002), 209–27.
56. Mendelson and Crawford, *Women in Early Modern England*, pp. 110–23.
57. M. Jackson, 'The Trial of Harriet Vooght: Continuity and Change in the History of Infanticide', in M. Jackson (ed.), *Infanticide: Historical Perspectives on Child Murder and Concealment, 1550–2000* (Aldershot: Ashgate, 2002), pp. 1–17.
58. M. L. Arnot, 'Understanding Women Committing Newborn Child Murder in Victorian England', in S. D'Cruze, *Everyday Violence in Britain, 1850–1950. Gender and Class* (Harlow: Longman, 2000), pp. 55–69, here p. 58.
59. C. Alder and K. Polk, *Child Victims of Homicide* (Cambridge: Cambridge University Press, 2001).

60. J. McDonagh, *Child Murder and British Culture, 1720–1900* (Cambridge: Cambridge University Press, 2003), p. 123, quoting Rev Henry Humble, 'Infanticide, Its Cause and Cure', *The Church and the World: Essays on Questions of the Day*, ed. Rev. Orby Shipley (1866), pp. 51–69, 57.

61. McDonagh, *Child Murder*, pp. 122–30; A. R. Higginbotham, 'Sin of the Age: Infanticide and Illegitimacy in Victorian London', *Victorian Studies*, 32 (1989), 319–37; M. L. Arnot, 'Understanding Women Committing Newborn Child Murder'.

62. J. Wheelwright, ' "Nothing In Between": Modern Cases of Infanticide', in Jackson (ed.), *Infanticide*, pp. 270–85.

63. J. M. Beattie, 'The Criminality of Women in Eighteenth-Century England', *Journal of Social History*, 8 (1974–5), 80–116, here p. 84; J. R. Dickinson and J. A. Sharpe, 'Infanticide in Early Modern England: The Court of Great Sessions at Chester, 1650–1800', in Jackson (ed.), *Infanticide*, pp. 35–51.

64. M. Francus, 'Monstrous Mothers, Monstrous Societies: Infanticide and the Role of Law in Restoration and Eighteenth-Century England', *Eighteenth-Century Life*, 21 (1997), 133–56; J. A. Sharpe, *Crime in Early Modern England 1550–1750*, 2nd edn. (Harlow: Longman, 1998), pp. 61–2.

65. P. C. Hoffer and N. E. H. Hull, *Murdering Mothers: Infanticide in England and New England, 1558–1803* (New York: New York University Press), p. 74; R. W. Malcolmson, 'Infanticide in the Eighteenth Century', in J. Cockburn (ed.), *Crime in England, 1550–1800* (London: Methuen, 1997), pp. 187–209, here p. 197.

66. Francus, 'Monstrous Mothers'; D. Rabin, 'Bodies of Evidence, States of Mind: Infanticide, Emotion and Sensibility in Eighteenth-Century England', in Jackson (ed.), *Infanticide*, pp. 73–92; and see also articles by M. Arnot and C. Quin in this volume.

67. M. Wiener, *Men of Blood: Violence, Manliness and Criminal Justice in Victorian England* (Cambridge: Cambridge University Press, 2004).

68. Higginbotham's sample comprises all murder cases in 12 sample years between 1839 and 1906 at the Old Bailey producing '42 cases of mothers accused of murdering illegitimate children under 5 years old as well as 90 other cases involving crimes relating to the deaths of illegitimate infants', Higginbotham, 'Sin of the Age', p. 324.

69. 68.1 per cent, compared to 9.8 per cent murder and 38.51 per cent manslaughter in Higginbotham's sample which, however, includes the killing of children up to seven years of age; Higginbotham, 'Sin of the Age'.

70. Ibid., pp. 332–3.

71. H. Marland, 'Getting Away With Murder? Puerperal Insanity, Infanticide and the Defence Plea', in Jackson (ed.), *Infanticide*, pp. 168–92; T. Ward, 'The Sad Subject of Infanticide: Law, Medicine and Child Murder, 1860–1938', *Social and Legal Studies*, 8 (1999), 163–80; T. Ward, 'Legislating for Human Nature: Legal Responses to Infanticide, 1860–1938', in Jackson (ed.), *Infanticide*, pp. 249–69.

72. Evans, ' "Unfortunate Objects" '

73. Arnot, 'Understanding Women Committing Newborn Child Murder', p. 61.

74. Margaret Waters was hung. M. L. Arnot, 'Infant Death, Child Care and the State: The Baby-Farming Scandal and the First Infant Life Protection Legislation of 1872', *Continuity and Change*, 9 (1994), 271–311.

75. W. Seccombe, 'Starting to Stop: Working-Class Fertility Decline in Britain', *Past and Present*, 126 (1990), 151–88 and subsequent debate in *Past and Present*, 134 (1992).

76. A. McLaren, *A History of Contraception: From Antiquity to the Present* (Oxford: Blackwell, 1990); Mendelson and Crawford, *Women in Early Modern England*, pp. 27–8; H. Cook, *The Long Sexual Revolution: English Women, Sex, and Contraception, 1800–1975* (Oxford: Oxford University Press, 2004).

77. Gowing, 'Secret Births'.

78. B. Brookes, *Abortion in England, 1900–1967* (London: Croom Helm, 1988), pp. 1–22; Cook, *The Long Sexual Revolution*, ch. 4; J. Thompson and A. S. Williams, 'Women and Abortion in 1930s Britain: A Survey and its Data', *Social History of Medicine*, 11 (1998), 283–309.

79. E. Ross, *Love and Toil: Motherhood in Outcast London, 1870–1918* (New York and Oxford: Oxford University Press, 1993).

80. Thompson and Williams, 'Women and Abortion in 1930s Britain'.

81. S. Brooke, ' "A New World for Women"? Abortion Law Reform in Britain During the 1930s', *American Historical Review*, 106 (2001), 431–59; Brookes, *Abortion in England*, ch. 3; L. A. Hall, ' "I-Have-Never-Met-the-Normal-Woman" – Stella Browne and the Politics of Womanhood', *Women's History Review*, 6 (1997), 157–82; see also K. Fisher, ' "Clearing Up Misconceptions": The Campaign to Set Up Birth Control Clinics in South Wales Between the Wars', *Welsh History Review*, 19 (1998), 103–29.

82. G. Davis and R. Davidson, ' "A Fifth Freedom" or "Hideous Atheistic Expediency"? The Medical Community and Abortion Law Reform in Scotland, c.1960–1975', *Medical History*, 50 (2006), 29–48.

83. G. Davis and R. Davidson, ' "Big White Chief", "Pontius Pilate" and the "Plumber": The Impact of the 1967 Abortion Act on the Scottish Medical Community, c.1967–1980', *Social History of Medicine*, 18 (2005), 283–306.

84. A. Wivel, 'Abortion Policy and Politics on the Lane Committee of Enquiry, 1971–1974', *Social History of Medicine*, 11 (1998), 109–35.

85. Davis and Davidson, 'Big White Chief'.

5 Women, Social Protest and Political Activism

1. On riot, established sources include, E. P. Thompson, 'The Moral Economy of the English Crowd in the Eighteenth Century', *Past and Present*, 50 (1971), 76–136; J. Walter and K. Wrightson, 'Dearth and the Social Order in Early Modern England', *Past and Present*, 71 (1976), 22–42; J. Bohstedt, *Riots and Community Politics in England and Wales 1790–1810* (Cambridge, MA: Harvard University Press, 1983);

J. Bohstedt, 'Gender Household and Community Politics: Women in English Riots, 1790–1810', *Past and Present*, 120 (1988), 88–122. More recently, articles in A. Randall and A. Charlesworth (eds), *Markets, Market Culture and Popular Protest in Eighteenth-Century Britain and Ireland* (Liverpool: Liverpool University Press, 1996); M. I. Thomis and J. Grimmett, *Women in Protest, 1800–1850* (London: Croom Helm, 1982), pp. 32–4.

2. J. Bohstedt, 'The Myth of the Feminine Food Riot: Women as Proto-Citizens in English Community Politics, 1790–1810', in H. V. Applewhite and D. G. Levy (eds), *Women and Politics in the Age of the Democratic Revolution* (Ann Arbor: University of Michigan Press, 1992), pp. 21–60.

3. Deposition of Edward Greenleaf, cordwainer and constable, Colchester Petty Sessions, Essex Record Office, P/CoR13, 29 July 1789.

4. Bohstedt, 'Gender, Household and Community Politics', p. 92.

5. Ibid., p. 95.

6. Bohstedt, *Riots and Community Politics*.

7. Deposition of Peter Hardon, corporal second division of marines, Colchester Petty Sessions, Essex Record Office, P/CoR8, 24 July 1779.

8. Bohstedt, 'Gender, Household and Community Politics'.

9. L. Taylor, 'Food Riots Revisited', *Journal of Social History*, 30 (1996), 483–98.

10. E. J. Hobsbawn and G. Rudé, *Captain Swing* (London: Lawrence & Wishart, 1969); Bohstedt, 'Gender, Household and Community Politics', p. 99.

11. P. King, 'Gleaners, Farmers and the Failure of Legal Sanctions in England, 1750–1850', *Past and Present*, 125 (2001), 116–50, here p. 120, from Epping Petty Sessions, 1785.

12. Ibid., p. 127.

13. D. J. V. Jones, 'The Rebecca Riots, 1839–1844', in A. Charlesworth (ed.), *An Atlas of Rural Protest in Britain, 1548–1900* (London: Croom Helm, 1989), pp. 165–9.

14. P. A. Custer, 'Refiguring Jemima: Gender, Work and Politics in Lancashire 1770–1820', *Past and Present*, 195 (2007), 127–58.

15. I. J. M. Robertson, 'The Role of Women in Social Protest in the Highlands of Scotland, c.1880–1939', *Journal of Historical Geography*, 23 (1997), 187–200.

16. K. Hunt, 'Negotiating the Boundaries of the Domestic: British Socialist Women and the Politics of Consumption', *Women's History Review*, 9 (2000), 389–410; M. Hilton, 'The Female Consumer and the Politics of Consumption in Twentieth-Century Britain', *Historical Journal*, 45 (2002), 103–28.

17. The established constitutional protection against arbitrary imprisonment.

18. Of a very extensive literature, see, for example, C. Tilly, *Popular Contention in Great Britain, 1758–1834*, (Cambridge, MA; Harvard University Press, 1995).

19. This was known as the Blanketeers' march since each man carried his blanket for bedding on the way.

20. R. Poole, ' "By the Law or the Sword", Peterloo Revisited', *History*, 91 (2006), 253–76, here p. 254; R. Poole, 'The March to Peterloo: Politics and Festivity in Late Georgian England', *Past and Present*, 192 (2006), 109–53.
21. M. Bush, 'The Women at Peterloo: The Impact of Female Reform on the Manchester Meeting of 16 August 1819', *History*, 89 (2004), 209–34. For a rather different interpretation of the gender issues at Peterloo, see Custer, 'Reconfiguring Jemima.'
22. Bush, 'The Women at Peterloo', pp. 228–9.
23. Ibid., pp. 224, 226.
24. A. Clark, *The Struggle for the Breeches: Gender and the Making of the British Working Class* (London: California University Press, 1997). For a recent critique, see Custer, 'Reconfiguring Jemima'.
25. H. I. Dutton and J. E. King, *Ten Per Cent and No Surrender* (Cambridge: Cambridge University Press, 1981), p. 52.
26. J. Jordan, *Josephine Butler* (London: John Murray, 2001); B. Caine, *Victorian Feminists* (Oxford: Oxford University Press, 1992).
27. Match-making was a dangerous trade, since the phosphorous used in the match heads caused a cancerous decay of the jaw.
28. J. Walkowitz, *City of Dreadful Delight: Narratives of Sexual Danger in Late-Victorian London* (London: Virago, 1992), pp. 66–7, 76-80. Extracts from the *East London Observer* from 30 June to 21 July 1888, at: http://www.mernick.co.uk/thol/matchgirls.html.
29. Of the extensive literature on women's suffrage, a recent useful collection of essays is, J. Purvis and S. Stanley Holton (eds), *Votes for Women* (London: Routledge, 2000); overviews can be found in S. Stanley Holton, 'The Women's Movement, Politics and Citizenship from the Late Nineteenth Century until 1918', in I. Bargielowska (ed.), *Women in Twentieth Century Britain* (Harlow: Longman, 2001), pp. 248–61, which provides a useful guide to further reading, also the following chapter in the same volume, by C. Beaumont; J. Hannam, 'Women and Politics', in J. Purvis (ed.), *Women's History: Britain, 1850–1945* (London: UCL Press, 1995); K. Cowman, *Women of the Right Spirit: Paid Organisers of the Women's Social and Political Union 1904–18* (Manchester: Manchester University Press, 2007); R. Strachey, *The Cause: A Short History of the Women's Movement in Great Britain* (London: Virago, 1978 (reprint), 1928) is a key early history; see also P. Bartley, *Emmeline Pankhurst* (London: Routledge, 2002); for an interpretation outside women's history, M. Pugh, *The March of the Women: A Revisionist Analysis of the Campaign for Women's Suffrage, 1886–1914* (Oxford: Oxford University Press, 2002).
30. Compare, for example, the essays in Purvis and Holton (eds), *Votes for Women*; and Pugh, *The March of the Women*.
31. Quoted by P. Bartley, 'Emmeline Pankhurst', *History Review*, March (2003), 42.
32. Ibid., p. 43.

33. S. Stanley Holton, 'In Sorrowful Wrath: Suffrage Militancy and the Romantic Feminism of Emmeline Pankhurst', in H. Smith (ed.), *British Feminism in the Twentieth Century* (Aldershot: Edward Elgar, 1990); C. J. Bearman, 'An Examination of Suffragette Violence', *English Historical Review*, 120 (2005), 365–97; Bartley, 'Emmeline Pankhurst', p. 43.

34. Published April 1913, quoted by Bearman, 'An Examination of Suffragette Violence', p. 375.

35. Bearman, 'An Examination of Suffragette Violence', p. 374, n. 29; Bartley, 'Emmeline Pankhurst', p. 43; L. Stanley and A. Morley, *The Life and Death of Emily Wilding Davison: A Biographical Detective Story* (London: Women's Press, 1988).

36. Bearman, 'An Examination of Suffragette Violence', pp. 368, 371; B. Harrison, 'The Act of Military Violence and the Suffragettes, 1904–14', in his *Peaceable Kingdom: Stability and Change in Modern Britain* (Oxford: Clarendon, 1982), pp. 24–81.

37. Bearman, 'An Examination of Suffragette Violence', pp. 377, 380; Cowman, *Women of the Right Spirit*.

38. Emmeline Pankhurst broke with her second daughter, Sylvia, whose feminism was combined with socialism and who had a child outside marriage.

39. J. Purvis, 'The Prison Experience of the Suffragettes in Edwardian Britain', *Women's History Review*, 4 (1995), 103–14, here pp. 111–12.

40. Ibid., p. 110.

41. A. Brown, 'Conflicting Objectives: Suffragette Prisoners and Female Prison Staff in Edwardian England', *Women's Studies*, 31 (2002), pp. 627–44, here p. 634.

42. Purvis, 'The Prison Experiences of the Suffragettes', p. 120.

43. Brown, 'Conflicting Objectives', p. 640.

44. Ibid.

45. Purvis, 'The Prison Experiences of the Suffragettes', p. 122.

46. Brown, 'Conflicting Objectives', p. 637.

47. M. Durham, *Women and Fascism* (London: Routledge, 1998), p. 54; J. Gottlieb, *Feminine Fascism: Women in Britain's Fascist Movement, 1923–45* (London: I. B. Tauris, 2003), p. 151; H. Kean, 'Some Problems of Constructing and Reconstructing a Suffragette's Life: Mary Richardson, Suffragette, Socialist and Fascist', *Women's History Review*, 7 (1998), 475–93; K. Cowman, ' "Incipient Toryism"? The Women's Social and Political Union and the Independent Labour Party, 1903–14', *History Workshop Journal*, 53 (2002), 129–48.

48. R. C. Thurlow, *Fascism in Britain from Oswald Mosley's Blackshirts to the National Front* (London: I. B, Tauris, 1998), pp. iii, 96.

49. Durham, *Women and Fascism*, p. 48.

50. Durham, *Women and Fascism.*, pp. 54, 55; Gottlieb, *Feminine Fascism*, pp. 66, 67.

51. Gottlieb, *Feminine Fascism*, ch. 6, pp. 228, 243, 245.

52. S. Rowbotham, *A Century of Women: The History of Women in Britain and the United States* (London: Viking, 1997), chs 7 and 8, here especially pp. 401–2.

53. J Liddington, *The Road to Greenham Common: Feminism and Anti-Militarism in Britain since 1820* (Syracuse: Syracuse University Press, 1991).

54. S. Roseneil, *Disarming Patriarchy: Feminism and Political Action at Greenham* (Milton Keynes: Open University Press, 1995); S. Roseneil, 'Transgressions and Transformations: Experience, Consciousness and Identity at Greenham Common', in N. Charles and F. Hughes Freeland (eds), *Practising Feminism: Identity, Difference and Power* (London: Routledge, 1996), pp. 86–108, here p. 86.

55. A. Young, *Femininity in Dissent* (London: Routledge, 1990), pp. 17–18; B. Harford and S. Hopkins, *Greenham Common: Women at the Wire* (London: Women's Press, 1984).

56. Roseneil, 'Transgressions', pp. 95–6; L. Segal, *Is the Future Female? Troubled Thoughts on Contemporary Feminism* (London: Random House, 1987); S. Roseneil, *Common Women, Uncommon Practices: The Queer Feminisms of Greenham* (London and New York, Cassell, 2000).

57. Roseneil, 'Transgressions', pp. 104–5.

58. Young, *Femininity in Dissent*, p. 40.

59. *The Guardian* and *The Observer*, 6 and 7 August 1989.

60. Young, *Femininity in Dissent*, pp. 24–5; S. Hipperson, 'Greenham Common Between the Years 1981–2000', at: http://www.greenhamwpc.org.uk/.

61. New by-laws of 1985 (RAF Greenham Common By-laws 1985, S.I. 1985 No. 485) made under the Military Lands Act of 1892, made it an offence for any person without authority to 'enter, pass through or over or remain in or over' the land that had been requisitioned for the base. Young, *Femininity in Dissent*, pp. 27–8; and Hipperson, 'Greenham Common.'

62. Young, *Femininity in Dissent*, p. 23.

63. Ibid., p. 24. Half of this was, however, suspended after appeal to the High Court.

64. Ibid., pp. 20–1.

65. H. Poulsen, 'Que(e)rying Conventional Political Protest', *European Journal of Women's Studies*, 9 (2002), 495–7, here p. 497.

66. For Wilmette Brown and Wages for Housework's involvement in the Greenham Camp, see, M. Chittenden and E. Grice, 'Greenham Peace Women Go to War', *The Times*, 18 October 1987; S. Boseley, ' "Yellow Peril" Splits Meeting: The Annual Conference of Nuclear Disarmament', *The Guardian*, 23 November 1987; A. Johnson, 'Wednesday Women: Sister Under the Skin – Wilmette Brown', *The Guardian*, 23 December 1987.

67. Of the now growing literature in this area, see M. Alison, 'Women as Agents of Political Violence: Gendering Security', *Security Dialogue*, 35 (2004), 447–63; R. Sales, *Women Divided: Gender, Religion and Politics*

in Northern Ireland (London: Routledge, 1997); L. Ryan, *Gender, Identity and the Irish Press: Embodying the Nation* (Lampeter: Edwin Mellen, 2001); B. Aretxaga, *Shattering Silence: Women, Nationalism and Political Subjectivity in Northern Ireland* (Princeton NJ: Princeton University Press, 1997); M. S. Corcoran, *Out of Order: the Political Imprisonment of Women in Northern Ireland, 1972–98*, (Cullompton: Willan, 2006).

6 Women in Control?

1. Quoted in P. Levine, *Feminist Lives in Victorian England: Private Roles and Public Commitment* (Oxford: Blackwell, 1990).
2. E. Blackwell, 'Rescue Work in Prostitution and Disease', reprinted in S. Jeffreys (ed.), *The Sexuality Debates* (London: Routledge, 1987), pp. 100–10.
3. M. Murray, *The Law of the Father? Patriarchy in the Transition from Feudalism to Capitalism* (New York: Routledge, 1995).
4. J. Sharpe, 'Women, Witchcraft and the Legal Process', in J. Kermode and G. Walker (eds), *Women, Crime and the Courts in Early Modern England* (London: UCL Press, 1994), pp. 106–24.
5. C. Holmes, 'Women: Witnesses and Witches', *Past and Present*, 140 (1993), 45–78.
6. J. C. Oldham, 'On Pleading the Belly: A History of the Jury of Matrons', *Criminal Justice History*, 6 (1985), 1–64.
7. *Medical Times and Gazette*, 27 January 1872, quoted in ibid., p. 25.
8. For example, London Metropolitan Archives, Middlesex Quarter Sessions, MJ/SPE/1885/31, Deposition 39.
9. P. Corfield, *Power and the Professions in Britain 1700–1850* (London: Routledge, 1989); J. Donnison, *Midwives and Medical Men* (London: Heinemann, 1977).
10. K. Michaelsen, ' "Union is Strength": The Medical Women's Federation and the Politics of Professionalism, 1917–30', in K. Cowman and L. A. Jackson (eds), *Women and Work Culture: Britain c.1860–1950*, (Aldershot: Ashgate, 2005), pp. 141–60.
11. Wellcome Library, London, Records of the Medical Women's Federation, SA/MWF Box 10, file E64, letter from Dr Marion Elford to Dr Elizabeth Haslam, 6 November 1913.
12. L. A. Jackson, 'Women Professionals and the Regulation of Violence in Interwar Britain', in S. D'Cruze, *Everyday Violence in Britain, 1850–1950: Gender and Class* (Harlow: Longman, 2000), pp. 119–35.
13. Women could own certain forms of property. See E. K. Helsinger, R. Lauterbach Sheets and W. Veeder, *The Woman Question: Society and Literature in Britain and America 1837–83*, Volume 2, *Social Issues*, ch. 1, 'The Law' (New York: Garland, 1983), pp. 3–55.
14. Quoted in Helsinger et al., *The Woman Question*, vol. 2, p. 13.
15. Parliamentary petition of 1856, allegedly signed by 26,000 women, quoted in Helsinger et al., *The Woman Question*, vol. 2, p. 14.
16. Quoted in Helsinger et al., *The Woman Question*, vol. 2, p. 48.

17. A. van Drenth and F. de Haan, *The Rise of Caring Power: Elizabeth Fry and Josephine Butler in Britain and the Netherlands* (Amsterdam: Amsterdam University Press: 1999).

18. F. Power Cobbe, 'Wife-Torture in England', *Contemporary Review*, 32 (1878), 55–87, reprinted in Jeffreys, *Sexuality Debates*, pp. 222 and 224.

19. C. Euler (2000) ' "The Iron Fetters of Our Souls": Nineteenth-Century Feminist Strategies to Get our Bodies into the Political Agenda', in D'Cruze (ed.), *Everyday Violence*, pp. 198–212.

20. J. Butler, 'An Appeal to the People of England on the Recognition and Superintendance of Prostitution by Governments' (first published 1870), reprinted in Jeffreys, *Sexuality Debates*, pp. 111–46.

21. A. Witz, *Professions and Patriarchy* (London: Routledge, 1992).

22. Levine, *Feminist Lives*.

23. Ibid., pp. 2–3.

24. M. Wrench (ed.) *Visits to Female Prisoners at Home and Abroad* (London, 1852), quoted in van Drenth and de Haan, *Rise of Caring Power*, p. 18.

25. Blackwell, 'Rescue work', p. 108.

26. Ibid.

27. Butler, 'An Appeal', p. 172.

28. C. Pankhurst, *The Great Scourge and How to End it* (London: Pankhurst, 1913).

29. H. Sommerlad and P. Sanderson, *Gender, Choice and Commitment: Women Solicitors in England and Wales and the Struggle for Equal Status* (Aldershot: Ashgate, 1998), p. 24.

30. Ibid., p. 64.

31. Ibid., p. 84.

32. Rose Heilbron and Helena Normanton were the first women to be appointed King's Counsel in 1949.

33. P. Polden, 'The Lady of Tower Bridge: Sybil Campbell, England's First Woman Judge', *Women's History Review*, 8 (1999), 505–26, here p. 516.

34. Sommerlad and Sanderson, *Gender, Choice and Commitment*, p. 84.

35. Michaelsen, ' "Union is Strength" '.

36. S. Becke, 'The First 50 Years', *Police Review*, 3 October 1969.

37. L. Bland, 'In the Name of Protection: The Policing of Women in the First World War', in J. Brophy and C. Smart (eds), *Women in Law* (London: Routledge, 1985), pp. 23–49; P. Levine, 'Walking the Streets in a Way no Decent Woman Should', *Journal of Modern History*, 66 (1994), 34–78; A. Woodeson, 'The First Women Police: A Force for Equality or Infringement', *Women's History Review*, 2 (1993), 217–32.

38. L. A. Jackson, *Women Police: Gender, Welfare and Surveillance in the Twentieth Century* (Manchester: Manchester University Press, 2006), p. 24.

39. E. Wilkinson, MP, 'Urgent Need for Women Police', *Pearson's Weekly*, 13 October 1928.

40. Jackson, *Women Police*, p. 141.

41. L. Wyles, *A Woman at Scotland Yard* (London: Faber & Faber, 1952).

42. Quoted in Jackson, *Women Police*, p. 187.

43. A. Logan, 'Professionalism and the Impact of England's First Women Justices, 1920–1950', *The Historical Journal*, 49.3 (2006), 833–50.
44. A. Logan, 'In Search of Equal Citizenship: The Campaign for Women Magistrates in England and Wales, 1910–1939', *Women's History Review*, 16 (2007), 501–18.
45. M. Llewelyn Davies (ed.), *Life as We Have Known it by Co-Operative Working Women* (London: Virago, 1977), first published 1931, pp. 98–9.
46. A. Logan, ' "A Suitable Person for Suitable Cases": The Gendering of Juvenile Courts in England c.1919–39', *Twentieth Century British History*, 16 (2005), 129–45; quote, p. 145.
47. Imperial War Museum, Manuscripts Collection, 77/156/1, Diary of Miss G. M. West, 10 March 1917.
48. Ibid., 10 April 1917.
49. J. Sparrow, *Diary of a Delinquent Episode* (London: Routledge, 1976), p. 34.
50. Ibid., p. 73.
51. H. Richardson, *Adolescent Girls in Approved Schools* (London: Routledge, 1969), p. 42.
52. Sparrow, *Diary*, p. 13.
53. Richardson, *Adolescent* Girls, p. 70.
54. West, Diary, 17 January 1917.
55. Ibid, 22 March 1916; 10 June 1917.
56. Wyles, *Woman at Scotland* Yard, pp. 40–1.
57. J. Lock, *Lady Policeman* (London: Michael Joseph, 1968).
58. Richardson, *Adolescent Girls*, p. 57.
59. Ibid., p. 67.
60. Ibid., pp. 58–9.
61. M. Todd, *Ever Such a Nice Lady* (London, Victor Gollancz, 1964), p. 16.
62. Ibid.
63. Sparrow, *Diary*, p. 123.
64. Lock, *Lady Policeman*, p. 102.
65. Wyles, *Woman at Scotland Yard*, p. 118.
66. Todd, *Nice Lady*, p. 101.

7 Women and Punishment

1. J. A. Sharpe, *Crime in Early Modern England 1550–1750*, 2nd edn (Harlow: Longman, 1999), ch. 8; C. Emsley, *Crime and Society in England, 1750–1900*, 3rd edn (Harlow: Longman, 2005), ch. 10.
2. M. Foucault, *Discipline and Punish: The Birth of the Prison*, trans. Alan Sheridan (Harmondsworth: Penguin, 1977).
3. C. Pateman, *The Sexual Contract* (Stanford, CA: Stanford University Press, 1988).
4. J. Cooper et al., *The Borough of Colchester*, Volume 9, *The Victoria County History of Essex* (Woodbridge: Boydell, 1994), p. 166. Essex Record Office, Colchester Borough Sessions Roll, D/Db5 Sr 243 January 1764.

5. K. Harvey, 'The Century of Sex? Gender, Bodies, and Sexuality in the Long Eighteenth Century', *Historical Journal*, 45 (2002), 899–916.

6. V.A.C. Gatrell, *The Hanging Tree: Execution and the English People 1770–1868* (Oxford: Oxford University Press, 1994), pp. 334–6.

7. S. Carroll, 'Introduction', in S. Carroll (ed.), *Cultures of Violence: Interpersonal Violence in Historical Perspective* (Basingstoke: Palgrave Macmillan, 2007), pp. 1–46, here p. 24.

8. D. Hay, P. Linebaugh and E. P. Thompson (eds), *Albion's Fatal Tree: Crime and Society in Eighteenth-Century England* (London: Allen Lane, 1975).

9. Emsley, *Crime and Society*, pp. 246, 249.

10. Sharpe, *Crime in Early Modern England*, p. 97.

11. J. C. Oldham, 'On Pleading the Belly: A History of the Jury of Matrons', *Criminal Justice History*, 6 (1985), 1–64.

12. Emsley, *Crime and Society*, pp. 261–2.

13. A. McKenzie, *Tyburn's Martyrs* (London: Hambledon Continuum, 2007).

14. E. Osborne, *The Last Dying Words, Speech, and Confession of Eliz. Osborne, Who Was Executed . . ., for the Cruel Murder of Her Mother-in-Law* (London?, c.1750): http://galenet.galegroup.com/servlet/ECCO Gale Document Number: CW3302760563.

15. G. Walker, *Crime, Gender and Social Order in Early Modern England* (Cambridge: Cambridge University Press, 2003).

16. M. Gaskill, *Crime and Mentalities in Early Modern England* (Cambridge: Cambridge University Press, 2000), pp. 127–42, 174–6, 286; N. Tosney, 'Women and "False Coining" in Early Modern London', *The London Journal*, 32 (2007), 103–23.

17. J. Humphries, 'Standards of Living and Quality of Life', in C. Williams (ed.), *The Blackwell Companion to the Nineteenth Century* (Oxford: Blackwell, 2004), pp. 287–304.

18. Emsley, *Crime and Society*, pp. 271–2, 262–6.

19. Gatrell, *The Hanging Tree*, p. 8; *Annual Register* (1829), p. 73, quoted in Ibid., p. 68.

20. M. Alpert, *London 1849: A Victorian Murder Story* (London: Longman, 2004); *The Examiner*, 17 November 1849.

21. M. J. Wiener, 'Alice Arden to Bill Sikes: Changing Nightmares of Intimate Violence in England, 1558–1869', *Journal of British Studies*, 40 (2001), 184–212; M. Wiener, *Men of Blood: Violence, Manliness and Criminal Justice in Victorian England* (Cambridge: Cambridge University Press, 2004).

22. M. Arnot, 'Infant Death, Child Care and the State: The Baby-Farming Scandal and the First Infant Life Protection Legislation of 1872', *Continuity and Change*, 9 (1994), 271–311; L. Rose, *The Massacre of the Innocents: Infanticide in Britain, 1800–1939* (London: Routledge, 1986), pp. 53, 64, 82–4, 91–109.

23. J. B. Christoph, *Capital Punishment and British Politics: The British Movement to Abolish the Death Penalty* (London: Allen & Unwin, 1962), p. 46;

A. Ballinger, *Dead Woman Walking: Executed Women in England and Wales, 1900*–1955 (Aldershot: Ashgate, 2000), p. 328.

24. Ibid., pp. 329–30.

25. L. Marks and T. Van den Bergh, *Ruth Ellis: A Case of Diminished Responsibility?* (London: Macdonald & Jane's, 1977); Christoph, *Capital Punishment*; T. Morris, *Crime and Criminal Justice since 1945* (Oxford: Blackwell, 1989).

26. J. M. Beattie, *Crime and the Courts in England, 1660–1800* (Oxford: Clarendon, 1986), pp. 506–7.

27. G. Morgan and P. Rushton, *Eighteenth-Century Criminal Transportation: The Formation of the Criminal Atlantic* (Basingstoke: Palgrave Macmillan, 2004).

28. K. McCabe, 'Assignment of Female Convicts on the Hunter River, 1831–1840', *Australian Historical Studies*, 30 (1999), 286–302, here note 1; D. Oxley, *Convict Maids: The Forced Migration of Women to Australia* (Cambridge: Cambridge University Press, 1996); P. Byrne, *Criminal Law and Colonial Subject: New South Wales, 1810–1830* (Cambridge: Cambridge University Press, 1993); J. Damousi, *Depraved and Disorderly: Female Convicts, Sexuality and Gender in Colonial Australia* (Cambridge: Cambridge University Press, 1997); K. Daniels, *Convict Women* (Sydney: Allen & Unwin, 1998).

29. Oxley, *Convict Maids*, p. 3.

30. Beattie, *Crime and the Courts*, p. 479.

31. J. Damousi, 'Beyond the "Origins Debate": Theorising Sexuality and Gender Disorder in Convict Women's History', *Australian Historical Studies*, 27 (1996), 1031461X, Academic Search Elite, here note 23, citing Report of the Committee into Convict Discipline, 24 March 1842, CSO 22/50, Archives Office of Tasmania, Hobart.

32. Daniels, *Convict Women*, p. 145; Damousi, 'Beyond the "Origins Debate"'.

33. G. P. Walsh, 'Reibey, Mary (1777–1855)', *Australian Dictionary of Biography*, Volume 2 (Melbourne: Melbourne University Press, 1967), pp 373–4.

34. McCabe, 'Assignment'.

35. R. Frances, 'Sex Workers or Citizens? Prostitution and the Shaping of "Settler" Society in Australia', *International Review of Social History*, 44, Supplement 7 (1999), 101–22; P. J. Byrne, 'A Colonial Female Economy: Sydney, Australia', *Social History* 24 (1999), 287–93.

36. Daniels, *Convict Women*, pp. 71–7, 62, 70, 80–5.

37. Ibid., pp. 51, 65.

38. Ibid., pp. 110–27.

39. E. Conlin Casella, ' "Doing Trade": A Sexual Economy of Nineteenth-Century Australian Female Convict Prisons', *World Archaeology*, 32 (2000), 209–21; E. Conlin Casella, 'To Watch or Restrain: Female Convict Prisons in 19th-Century Tasmania', *International Journal of Historical Archaeology*, 5 (2001), 51; A. Howe, *Punish and Critique: Towards a Feminist Analysis of Penality* (London: Routledge, 1994), p. 156.

40. Daniel, *Women Convicts*, pp. 147–8.

41. J. J. Willis, 'Transportation versus Imprisonment in Eighteenth- and Nineteenth-Century Britain: Penal Power, Liberty, and the State', *Law and Society Review*, 39 (2005), 171–210.

42. J. Innes, 'Prisons for the Poor: English Bridewells, 1555–1800', in F. Snyder and D. Hay (eds), *Labour, Law and Crime: An Historical Perspective* (London: Tavistock, 1987), pp. 42–122; here p. 47.

43. Sharpe, *Crime in Early Modern England*, pp. 257–8; P. Dillon, *The Much-Lamented Death of Madam Geneva: The Eighteenth-Century Gin Craze* (London: Review, 2002), p. 159; M. Jackson (ed.), *Infanticide: Historical Perspectives on Child Murder and Concealment, 1550–2000* (Aldershot: Ashgate, 2002), p. 30; R. Shoemaker, 'Reforming the City: The Reformation of Manners Campaign in London, 1690–1738', in L. Davison, T. Hitchcock et al. (eds), *Stilling the Grumbling Hive: The Response to Social and Economic Problems in England, 1688–1750* (Stroud: Alan Sutton, 1992), pp. 99–120; J. Boulton, 'Going on the Parish: The Parish Pension and its Meaning in the London Suburbs 1640–1724', in T. Hitchcock, P. Sharpe and P. King (eds), *Chronicling Poverty: The Voices and Strategies of the English Poor 1640–1840* (London, 1997); Beattie, *Crime and the Courts*, p. 566.

44. T. Hitchcock, *Down and Out in Eighteenth-Century London* (London: Hambledon, 2004), p. 158.

45. Colchester, St Leonard's overseers' correspondence, Essex Record Office D/P 245, 20 March 1765.

46. L. Forman Cody, 'Living and Dying in Georgian London's Lying-In Hospitals', *Bulletin of the History of Medicine*, 78 (2004), 309–48.

47. D. T. Andrew, *Philanthropy and Police: London Charity in the Eighteenth Century* (Princeton, NJ: Princeton University Press, 1989); T. Hitchcock, *English Sexualities, 1700–1800* (Basingstoke: Macmillan, 1997).

48. P. Cox, 'Review of *Fragile Moralities and Dangerous Sexualities: Two Centuries of Semi-Penal Institutionalisation for Women* by A. Barton', *The Howard Journal of Criminal Justice*, 45 (2006), 559–60.

49. S. Halliday, *Newgate: London's Prototype of Hell* (Stroud: Sutton, 2006), pp. 32, 46.

50. *Memoirs of the Right Villainous John Hall* (1708), quoted in Halliday, *Newgate*, pp. 42–3.

51. Cited in Halliday, *Newgate*, p. 173.

52. John Howard, *The State of the Prisons in England and Wales, with Preliminary Observations, and an Account of Some Foreign Prisons* (Warrington, 1777), pp. 15–16, 33–4.

53. Cited in Halliday, *Newgate*, p. 174.

54. Cited in ibid., p. 181.

55. See, for example, H. Johnston, 'Discovering the Local Prison: Shrewsbury Prison in the Nineteenth Century', *The Local Historian*, 35 (2005), 230–42.

56. B. Forsythe, 'Women Prisoners and Women Penal Officials 1840–1921', *British Journal of Criminology*, 33 (1993), 525–40, here p. 526–7; D. Wilson, 'Millbank, the Panopticon, and their Victorian Audiences', *The*

Howard Journal of Criminal Justice, 41 (2002), 364–81, here p. 370; R. Dobash, R. D. Dobash, and S. Gutteridge, *The Imprisonment of Women* (Oxford: Blackwell, 1986), p. 86; A. Brown, 'The Amazing Mutiny at the Dartmoor Convict Prison', *British Journal of Criminology*, 47 (2007), 276–92.

57. L. Zedner, *Women, Crime and Custody in Victorian England* (Oxford: Clarendon Press, 1991), p. 135; S. McConville, *Next Only to Death: English Local Prisons, 1860–1900* (London: Routledge, 1995), pp. 206–9, 336.

58. N. Walker, 'Crime and Penal Measures', in A. H. Halsey (ed.), *British Social Trends Since 1900* (Basingstoke: Macmillan, 1988), p. 627.

59. Forsythe, 'Women Prisoners', p. 526.

60. P. Priestley (ed.), *Victorian Prison Lives: English Prison Biography, 1830–1914* (London: Methuen, 1985), p. 336.

61. Zedner, *Women, Crime and Custody in Victorian England*; Y. Jewkes and H. Johnston (eds), *Prison Readings: A Critical Introduction to Prisons and Imprisonment* (Cullompton: Willan, 2006), pp. 30–8, here pp. 32–3.

62. Forsythe, 'Women Prisoners'.

63. McConville, *Next Only to Death*, p. 343.

64. J. Long, *Conversations in Cold Rooms: Women, Work and Poverty in Nineteenth-Century Northumberland* (Woodbridge: Boydell, 1999), pp. 148–51.

65. Forsythe, 'Women Prisoners', pp. 533–4.

66. J. Purvis, 'The Prison Experience of the Suffragettes in Edwardian Britain', *Women's History Review*, 4 (1995), 103–34.

67. Gladstone Committee, Minutes of Evidence, p. 175, quoted in McConville, *Next Only to Death*, p. 350.

68. McConville, *Next Only to Death*, p. 337.

69. Zedner, *Women, Crime and Custody*, p. 6.

70. Ibid., pp. 264–7.

71. C. Leeson, *The Probation System* (London, 1914). pp. 64–5.

72. P. Dale, 'Implementing the 1913 Mental Deficiency Act: Competing Priorities and Resource Constraint Evident in the South West of England before 1948', *Social History of Medicine*, 16 (2003), 403–18, here pp. 405, 406, 409, 411, 412.

73. P. Dale, 'Training for Work: Domestic Service as a Route Out of Long-Stay Institutions Before 1959', *Women's History Review*, 13 (2004), 387–405.

74. Forsythe, 'Women Prisoners', p. 526.

75. A. D. Smith, *Women in Prison: A Study in Penal Methods* (London: Stevens & Sons, 1962), p. 170.

76. Ibid., pp. 129, 141–2; W. A. Elkin, *The English Penal System* (Harmondsworth: Penguin, 1957), p 145.

77. F. Heidensohn 'Gender and Crime', in M. MacGuire et al., *Oxford Handbook of Criminology* (Oxford: Clarendon, 1994), p. 1022.

78. Elkin, *The English Penal System*, p. 142; Sir H. Scott, 'Minimum Security Prisons', in 'Prisons Today and Tomorrow', reprinted from the *Howard Journal* (London, 1946), p. 8.

79. Elkin, *The English Penal System*, p. 146.

80. Smith, *Women in Prison*, p. 172.
81. I. Zweiniger-Bargielowska, *Austerity in Britain: Rationing, Controls and Consumption, 1939–1955* (Oxford: Oxford University Press, 2001).
82. J. Henry, *Who Lie in Gaol* (London: Victor Gollancz, 1952).
83. M. Size, *Prisons I Have Known* (London, George Allen & Unwin: 1957), p. 155.
84. Ibid., p. 162. Figures calculated from Annual Governor's Reports to the Prison Commissioners for 1947, 1948 and 1949. Original documents viewed at Askham Grange.
85. Calculated from Prison Receptions Registers for 1947.
86. Governor's Annual Reports to the Prison Commissioners (GovPC) for 1947 and 1950.
87. Governor's Reports to the Boards of Visitors, including 4 April 1950, 2 April 1951, 2 June 1951.
88. Walker, 'Crime and Penal Measures', p. 629; J. Hall Morton, 'Alcoholics in Prison', *Howard Journal*, 2 (1929), p. 307; M. Woodside, 'Women Drinkers Admitted to Holloway Prison During February, 1960', *British Journal of Criminology*, I (1960), 221–35; X. Field, *Under Lock and Key* (London: Max Parrish, 1963), p. 8.
89. C. Rowett and P. J. Vaughn, 'Women and Broadmoor: Treatment and Control in a Special Hospital', in B. Hutter and G. Williams (eds), *Controlling Women: The Normal and the Deviant* (London: Routledge, 1981), pp. 131–53, here p. 133; P. Carlen and A. Worrall, 'Analyzing Women's Imprisonment', in Y. Jewkes and H. Johnston (eds), *Prison Readings: A Critical Introduction to Prisons and Imprisonment* (Cullompton: Willan, 2006), pp. 121–9.
90. P. Carlen (ed.), *Criminal Women: Autobiographical Accounts* (Cambridge: Polity, 1985), p. 178; P. Carlen, 'Introduction: Women and Punishment', in P. Carlen (ed.), *Women and Punishment*, pp. 3–20 (Cullompton: Willan, 2002); Henry, *Who Lie In Gaol*, p. 20; Josie O'Dwyer, 'Surviving Holloway', in Carlen (ed.), *Criminal Women*, p. 167; Rowett and Vaughn, 'Women in Broadmoor', p. 131.
91. Carlen (ed.), *Criminal Women*, p. 183; Forsythe, 'Women Prisoners', p. 534; P. Carlen, 'Death and the Triumph of Governance?: Lessons from the Scottish Women's Prison', *Punishment and Society*, 3 (2001), 459–70; Wilson, 'Millbank', p. 378; E. Genders and E. Player, *Women in Prison: The Treatment, the Control and the Experience* (Milton Keynes: Open University Press, 1987), p. 165.
92. A. Barton, *Fragile Moralities and Dangerous Sexualities: Two Centuries of Semi-Penal Institutionalisation for Women* (Aldershot: Ashgate, 2005), p. 152.
93. Ibid., p. 155, quoting Pat Carlen, 'A Strategy for Women Offenders? Lock Them Up, Programme Them, ... and Then Send Them Out Homeless', *Criminal Justice Matters*, 53 (2003), pp. 34–5, here p. 34.
94. Ibid., p. 179; P. Carlen, *Women's Imprisonment* (London: Routledge & Kegan Paul, 1983), p. 85; Forsythe, 'Women Prisoners', pp. 529–30.
95. Genders and Player, *Women in Prison*, p. 177.

96. A. Ballinger, 'Masculinity in the Dock: Legal Responses to Male Violence and Female Retaliation in England and Wales, 1900 to 1965', *Social Legal Studies*, 16 (2007), 459–81, formulates this argument in relation to sentences in murder trials but it is equally applicable to penal regimes.

8   Girls and Delinquency

1. S. Shesgreen (ed.), *Engravings by Hogarth* (New York: Dover, 1975).
2. P. Griffiths, 'Juvenile Delinquency in Time', in P. Cox and H. Shore (eds), *Becoming Delinquent: British and European Youth, 1650–1950* (Aldershot: Ashgate, 2002).
3. 1815 Committee for Investigating the Causes of the Alarming Increase of Juvenile Delinquency in the Metropolis, cited in H. Shore, *Artful Dodgers: Youth and Crime in Early Nineteenth-Century London* (London: Boydell, 1999).
4. Shore, *Artful Dodgers*, p. 17.
5. P. King and J. Noel, 'The Origins of "The Problem of Juvenile Delinquency": The Growth of Juvenile Prosecutions in London in the Late Eighteenth and Early Nineteenth Centuries', *Criminal Justice History* 15 (1993), 17–41, here p. 21.
6. P. King 'The Rise of Juvenile Delinquency in England, 1780–1840', *Past and Present*, 160 (1999), 116–66.
7. H. Hendrick, *Child Welfare. England 1872–1989* (London: Routledge, 1994).
8. J. Donzelot, *The Policing of Families*, trans. Robert Hurley (Baltimore, MD: Johns Hopkins University Press, 1997), first published 1977; D. Garland, *Punishment & Welfare* (Aldershot: Gower, 1985).
9. M. Rahikainen, *Centuries of Child Labour: European Experiences from the Seventeenth to the Twentieth Century* (Aldershot: Ashgate, 2004).
10. The legal age of criminal responsibility was raised from seven in 1908 to eight in 1933 and ten in 1963. A 'young person' was defined as someone under the age of 16 in 1908; this rose to 17 in 1933; thus from 1933 the term 'juvenile' referred to all those under 17.
11. H. Taylor, 'The Politics of the Rising Crime Statistics of England and Wales, 1914–1960', *Crime, Histoire & Sociétés/Crime, History & Societies*, 1 (1998), 5–28.
12. Shore, *Artful Dodgers*, p. 172.
13. *OBP* (accessed 10 Oct. 2008), 14 May 1766, Sarah Waldern, t17660514-13.
14. *OBP*, 18 September 1765, Elizabeth Gould, t17650918-14.
15. *OBP*, 3 September 1690, Mary Beard, t16900903-26; 27 May 1691, Mary Beard, t16910527-14; list of pardons 15 Jan 1692, s16920115-1.
16. *OBP*, 15 December 1845, Louisa Baker, t18451215-350.
17. *OBP*, 2 February 1846, Mary Ann Booth, t18460202-650.
18. *OBP* 15 May 1834, Caroline Beaton and Mary Ann Cain, 15 May 1834, t18340515-42.

19. Manchester City Archives, M117, Juvenile Court Registers, 22 December 1960.
20. K. Peiss, 'Making Up, Making Over: Cosmetics, Consumer Culture, and Women's Identity', in V. De Grazia (ed.), *The Sex of Things: Gender and Consumption in Historical Perspective* (Berkeley: University of California Press, 1996), pp. 311–36.
21. A. Davis, ' "These Viragos Are No Less Cruel Than the Lads": Young Women, Gangs and Violence in Late Victorian Manchester and Salford', *British Journal of Criminology*, 39 (1999), 72–89.
22. J. Knelman, *Twisting in the Wind: The Murderess and the English Press* (Toronto: University of Toronto Press, 1998), p. 143. See also B. Taylor, *Cruelly Murdered: Constance Kent and the Killing at Road Hill House* (London: Souvenir, 1979); K. Summerscale, *The Suspicions of Mr Whicher: or the Murder at Road Hill House* (London: Bloomsbury, 2008).
23. H. Shore, 'The Trouble with Boys: Gender and the "Invention" of the Juvenile Offender in Early Nineteenth-Century Britain', in Arnot and Usborne, *Gender and Crime in Modern Europe*, pp. 75–92; L. Mahood and M. Littlewood, 'The "Vicious" Girl and the "Street-Corner" Boy: Sexuality and the Gendered Delinquent in the Scottish Child-Saving Movement, 1850–1914', *Journal of the History of Sexuality*, 4 (1994), 549–78; S. Rose, ' "Good Time" Girls and Quintessential Aliens', in her *The People's War* (Oxford: Oxford University Press, 2003), pp. 71–106.
24. T. R. Fyvel, *The Insecure Offender: Rebellious Youth in the Welfare State* (London: Pelican, 1963; 1st edn 1961), p. 97.
25. P. Cox, *Gender, Justice and Welfare: Bad Girls in Britain, 1900–1950* (Basingstoke: Palgrave Macmillan, 2003), p. 15.
26. S. Cohen, *Folk Devils and Moral Panics* (London: 1972), p. 9.
27. *Pall Mall Gazette*, 8 July 1885.
28. L. A. Jackson, *Child Sexual Abuse in Victorian England* (London: Routledge, 2000), p. 106.
29. A. M. Woollacott, ' "Khaki Fever" and its Control: Gender, Class, Age and Sexual Morality on the British Homefront in the First World War', *Journal of Contemporary History*, 29 (1994), 325–47.
30. *News Chronicle*, 8 December 1943; NA, MH 102/1150, Girls who come before the juvenile court and soldiers in uniform.
31. NA, MH 102/895, Absconders from Approved Schools Soliciting American Soldiers in the Streets and Spreading Venereal Disease, letter from D. Peto to Miss Good of the Home Office, 17 May 1943.
32. S. Rose, ' "Good Time" Girls'.
33. *Liverpool Post*, 25 March 1943; South *Wales Weekly Argus*, 27 May 1944.
34. Cox, *Gender, Justice and Welfare*, p. 55.
35. Ibid., p. 42.
36. C. Rolph (ed.), *Women of the Streets: A Sociological Study of the Common Prostitute* (London: Secker & Warburg, 1955), p. 106.
37. M. Cale, 'Girls and the Perception of Sexual Danger in the Victorian Reformatory System', *History*, 78 (1993), 201–17.

38. Cox, *Gender, Justice and Welfare*, p. 86.
39. M. Cale, 'Working for God? Staffing the Victorian Reformatory and Industrial School System', *History of Education*, 21 (1992), 113–27, p. 114.
40. L. Mahood, *Policing Gender, Class and Family* (London: UCL Press, 1995); Cox, *Gender, Justice and Welfare*.
41. Ibid.; Jackson, *Child Sexual Abuse*, p. 140.
42. *Our Waifs and Strays*, vol. 8, no. 202 (February 1901), pp. 1–2.
43. P. Cox, 'Girls, Deficiency and Delinquency', in D. Wright and A. Digby (eds), *From Idiocy to Mental Deficiency: Historical Perspectives on People with Learning Difficulties* (London: Routledge, 1996), pp. 184–206.
44. NA, MEPO 2/8710/94821 The Liverpool Police and Juvenile Crime. A memorandum prepared by the Chief Constable of Liverpool.
45. *Picture Post*, 3 May 1947, pp. 18–20.
46. NA, CRIM 1/482 Rex v. Jones, statement of Hulten, 12 October 1944. For the trial proceedings, see C. E. Bechofer Roberts (ed.), *The Trial of Jones and Hulten* (London: Jarrolds, 1945).
47. G. Orwell, 'Decline of the English Murder', *Tribune*, 15 February 1946.
48. R. Alwyn Raymond, *The Cleft Chin Murder* (London: Claud Morris, 1945).
49. A. La Bern, *Night Darkens the Street* (London: Nicholson & Watson, 1947).
50. NA, MH102/1137 – Publicity about Home Office schools, Film Based on the 'Cleft Chin' Murder Case; and MH102/1138 Publicity about Home Office schools, 'Good Time Girl', Harmful Effect on the Young.
51. NA, MH 102/1139, 'Publicity about Home Office Schools'.
52. *Newcastle Journal*, 23 June 1948.
53. *Newcastle Journal*, 14 May 1948.
54. *Monthly Film Bulletin*, 15, no. 173 (May 1948), p. 59.
55. *Daily Mirror*, 30 April 1948; *Sunday Pictorial*, 2 May 1948.
56. NA, MH102/1140 Film – Publicity about Home Office schools, *Good Time Girl*. Release, letter to Home Secretary, 16 October 1948.
57. MH 102/1139 Publicity about Home Office schools.
58. *Newcastle Journal*, 28 June 1948.
59. NA, MEPO 3/2280 Murder of George Heath, Police report, Divisional Detective Inspector, 4 November 1944.
60. P. Carlen (ed.), *Criminal Women: Autobiographical Accounts* (Cambridge: Polity, 1985), see especially 'Christina: In Her Own Time' by Diana Christina and Pat Carlen, pp. 59–79.
61. Ibid, p. 142; P. Carlen, *Women, Poverty and Social Control* (Milton Keynes: Open University, 1988), p. 106.
62. NA, MH102/895 Girl Absconders.
63. J. Sparrow, *Diary of a Delinquent Episode* (London: Routledge, 1976).
64. Carlen, *Criminal Women*, p. 67.
65. NA, CRIM 1/482.
66. G. Sereny, *Cries Unheard: Why Children Kill; The Story of Mary Bell* (London: Holt, 2000), p. 45.

67. A. Worrall, 'Girls at Risk? Reflections on Changing Attitudes to Young Women's Offending', *Probation Journal*, 48 (2001), 86–92, p. 86.

68. Ibid.

Afterword

1. *Sun*, 23 January 2008, 'How Do We Mend Broken Britain?'

2. F. Heidensohn, 'The Deviance of Women: A Critique and an Enquiry', *British Journal of Sociology*, 19 (1968), 160–75; F. Heindensohn, 'Women and the Penal System', in A. Morris (ed.), *Women and Crime: Papers Presented to the Cropwood Round Table Conference* (Cambridge, 1981), p. 127; A. Worrall, *Offending Women* (London: Routledge, 1990); P. Cox, *Gender, Justice and Welfare: Bad Girls in Britain, 1900–1950* (Basingstoke: Palgrave Macmillan, 2003), p. 2.

3. *Sun*, 15 April 2008. The Metropolitan Police identified 3 'girl gangs' amongst a tally of almost 200 gangs in London in 2007. *Guardian*, 3 May 2007.

4. See, for example, the case of 18-year-old Sian Simpson, stabbed and killed by another young woman in June 2007. *Sun*, 21, 22 and 27 June 2007; *Telegraph*, 21 June 2007; *Daily Mail*, 21 June 2007.

5. Psychologist Cynthia McVeigh of Glasgow Caledonian University, quoted in 'Girl Gangs Muscling in on Street Violence', *Daily Mail*, 23 August 2007.

6. J. Pullinger and C. Summerfield (eds), *Social Focus on Men and Women* (London: Stationery Office, 1998), p. 71.

7. L. Snider, 'Constituting the Punishable Woman: Atavistic Man Incarcerates Postmodern Woman', *British Journal of Criminology*, 43 (2003), 354–78, here p. 368.

8. Report of Department of Public Health, University of Oxford, quoted by Baroness Jean Corston, *The Corston Report Executive Summary* (London: Stationery Office, 2007), p. 14.

9. Snider, 'Constituting the Punishable Woman', p. 369.

10. Recent press comment includes, Pauline Campbell et al., 'Prison Suicides', *Observer*, 6 April 2008; Amelia Hill, 'Sick and Suicidal' and other leading articles, case studies of recent suicides and comment, *The Observer*, 30 and 31 March 2008; Jamie Doward, 'The Short and Desperate Life of Petra', *The Observer*, 3 February 2008.

11. Amelia Hill, 'Sick and Suicidal'; Baroness Jean Corston, *The Corston Report*, available at: http://www.homeoffice.gov.uk/documents/corston-report/and the government's response downloadable at: http://www.official-documents.gov.uk/document/cm72/7261/7261.pdf.

12. D. Garland, *Punishment and Modern Society: A Study in Social Theory* (Oxford: Clarendon, 1990).

13. L. Agustin, *Sex on the Margins: Migration, Labour Politics and the Rescue Industry* (London: Zed Books, 2007).

14. Reported in *The Independent*, 23 April 2008.

Suggested Reading

General

Most of the topics discussed in this book can be explored further using the Old Bailey Sessions Papers Online (http://www.oldbaileyonline.org/).

The following works are excellent further reading suggestions in relation to all themes:

Arnot, M. and C. Usborne eds. *Gender and Crime in Modern Europe*. London: UCL Press, 1999.

Emsley, C. *Crime and Society in England, 1750–1900*. Harlow: Longman, 3rd edn, 2005.

Godfrey, B., D. Cox and S. Farrall. *Criminal Lives: Family Life, Employment and Offending*. Oxford: Oxford University Press, 2007.

Kermode, J. and G. Walker eds. *Women, Crime and the Courts in Early Modern England*. London: UCL Press, 1994.

King, P. *Crime and Law in England, 1750–1840*. Cambridge: Cambridge University Press, 2006.

Sharpe, J. A. *Crime in Early Modern England 1550–1750*. Harlow: Longman, 2nd edn, 1998.

Shoemaker, R. B. *Gender in English Society 1650–1850*. Harlow: Longman, 1998.

Smart, C. ed. *Regulating Womanhood: Historical Essays on Marriage, Motherhood and Sexuality*. London: Routledge, 1992.

Walker, G. *Crime, Gender and Social Order in Early Modern England*. Cambridge: Cambridge University Press, 2003.

Zedner, Z. *Women, Crime and Custody in Victorian England*. Oxford: Oxford University Press, 1991.

Chapter 1

Beattie, J. M. 'The Criminality of Women in Eighteenth-Century England', *Journal of Social History*, 8 (1974–75), 80–116.

Beattie, J. M. *Crime and the Courts in England, 1660–1800*. Princeton, NJ: Princeton University Press, 1986.

Davis, J. 'A Poor Man's System of Justice: The London Police Courts in the Second Half of the Nineteenth Century', *Historical Journal*, 27 (1984), 309–35.

Davies, O. *Witchcraft, Magic and Culture 1736–1951*. Manchester: Manchester University Press, 1999.

Feeley, M. and D. Little. 'The Vanishing Female: The Decline of Women in the Criminal Process, 1687–1912'. *Law and Society Review*, 25 (1991), 719–57.

Godfrey, B., S. Farrall and S. Karstedt. 'Explaining Gendered Sentencing Patterns for Violent Men and Women in the Late Victorian and Edwardian Period', *British Journal of Criminology*, 45.5 (2005), 696–720.

Gowing, L. *Domestic Dangers: Women, Words and Sex in Early Modern London*. Oxford: Clarendon Press, 1996.

King, P. 'Gender, Crime and Justice in Late-Eighteenth and Early-Nineteenth-Century England', in M. Arnot and C. Usborne eds. *Gender and Crime in Modern Europe*. London: UCL Press, pp. 44–74.

Meldrum, T. 'A Women's Court in London: Defamation at the Bishop of London's Consistory Court, 1700–1745', *London Journal*, 19 (1994), 1–20.

Wiener, M. J. 'The Victorian Criminalisation of Men', in P. Spierenburg ed. *Men of Violence: Gender, Honour and Rituals in Modern Europe and America*. Columbus: Ohio State University Press, 1998.

Chapter 2

Carlen, P. *Women, Crime and Poverty*. Oxford: Oxford University Press, 1988.

Gibbens, T. C. N. and J. Prince. *Shoplifting*. London: Institute for the Study and Treatment of Delinquency, 1962.

Godfrey, B. 'Workplace Appropriation and the Gendering of Factory "Law" West Yorkshire, 1840–80', in M. Arnot and C. Usborne eds. *Gender and Crime in Modern Europe*. London: UCL Press, 137–150.

King, P. 'Female Offenders, Work and Life-Cycle Change in Late-Eighteenth-Century London', *Continuity and Change*, 11 (1996), 61–90.

Lemire, B. 'The Theft of Clothes and Popular Consumerism in Early Modern England', *Journal of Social History*, 24 (1990), 255–76, 257.

MacKay, L. 'Why They Stole: Women in the Old Bailey, 1779–89', *Journal of Social History*, 32 (1999), 623–39.

Morgan, G. and P. Rushton. *Rogues, Thieves and the Rule of Law. the Problem of Law Enforcement in the North-East of England, 1718–1800*. London: UCL Press, 1998.

Palk, D. *Gender, Crime and Judicial Discretion, 1780–1830*. London: Boydell Press, 2006.

Walker, G. 'Women, Theft and the World of Stolen Goods', in J. Kermode and G. Walker, *Women, Crime and the Courts*. London and Durham, NC: UCL Press and University of North Carolina Press, 1994, pp. 81–105.

Whitlock, T. C. *Crime, Gender and Consumer Culture in Nineteenth-Century England*. Aldershot: Ashgate, 2005.

Chapter 3

Ballinger, A. *Dead Woman Walking: Executed Women in England and Wales, 1900–1955*. Dartmouth: Ashgate, 2000.

Birch, H. ed. *Moving Targets: Women, Murder and Representation*. London: Virago, 1993.

Carroll, S. 'Introduction', S. Carroll ed., *Cultures of Violence: Interpersonal Violence in Historical Perspective*. Basingstoke: Palgrave Macmillan, 2007, pp. 1–46.

D'Cruze, S. ed. *Everyday Violence in Britain, 1850–1950*. Harlow: Pearson, 2000; contains several relevant articles.

D'Cruze, S. *Crimes of Outrage: Sex, Violence and Victorian Working Women*. London: UCL Press, 1998, ch. 3.

Davies, O. *Witchcraft, Magic and Culture, 1736–1951*. Manchester: Manchester University Press, 1999.

Davis, A. ' "These Viragoes Are No Less Cruel Than the Lads" Young Women, Gangs and Violence in Late Victorian Manchester and Salford', *British Journal of Criminology*, 39 (1999), 72–89.

Frost, G., ' "She is But a Woman": Kitty Byron and the English Edwardian Criminal Justice System, in S. D'Cruze and A. Rao eds. *Violence, Vulnerability and Embodiment*. Special Issue of *Gender and History*, 16 (2004), 538–60.

Godfrey, B. S., S. Farrall, S. Karstedt. 'Explaining Gendered Sentencing Patterns for Violent Men and Women in the Late-Victorian and Edwardian Period', *British Journal of Criminology*, 45.5 (2005), 696–720.

Gowing, L. *Domestic Dangers: Women, Words and Sex in Early Modern London*. Oxford: Clarendon Press, 1996.

Rediker, M. *Villains of all Nations: Atlantic Pirates in the Golden Age, 1716–1726*. London: Verso, 2004.

Robb, G. and N. Erber eds. *Disorder in the Court: Trials and Sexual Conflict at the Turn of the Century*. Basingstoke: Macmillan, 1999.

Watson, K. *Poisoned Lives: English Poisoners and their Victims*, London and New York: Hambledon, 2004.

Robb, G. 'Circe in Crinoline: Domestic Poisonings in England', *Journal of Family History*, 22 (1997), 176–90.

Sharpe, J. A. *Instruments of Darkness: Witchcraft in England 1550–1750*. London: Hamish Hamilton, 1996.

Stanley, J. ed. *Bold in her Breeches: Women Pirates Across the Ages*. London: Pandora, 1995.

Waddams, S. M. *Sexual Slander in Nineteenth-Century England: Defamation in the Ecclesiastical Courts, 1815–1855*. Toronto and London: University of Toronto Press, 2000.

Weiner, M. *Men of Blood: Violence, Manliness, and Criminal Justice in Victorian England*. Cambridge: Cambridge University Press, 2004.

Chapter 4

Arnot, M. L. 'Understanding Women Committing Newborn Child Murder in Victorian England', in Shani D'Cruze ed. *Everyday Violence in Britain, 1850–1950*. Harlow: Pearson, 2000, pp. 55–69.

Arnot, M. L. 'Infant Death, Child Care and the State: The Baby-Farming Scandal and the First Infant Life Protection Legislation of 1872', *Continuity and Change*, 9 (1994), 271–311.

Bartley, P. and B. Gwinnett. 'Prostitution', in Ina Zweiniger Bargielowska ed. *Women in Twentieth-Century Britain*. Harlow: Longman, 2001, pp. 214–28.

Bartley, P. *Prostitution: Prevention and Reform in England, 1860–1914*. London: Routledge, 2000.

Bland, L. *Banishing the Beast: English Feminism and Sexual Morality, 1885–1914*. London: Penguin, 1995.

Brookes, B. *Abortion in England, 1900–1967*. London: Croom Helm, 1988.

Brown, A. and D. Barrett. *Knowledge of Evil: Child Prostitution and Child Sexual Abuse in Twentieth-Century England*. Cullompton: Willan, 2002.

Cook, H. *The Long Sexual Revolution: English Women, Sex, and Contraception, 1800–1975*. Oxford: Oxford University Press, 2004.

Finnegan, F. *Poverty and Prostitution: A Study of Victorian Prostitutes in York*. Cambridge: Cambridge University Press, 1979.

Gowing, L. 'Secret Births and Infanticide in Seventeenth-Century England', *Past and Present*, 156 (1997), 87–115.

Henderson, T., *Disorderly Women in Eighteenth-Century London: Prostitution and Control in the Metropolis, 1730–1830*. London and New York: Longman, 1999.

Higginbotham, A. R. 'Sin of the Age: Infanticide and Illegitimacy in Victorian London', *Victorian Studies*, 32 (1989), 319–37.

Jackson, M. ed. *Infanticide: Historical Perspectives on Child Murder and Concealment, 1550–2000*. Aldershot: Ashgate, 2002.

Karras, R. Mazo. *Common Women: Prostitution and Sexuality in Medieval England*. Oxford: Oxford University Press, 1996.

Kohn, M. *Dope Girls: The Birth of the British Drugs Underground*. London: Lawrence & Wishart, 1992.

Levine, P. *Prostitution, Race and Politics: Policing Venereal Disease in the British Empire*. London and New York: Routledge, 2003.

Mahood, L. *The Magdalenes: Prostitution in the Nineteenth Century*. London: Routledge, 1990.

McDonagh, J. *Child Murder and British Culture, 1720–1900*. Cambridge: Cambridge University Press, 2003.

Mort, F. *Dangerous Sexualities: Medico-Moral Politics in England since 1830*. London: Routledge & Kegan Paul, 1987.

Self, H. *Prostitution, Women and Misuse of the Law: The Fallen Daughters of Eve*. London: Frank Cass, 2003.

Walkowitz, J. R. *City of Dreadful Delight: Narratives of Sexual Danger in the Victorian City*. London: Virago, 1994.

Walkowitz, J. R. *Prostitution and Victorian Society: Women, Class and the State*. Cambridge: Cambridge University Press, 1980.

Chapter 5

Bartley, P. *Emmeline Pankhurst*. London: Routledge, 2002.

Bearman, C. J. 'An Examination of Suffragette Violence', *English Historical Review*, 120 (2005), 365–97.

Bohstedt, J. 'Gender Household and Community Politics: Women in English Riots, 1790–1810', *Past and Present*, 120 (1988), 88–122.

Bohstedt, J. 'The Myth of the Feminine Food Riot: Women as Proto-Citizens in English Community Politics, 1790–1810', in Harriet V. Applewhite and Darline G. Levy eds. *Women and Politics in the Age of the Democratic Revolution*. Ann Arbor: University of Michigan Press, 1992, pp. 21–60.

Bohstedt, J. *Riots and Community Politics in England and Wales 1790–1810*. Cambridge, MA: Harvard University Press, 1983.

Bush, M. 'The Women at Peterloo: The Impact of Female Reform on the Manchester Meeting of 16 August 1819', *History*, 89 (2004), 209–34.

Clark, A. *The Struggle for the Breeches: Gender and the Making of the British Working Class*. London: California University Press, 1997.

Cowman, K. *Women of the Right Spirit: Paid Organisers of the Women's Social and Political Union 1904–18*. Manchester: Manchester University Press, 2007.

Custer, A. 'Refiguring Jemima: Gender, Work and Politics in Lancashire 1770 1820', *Past and Present*, 195 (2007), 127–58.

Durham, M. *Women and Fascism*. London: Routledge, 1998.

Gottlieb, J. *Feminine Fascism: Women in the British Fascist Movement, 1923–45*. London: I. B. Tauris, 2003.

Holton, S. Stanley. 'The Women's Movement, Politics and Citizenship from the Late Nineteenth Century until 1918', in Ina Zweiniger Bargielowska ed. *Women in Twentieth Century Britain*. Harlow: Pearson Education, 2001, pp. 248–61.

King, P. 'Gleaners, Farmers and the Failure of Legal Sanctions in England, 1750–1850', *Past and Present*, 125 (2001), 116–50.

Liddington, J. *The Road to Greenham Common: Feminism and Anti-Militarism in Britain since 1820*. Syracuse: Syracuse University Press, 1991.

Pugh, M. *The March of the Women: A Revisionist Analysis of the Campaign for Women's Suffrage, 1886–1914*. Oxford: Oxford University Press, 2002.

Purvis, J. and S. Stanley Holton eds. *Votes for Women*. London: Routledge, 2000.

Roseneil, S. *Common Women, Uncommon Practices: The Queer Feminisms of Greenham*. London and New York, Cassell, 2000.

Roseneil, S. *Disarming Patriarchy: Feminism and Political Action at Greenham*. Milton Keynes: Open University Press, 1995.

Thomis, M. I. and J. Grimmett. *Women in Protest, 1800–1850*. London: Croom Helm, 1982.

Thompson, E. P. 'The Moral Economy of the English Crowd in the Eighteenth Century', *Past and Present*, 50 (1971), 76–136.

Tilly, C. *Popular Contention in Great Britain, 1758–1834*. Cambridge, MA: Harvard University Press, 1995.

Young, A. *Femininity in Dissent*. London: Routledge, 1990.

Chapter 6

Bland, L. 'In the Name of Protection: The Policing of Women in the First World War', in J. Brophy and C. Smart eds. *Women in Law*. London: Routledge, 1985, pp. 23–49.

Carrier, J. *The Campaign for the Employment of Women as Police Officers*. Aldershot: Avebury, 1988.

Jackson, L. A. *Women Police: Gender, Welfare and Surveillance in the Twentieth Century*. Manchester: Manchester University Press, 2006.

Heidensohn, F. *Women in Control? The Role of Women in Law Enforcement*. Oxford: Oxford University Press, 1992.

Jones, S. *Policewomen and Equality*. Basingstoke: Macmillan, 1986.

Levine, P. *Feminist Lives in Victorian England: Private Roles and Public Commitment*. Oxford: Blackwell, 1990).

Levine, P. 'Walking the Streets in a Way No Decent Woman Should', *Journal of Modern History*, 66 (1994), 34–78.

Logan, A. *Feminism and Criminal Justice: A Historical Perspective*. Basingstoke: Palgrave Macmillan, 2008.

Oldham, J. C. 'On Pleading the Belly: A History of the Jury of Matrons', *Criminal Justice History*, 6 (1985), 1–64.

Polden, P. 'The Lady of Tower Bridge: Sybil Campbell, England's First Woman Judge', *Women's History Review*, 8 (1999), 505–26.

Sommerlad, H. and P. Sanderson. *Gender, Choice and Commitment: Women Solicitors in England and Wales and the Struggle for Equal Status*. Aldershot: Ashgate, 1998.

Witz, A. *Professions and Patriarchy*. London: Routledge, 1992.

Woodeson, A. 'The First Women Police: a Force for Equality or Infringement', *Women's History Review*, 2 (1993), 217–32.

Note: Biographical essays concerning many of the women mentioned in this chapter can be accessed though the Dictionary of National Biography Online, http://oxforddnb.com.

Chapter 7

Ballinger, A. *Dead Woman Walking: Executed Women in England and Wales, 1900–1955*. Dartmouth: Ashgate, 2000.

Barton, A. *Fragile Moralities and Dangerous Sexualities: Two Centuries of Semi-Penal Institutionalisation for Women*. Aldershot: Ashgate, 2005.

Brown, A. 'Conflicting Objectives: Suffragette Prisoners and Female Prison Staff in Edwardian England', *Women's Studies*, 31 (2002), 627–45.

Byrne, P. *Criminal Law and Colonial Subject: New South Wales, 1810–1830*. Cambridge: Cambridge University Press, 1993.

Carlen, P. ed. *Women and Punishment*. Cullompton: Willan, 2002.

Carlen, P. et al. ed. *Criminal Women: Autobiographical Accounts*. Cambridge: Polity, 1985.

Corston, Baroness J. *The Corston Report Executive Summary*. London: Stationery Office, 2007.

Damousi, J. *Depraved and Disorderly: Female Convicts, Sexuality and Gender in Colonial Australia*. Cambridge: Cambridge University Press, 1997.

Daniels, K. *Convict Women*. Sydney: Allen & Unwin, 1998.

Dobash, R., R. D. Dobash, and S. Gutteridge. *The Imprisonment of Women*. Oxford: Blackwell, 1986.

Forsythe, B. 'Women Prisoners and Women Penal Officials 1840–1921', *British Journal of Criminology*, 33 (1993), 525–40.

Godfrey, B. S., S. Farrall, S. Karstedt. 'Explaining Gendered Sentencing Patterns for Violent Men and Women in the Late-Victorian and Edwardian Period', *British Journal of Criminology*, 45.5 (2005), 696–720.

Gatrell, V. A. C. *The Hanging Tree: Execution and the English People, 1770–1868*. Oxford: Oxford University Press, 1994.

Johnston. H. ed. *Punishment and Control in Historical Perspective*. Basingstoke: Palgrave Macmillan, 2008.

McKenzie, A. *Tyburn's Martyrs*. London: Hambledon Continuum, 2007.

Oldham, J. C. 'On Pleading the Belly: A History of the Jury of Matrons', *Criminal Justice History*, 6 (1985), 1–64.

Oxley, D. *Convict Maids: The Forced Migration of Women to Australia*. Cambridge: Cambridge University Press, 1996.

Purvis, J. 'The Prison Experience of the Suffragettes in Edwardian Britain', *Women's History Review*, 4 (1995), 103–34.

Wiener, M. J. *Men of Blood: Violence, Manliness, and Criminal Justice in Victorian England*. New York: Cambridge University Press, 2004.

Wiener, M. J. 'Alice Arden to Bill Sikes: Changing Nightmares of Intimate Violence in England, 1558–1869', *Journal of British Studies*, 40 (2001), 184–212.

Chapter 8

Alder, C. and A. Worrall. *Girls' Violence*. New York: SUNY, 2004.

Cale, M. 'Girls and the Perception of Sexual Danger in the Victorian Reformatory System', *History*, 78 (1993), 201–17.

Cale, M. 'Working for God? Staffing the Victorian Reformatory and Industrial School System', *History of Education*, 21 (1992), 113–27.

Cox, P. 'Girls, Deficiency and Delinquency', in D. Wright and A. Digby eds. *From Idiocy to Mental Deficiency: Historical Perspectives on People with Learning Difficulties*. London: Routledge, 1996.

Cox, P. *Gender, Justice and Welfare: Bad Girls in Britain, 1900–1950*. Basingstoke: Palgrave Macmillan, 2003.

Cox, P. 'Girls in Trouble: Defining Female Delinquency, Britain, 1900–1950', in M. J. Maynes, B. Soland and C. Benninghaus eds. *Secret Gardens, Satanic Mills: Placing Girls in European History 1750–1960*. Bloomington: Indiana University Press, 2005, pp. 192–208.

Cox, P. and H. Shore eds. *Becoming Delinquent: British and European Youth, 1650–1950*. Aldershot: Ashgate, 2002.

Davies, A. ' "These Viragoes are no less Cruel than the Lads": Young Women, Gangs and Violence in Late-Victorian Manchester and Salford', *British Journal of Criminology*, 39 (1999), 72–89.

Jackson, L. A., ' "The Coffee Club Menace": Policing Youth, Leisure and Sexuality in Post-War Manchester', *Cultural and Social History*, 5 (2008), 289–308.

King, P. and J. Noel. 'The Origins of "The Problem of Juvenile Delinquency": The Growth of Juvenile Prosecutions in London in the Late Eighteenth and Early Nineteenth Centuries', *Criminal Justice History*, 15 (1993), 17–41.

L. Mahood and M. Littlewood. 'The "Vicious" Girl and the "Street-Corner" Boy: Sexuality and the Gendered Delinquent in the Scottish Child-Saving Movement, 1850–1914', *Journal of the History of Sexuality*, 4 (1994), 549–78.

Mahood, L. *Policing Gender, Class and Family*. London: UCL Press, 1995.

S. Rose, ' "Good Time" Girls and Quintessential Aliens', in S. Rose, *The People's War*. Oxford: Oxford University Press, 2003, pp. 71–106.

Shore, H. *Artful Dodgers: Youth and Crime in Early Nineteenth-Century London*. London: Boydell, 1999.

Afterword

Snider, L. 'Constituting the Punishable Woman: Atavistic Man Incarcerates Postmodern Woman', *British Journal of Criminology*, 43 (2003), 354–78.

Agustin, L. *Sex on the Margins: Migration, Labour Politics and the Rescue Industry*. London: Zed Books, 2007.

Index

COLEG MORGANNWG
LEARNING RESOURCES CENTRE
★ ABERDARE ★